Restoring the
KENNET & AVON CANAL

Restoring the
KENNET & AVON CANAL

PETER LINDLEY-JONES

TEMPUS

Acknowledgements

Penrose Associates, Bristol
Clew, Kenneth R., *The Kennet & Avon Canal* (David & Charles: 1968) ISBN 0 7153 8656 3
Bolton, David, *Race Against Time* (Methuen: 1990) ISBN 0 4136 3470 1
HM Stationery Office, *Report of the Committee of Inquiry into Inland Waterways (1658)*

British Waterways Publications:
Kennet & Avon Partnership Project, *Access to Your Working Waterway Heritage*
Water Appeal, *Making it Happen – Kennet & Avon Canal Waterway Access for All*
Kennet & Avon Canal, *A Leisure Strategy* (1987)
Funding Sources for Major Waterway Environmental and Economic Regeneration Schemes
– Creating a Sustainable Future, P.A.T.E.L Report (November 1991)

Special thanks to the following people who helped with information, editing and proof-reading:
Ian Broom; Clive and Helen Hackford; David Harris; Terry Kemp; Ray Knowles; John Laverick; David Lamb; Admiral Sir William O'Brien; Brian Oram; the staff of the Devizes office of British Waterways and the Kennet & Avon Canal Trust, Devizes. Finally, and most importantly, I would like to thank my wife Dorothy, who patiently read through every dot and comma of my final draft.

First published 2002
Reprinted 2006

Tempus Publishing Ltd
The Mill, Brimscombe Port
Stroud, Gloucestershire GL5 2QG
www.tempus-publishing.com

British Library Cataloguing in Publication Data.
A catalogue record for this book is available from the British Library.

ISBN 0 7524 2387 8

Typesetting and origination by Tempus Publishing.
Printed and bound in Great Britain.

Contents

Dedication

The original idea and much of the early history for this book was researched by Jack Dalby, who died before it could be completed and published.

John Gould MBE, who carried the Kennet & Avon Canal restoration torch in the darkest days of its history asked me, a few months before he died, to complete the task that Jack had begun, fearing that as the years rolled on much of the early chronicles would be forgotten.

This I have been pleased to do, with help and information gleaned from Government papers, Minutes of the Kennet & Avon Canal Association and its successor the Kennet & Avon Canal Trust, together with British Waterways, the Kennet & Avon Canal Trust and their magazine the *Butty*, and conversations with John Gould and many other Trust officers and colleagues.

This book is dedicated to John Gould and Jack Dalby but, as they both would wish, it is also dedicated to all who have assisted in the massive task of awakening this Sleeping Beauty.

Peter Lindley-Jones
Devizes 2002

Foreword

I am delighted and honoured to be invited to write a foreword to this wonderful record of achievement on our canal and I congratulate Peter Lindley-Jones on so splendidly taking on the task from Jack Dalby, whose baby it was and whose unflagging enthusiasm I recall when discussing the manuscript with him only weeks before his death.

I called it 'our canal' because that is, I know, how we all saw it. It is not ours, of course, but we worked on it, came to love it, became very possessive about it and, against the odds, helped to drag it from dereliction into life. As I read through this history many names came to mind of people who, along with thousands of other forgotten volunteers, do not get a mention but are just as much the architects of success as those who do. I salute them: the photo opportunity may have shown the General and the Admiral with spades in their hands, but they were not the ones who used them.

The Trust gave me seventeen years of interest and enjoyment as Chairman and I took enormous pride in standing beside Her Majesty at the re-opening but now, as I look in wonder at what has been achieved since I resigned, I realise that my pride can be nothing compared to those who have followed. She was no beauty while she slept; I was lucky to preside over the final re-awakening but the Trust made her beautiful again.

Admiral Sir William O'Brien KCB DSO
March 2002

I feel very privileged to be able to add my comments to those of the Admiral and would like to take this opportunity on behalf of British Waterways to thank those many, many individuals who, over a number of decades, have worked so hard to restore the Kennet & Avon Canal.

This book is a testament to many challenges, some of which may have seemed insurmountable, but nevertheless were overcome with passion and determination.

Operating the Kennet & Avon Canal in the twenty-first century presents many new challenges. Leisure and recreation activities have replaced freight. Today's visitors expect more and more facilities, whether they are part of the local community or the many visitors to the waterway, including those from overseas who visit one of the historic features or hire a boat for the week.

The future success of the Kennet & Avon Canal will continue to rely on input from the Kennet & Avon Canal Trust and local communities. I am very proud to have played my small part in this wonderful story

Michael Goodenough
Waterway Manager, The Kennet & Avon Canal, British Waterways
April 2002

Sustainability is one of the current 'in' words, particularly in considering the future of restored canals. What sustained the Kennet & Avon Canal Trust? The answer is simple – volunteers. Peter Lindley-Jones originates from one of our early volunteer bands and knew many of those whom you will read about in this book. The book has long needed writing. The basis was there in our records, written by Jack Dalby. The account needed editing, updating and turning into a readable account of what happened over the years. Having masterminded our adoption scheme, Peter mentioned the Jack Dalby papers in conversation with me and the inevitable happened. Once again he became a volunteer. Many reading this will know the feeling.

More than most I know the long hours, effort and dedication put into this by Peter. I have read most of it in sections but like you not the whole, complete with photographs, charts and other information. I believe it will take a needed space on our bookshelves and complete the story started many years ago by a band of people to whom we owe an immeasurable debt.

David L. Lamb
Kennet & Avon Canal Trust Chairman
April 2002

Introduction

The Kennet & Avon Canal, flowing as it does through some of the most attractive areas of southern England, can lay claim to being one of Britain's most picturesque waterways. So it is little wonder that the huge crowd that thronged the lock sides at Devizes for the canal's re-opening by Her Majesty The Queen in August 1990 saw it as an occasion for a grand celebration.

There were those within the crowd and watching from afar to whom the presence of Her Majesty was a most gracious nod of approval to all who had for so many years given freely of their time and effort despite official indifference, and at times rank opposition. That this happy culmination of many years of rejuvenation, perhaps the largest civil engineering restoration campaign ever undertaken by a voluntary organisation, was possible at all was entirely due to their determination and for displaying that most British characteristic – refusing to take 'no' for an answer.

After the Second World War a few people realised that without positive action the remnants of the canal system of this country, a memorial to the ingenuity of our forebears, would be lost forever. Not only were they convinced that eventually the value of canals as multi-purpose amenities would dawn on the powers that be, but they managed to pass their enthusiasm on to others to carry the idea forward.

Although the official re-opening of the Kennet & Avon Canal in 1990 was the outward pinnacle of success, it required another ten years of work and the expenditure of around £30 million before the canal's future could be truly said to be finally assured. This book attempts to trace the campaign spread over five decades by the Kennet & Avon Canal Association, which later became the Kennet & Avon Canal Trust, to save the Kennet & Avon Canal through all the disappointments and successes.

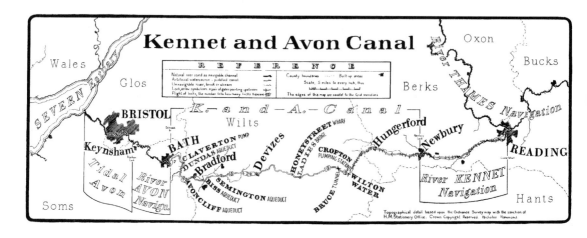

1 Brief Early History
1715-1948

The River Kennet was made navigable from the Thames at Reading to Newbury Wharf between 1715 and 1723; John Hore of Newbury being surveyor and engineer. The navigation comprised twenty-one locks and eleven and a half miles of artificial cut, only the most suitable seven miles of the river being incorporated into the waterway. The barges that were used could carry up to eighty tons, their main cargoes being agricultural products from Newbury to London with coal and other heavy goods from London to Newbury.

To the west, the River Avon was made navigable between Bristol and Bath, again under the direction of John Hore, in the period 1724 to 1727. Only six locks, plus one which gives entrance to the floating harbour, and a few artificial cuts were necessary. The principal cargoes were Bath stone and coal.

The two Hore navigations were linked by a fifty-six-mile, seventy-nine-lock canal built by the Kennet & Avon Canal Co. between 1794 and 1810. The engineer was John Rennie. In 1796 the company bought the majority of shares in the Avon Navigation and in 1812 it also purchased the Kennet Navigation. The total cost of the eighty-six-mile, 106-lock waterway, including these two purchases, was just over £1 million. Water was supplied with the aid of two steam-driven beam engine pumps from springs near Crofton, and from the Avon using a water-driven pump at Claverton near Bath. Locks were 14ft (4.3m) wide and could accommodate boats capable of carrying some sixty tons.

At Limpley Stoke, near Bath, the canal was joined to the rapidly developing Somerset coalfield by the Somersetshire Coal Canal, which was completed by a separate company in 1805. Throughout the useful life of the Kennet & Avon Canal, it provided a staple trading commodity – Somerset coal – distributed across a broad swathe of the south of England.

Trade gradually built up on the Kennet & Avon until the opening of the Great Western Railway between Bristol and London in 1841. This forced the canal company, in an attempt to combat the competition, to lower tariffs and reduce maintenance. Despite these measures trade continued to decline so that by 1851 the canal company, finding themselves in grave financial difficulties, offered the canal for sale to the GWR. The transfer was authorised by the 1852 GWR Act with the GWR paying the canal company the sum of £210,415. From then until 1947 the canal was a railway concern.

The coal trade was not immediately affected as the railways had not yet penetrated the Somerset coalfield. However this occurred in the early 1870s and by 1877 the Kennet & Avon began to lose money. The Somerset Coal Canal also began to suffer from the rail competition and this, combined with worked-out pits, forced the canal into liquidation in 1893.

Traffic on the Kennet & Avon continued to decline and the condition of the canal was allowed to deteriorate. Water supplies, never over sufficient, were reduced by the closure of the coal canal and still further by the closure of the Wiltshire & Berkshire Canal, both of which had supplied lockage water.

In 1926 the GWR, wishing to get rid of what was to them an unmitigated nuisance, announced that they were seeking to close the canal by a Ministry of Transport Order. A storm of protest from many sources was unleashed and not only was the GWR forced to withdraw the threat but was persuaded to restore the canal to a more satisfactory condition. This they did, with little enthusiasm, during the early 1930s. Sadly it was all to little avail as

Anti-tank gun pill-box. (K&ACT Archives)

extra traffic was not forthcoming and passage from one end to the other was soon only to be accomplished with great difficulty.

The sole activity on the canal during the Second World War was during the invasion 'scare' of 1940. The waterways across southern England, including the Thames, Pang and Kennet, were regarded as an excellent line of defence which explains the many pill-boxes and gun emplacements still to be found alongside the canal. Kenneth Clew, in his history of the Kennet & Avon, tells how preparations were made in such great haste that many lock balance beams had to be shortened because some pill-boxes were built too close to the lock gates, whilst others were erected at sites so far away from any road or track that bringing a gun into position would have posed a problem.

The Transport Act of 1947 nationalised the main line railways and on 1 January 1948 the control of the Kennet & Avon passed into the hands of the new Railway Executive.

A full and detailed account of the early history of the canal can be found in Kenneth Clew's *The Kennet & Avon Canal*, published by David and Charles (ISBN 0-7153-8656-5).

2 The Inland Waterways Association
1945-1948

The impetus for the restoration of the Kennet & Avon, as well as many other canals, was generated by the publication of L.T.C. Rolt's book *Narrow Boat* in 1944. This lovingly told story of a 1939/1940 cruise in a converted 72ft (21.6m) working boat, *Cressy*, was surprisingly rejected by a number of publishers as being of 'insufficient public interest'. Eventually it was accepted by Eyre & Spottiswoode and immediately became a resounding success. The text had been completed while *Cressy* was moored on the Kennet & Avon, just below the tail of Hungerford Lock at Woolridge's Wharf from March 1940 to the end of April 1941.

Tom Rolt, a mechanical engineer, had accepted a job with an agricultural foundry in nearby Aldbourne. As he later recalled in *Landscape with Canals*, he had brought *Cressy* up 'the disused and virtually derelict' canal from Reading with great difficulty, taking five days for the journey. He also records in the same book how, when he wished to move *Cressy* to the Midlands, the Great Western Railway, although prepared to facilitate his passage to Bath, advised him that the journey westward would be hazardous. So instead he proceeded to Bromsgrove via Reading finding, much to his relief, that in order to delay possible German invaders the many swing-bridges along the way had been refurbished and now opened with comparative ease.

Narrow Boat alerted public opinion to the possible imminent loss of a priceless national asset, a remarkable water highway system, bequeathed by the Industrial Revolution. Such was the success of *Narrow Boat* that a small avalanche of fan mail soon descended into *Cressy*'s cabin.

Amongst the enthusiastic replies was one from Robert Aickman, another canal enthusiast, who had written to Tom suggesting that some form of canal organization should be formed to attempt to arrest the decline of Britain's waterways and promote their use. Whilst *Cressy* was moored at Tardebigge on the Worcester & Birmingham Canal, the two men met together with their wives, Ray and Angela, and very soon became firm friends.

Some six months later they arranged a meeting at Robert's London home, the purpose of which was to form a canal association. Both Tom and Robert were anxious that the gathering should be restricted to those who were truly interested in canals and amongst the half dozen or so invited was Charles Hadfield who, like Robert, had made contact with Tom after the publication of *Narrow Boat*. Rarely can one pinpoint important turning points in fortune with great accuracy, but in the history of Britain's inland waterways that meeting held in Robert's book-lined third-floor sitting room in Gower Street was the catalyst which changed, for all time, the public's perception of canals.

Thus it was that the Inland Waterways Association (IWA) was formed on 15 February 1946 with Robert Aickman as chairman, Charles Hadfield as vice-chairman and Tom Rolt and Frank Eyre as honorary secretary and treasurer respectively. Tom undertook the task of keeping an eye on the Warwickshire Avon area, whilst Robert was to give his attention to the Kennet and Avon by taking charge of the campaign for its restoration to good order and full navigability; Robert pointed out that the canal, as well as being a work of great engineering importance, provided the only wide boat link between the Bristol Channel and the Thames, thus avoiding the long, and possibly dangerous, small boat passage around the south coast. IWA pressure soon produced welcome publicity with the *Newbury Weekly News* publishing a long article containing reminiscences of Mr Squires, the retiring Canal Inspector, together with the history of the Kennet & Avon and a plea for the restoration of boating facilities in the town.

John Gould, a Newbury resident, was an early *Narrow Boat* convert having received the book as a present from his wife Win whilst serving in India during the war. On his return, he not only became one of the earliest IWA members, but joined the canal maintenance staff and wrote to the *Newbury Weekly News* describing the Crofton pumps and berating the GWR for discouraging trade. He also criticised the public's lack of interest in seeing that the railway kept to its statutory maintenance obligations. Small wonder then that he was summoned to appear before the divisional engineer! IWA influence was also at work in the preliminary stages of the 1947 Transport Bill which was to nationalise transport. Two MPs, Elwyn Jones and Ian Mikardo, put down questions to the Minister of Transport seeking Ministerial assurance that no waterway, and specifically the Kennet & Avon, would be abandoned until the British Transport Commission, to be set up under the Bill, had fully examined each case. The Minister was unable to give such a general assurance but did inform the MPs that there was no question of abandoning the Kennet & Avon before the Commission had examined its case. Anthony Hurd, MP for Newbury, and Christopher Hollis, MP for Devizes, expressed sympathy with the IWA's views and concern at the state of the canal.

In the House of Lords, Lord Methuen put down a question concerning an obstruction at Reading which restricted entrance to the canal. He obtained a definite promise that girders placed under Bridge Street bridge would be removed and the bridge rebuilt.

In the meanwhile, it was stated that the girders were unlikely to impede the passage of ordinary pleasure craft. This strange obstacle in Reading, which was supposed to strengthen the bridge, was actually the responsibility of Reading Corporation and not the Great Western Railway who, nevertheless, used it as a rather weak excuse to deter passage. On being given notice, the Corporation could, within an hour, lower the level of the River Kennet to permit craft with 7.5ft (2.29m) headroom to pass under the bridge.

When the structure was examined around 1963 it was found that the wooden wedges,

Newbury Parkway bridge, c.1986. (Keith Pritchard)

Newbury, c.1960. (Michael Ware)

which should have formed the contact between the underside of the bridge and the girders, were, in fact, quite loose. The girders were not supporting the bridge in any way – the obstruction had clearly been unnecessary for years. However, doubts as to the strength of the bridge lingered on so it was not until 1966 that the obstruction was finally removed and unhindered passage was resumed.

While Parliament was discussing the legislation leading up to the Transport Act, the Newbury branch of the Worker's Educational Association organised a mock Parliamentary debate on the Bill in Newbury Town Hall. At John Gould's request, both Tom Rolt and Robert Aickman attended and addressed the meeting. The packed audience also listened to speeches given by MPs of all parties, together with representatives of other transport interests. The IWA's cause was the only contribution greeted with equal enthusiasm by members of all political parties and attracted prolonged applause.

Later, an IWA deputation to the Minister of Transport stressed, amongst other recommendations, that all existing navigations should be kept in first-class order for both commercial and pleasure traffic and that navigations no longer in use, owing to deterioration by neglect, should be restored.

A new threat appeared when Newbury Council was considering a replacement for the temporary bridge built over the canal beside Victoria Park. This bridge, with an air draught over the water which could be as low as 6.5ft (2m), had been erected in the early days of the war because of possible delays which would occur should the narrow Northbrook bridge, built in 1760, be damaged by war-time traffic; this was the only main road crossing of the canal for some miles in each direction. To save expense, the Finance and General Purposes Committee suggested that, as the canal was not now used for navigation, the council would be justified in urging that the existing statutory provisions should be amended to permit the construction of bridges over the waterway approximately 4ft (1.22m) above water level.

The IWA's and Newbury's opposition was swift and emphatic because, it was pointed out, the lowering of only one bridge would effectively close the waterway as a through route. The campaign was supported by the managing director of Hovis Ltd at West Mills, who argued that if the Kennet & Avon was more readily navigable, grain could be carried by water to

John Gould outside the Lock Cottage, Newbury.

Newbury from either Avonmouth or London, thus relieving the increasing congestion on roads and railways.

Bowing to the overwhelming opposition, the council's decision was reversed and the temporary auxiliary bridge was not replaced. The IWA was quick to take credit for the change of heart, stating that the struggle for the Kennet & Avon was of fundamental significance to the whole position of the country's waterways. When the proposed A34 relief road finally materialised in 1964, ample headroom was provided.

The low war-time bridge remained however, and it was not until late 1999/early 2000 that there were reports of West Berkshire County Council making British Waterways a proposal to reconstruct the bridge and increase the waterborne clearance. The final outcome depended on British Waterways and the council being able to find the necessary finance as the project was likely to be expensive, with the bridge containing many cables and services by that time.

In December 2000 British Waterways announced that during the period January to March 2001 the Parkway bridge would be refurbished and the headroom increased – over fifty years after the problem first became apparent!

As part of the IWA's campaign against the poor state of the canal, boat-owning members were invited to submit logs of through journeys. Philip Ogden, later to become the Canal Trust's honorary civil engineer, and Mrs Ogden canoed through in July 1947, submitting a lock by lock report. That same summer John Gould took an unofficial extended holiday to help bring the houseboat and cruiser *Tranquil* from Saltford on the Avon right through to the Thames. He did not risk reporting back for work on the canal! The IWA later published his comprehensive report.

Politicians were not slow to take advantage of public sentiment; the first item of the Labour Party policy in the November Newbury Municipal elections was to 'press for dredging and maintaining of the Kennet Canal [*sic*] in a decent state of repair for navigational purposes and also as a precaution against flooding'.

On 31 January 1948 a packed meeting was held in Newbury Public Library with John Gould in the chair, the speakers being supported by a comprehensive collection of interesting canal photographs which John and Win Gould had arranged around the walls. Robert Aickman addressed the meeting, referring to the greatly increased interest shown in Newbury. The former indifference, he said, had changed and restoration was being seriously considered. John Gould and W. Lester also made telling speeches and, apart from some objections raised by representatives of the former GWR, the meeting ended with great enthusiasm for the IWA cause. At about this time Lt Neville Davis, just retired from the RNVR, purchased the converted narrow boat *Callisto*, intending to live aboard with his family. Encouraged by enthusiasts at Newbury, he planned to navigate her from Wolvercote on the Oxford Canal. The Railway Executive at first refused *Callisto* entry to the Kennet & Avon on the spurious grounds that she was 70ft (21m) long while Kennet & Avon locks were only 69ft (20.7m) but when Neville quoted the passage of *Cressy* of similar dimensions in 1940 the authorities had to admit defeat.

The notorious Bridge Street girders were negotiated with only one inch to spare, with locks and swing-bridges requiring gangs of canal staff to operate them; it was not until a month later, in April 1948, that *Callisto* moored up just above West Mills swing-bridge in Newbury.

Accounts of craft through the canal at this period told how a large proportion of the canal staff were taken off their unending battle against time and decay to assist such passages. It is said that their enthusiasm far exceeded that of the canal authorities! Robert Aickman and Tom Rolt attended a meeting with the chairman of the Executive in May 1948, returning confident that co-operation between the IWA and the Executive was indeed possible and that at last a better future for the waterways seemed assured. The traditional discouragement and adverse treatment of applicants wishing to navigate the Kennet & Avon was to be a thing of the past and the case of everyone wishing to trade on the navigation would henceforth be sympathetically considered.

Fine as this first appeared, it soon became obvious that this sympathy did not apply to pleasure use; when Mrs Cavendish sought permission to row her skiff through the canal, every obstruction was placed in her way – prohibitive charges (an increase of 50% since November 1947), fearful stories of weed, a request that she should not use locks and finally the crippling information that she would not be allowed to navigate after 4pm on any weekday and 11am on a Saturday!

Despite this official opposition, and with IWA intervention, Mrs Cavendish persisted, rowing with her small son from Reading to Great Bedwyn and back to Newbury. She had nothing but praise for the help of all the lock-keepers and staff under Mr Carpenter, the local inspector.

Early in September 1948 the same gangs saw the narrow boat *Westminster*, the first trading craft on the canal for twelve years, on her way to Avonmouth to pick up a cargo of grain for the Hovis mill in Newbury. She arrived back late in October laden with ten tons of cargo, having taken eight working days on the journey. The most difficult section, due to low water and abundant weed, was the nine-mile pound from Bath to Bradford-on-Avon, but on the last day she covered the whole distance from Bedwyn to Newbury, accompanied by many small boats which escorted her return to a triumphal reception. A rather tongue-in-cheek letter from Charles Hulbert of Bristol commented on the voyage.

If only funds could be raised to cover the carriage of about a dozen such loads in succession over a period of three or four months, I am sure we would break down the opposition because nowadays the Railway Executive has to account to the Treasury for the money spent on hauling gangs. These, if continually employed for a few months, would soon set tongues wagging and

*initiate a series of newspaper comments, to say nothing of entirely disrupting normal mainte-
nance, because I understand carpenters, blacksmiths and stonemasons are all pressed into service.*

Messrs Robbins, Lane & Pinniger of Honey Street, the last remaining trader on the Kennet
& Avon, egged on by the IWA, had earlier claimed £18,000 for trade lost in the twelve years
up to December 1946 due to the condition of the canal. They also sought an injunction
restraining the Great Western Railway from impeding, obstructing or hindering the navigation and use of the canal between Hanham and Hungerford by failing to maintain it in the
condition agreed with the railway in 1929 to provide 3.5ft (1.07m) depth throughout. (It
should be noted that Section 17 of the Regulation of Railways Act of 1873 and the GWR
takeover agreement of 1852 placed an obligation on the owners to maintain navigation.)

They also asked for an order for the company to restore the canal to the condition stipulated in that undertaking. At the hearing on 11 January, Mr Justice Hilberry gave judgement
in favour of the plaintiffs, awarding them damages and costs but neither the injunction nor
order was granted.

The Railway Executive launched an appeal but meanwhile, on 28 February 1949, the canal
was transferred to the newly formed Docks & Inland Waterways Executive (DIWE) of the
British Transport Commission, who finally accepted responsibility for a full settlement
without a further court case.

Resisting the judgement, the Railway Executive had laid great stress on the alleged
shortage of water, but the IWA suggested that, although the water was short at times, levels
were deliberately kept down by the non-operation of pumps and a large unaccounted leak
on the summit level. Low water, they maintained, promoted weed growth and exposed the
clay puddle, which then cracked with the result that the general appearance of the canal
deterred anyone contemplating boating on it.

Mr W.G. Bennet, a solicitor and part-owner of *Westminster*, pointed out that the Railway
Executive had been able to escape from its obligation to maintain the canal for a payment of
£7,500, a very dangerous precedent, making it impossible to have questions asked in
Parliament relating to breaches of obligations to maintain canals.

3 The Kennet & Avon Branch of the IWA
1949–1951

Towards the end of 1948 there was a growing feeling amongst the Kennet & Avon Canal supporters in Newbury that although the IWA was the ideal forum for nationwide pressure on the Docks & Inland Waterways Executive, there was a need for a local body concerned mainly with the Kennet & Avon and its specific problems. In the *Newbury Weekly News* of 28 October 1948 the following notice appeared:

Inland Waterways

It is intended to form a local association to foster the navigation and use of the above with particular regard to the Kennet and Avon Navigation. Will those interested please write to the provisional Secretary, J.C. Lester.

At an inaugural meeting held in Newbury Library on 29 January 1949, Col. T.G. Clarke was in the chair and introduced Robert Aickman, who gave a concise 'history of the canal and its destruction [*sic*] by the Great Western Railway'. He stated that during the last twelve months the formerly hostile policy of the authorities had softened, maintenance had improved and several boats, including one commercial trader, had made the through passage.

Concerned lest fragmentation of the IWA into a number of local societies would considerably weaken its campaign, Aickman proposed that the local organization should be a branch of the main association and not a separate body. This was carried unanimously. John Lester was elected chairman and John Gould secretary. Other members of the executive committee were Neville Davis, Charles Hulbert representing the western end and J. Rogers representing the junior members. The objects of the branch were to foster interest in and use of the canal in the following manner:

1. Giving advice and help to would-be navigators.
2. Making representations, as occasion might arise, to the responsible authorities, it being felt that heretofore the efforts of individuals had carried insufficient weight and had been largely ineffective.
3. To compile a Kennet & Avon Pilot Book to be kept up to date by members and to circulate a Kennet & Avon newsheet.
4. To organise outings on the waterways.

Under the editorship of Neville Davis, the branch undertook the production of a regular typewritten newsletter to keep members informed of canal happenings. As the letter was to be the companion to the IWA bulletin, it seemed appropriate that it should be called the *Butty*, especially as the term 'butty' also related, in canal terms, to the companion vessel of a pair of canal narrow boats.

The *Butty* commented forthrightly on canal happenings as the following snippets show:

Issue 1, February 1949, reported that, after nearly one hundred years of GWR control, the canal had been transferred to the Docks & Inland Waterways Executive. As the Hovis grain run was not likely to be repeated, the narrow boat *Westminster* would leave for Reading the following weekend.

Issue 2, April 1949, stated that the Divisional Waterways Officer, South Western Division of the Docks & Inland Waterways Executive, had obtained the services of a geologist to study water supply problems on the canal summit; the branch offered to help.

Issue 3, May 1949, reported that a dredger was working on the long pound, just east of Devizes. Tyle Mill and some accommodation swing-bridges had been repaired or replaced. The Inland Waterways Executive were to standardise charges on the whole of the division's waterways.

Issue 4, June/July 1949, told how John Gould, encouraged by the improving state of the canal and wishing to see it used commercially, purchased three motor narrow boats and three butties from Harvey Taylor of Aylesbury, which, with the exception of the pair *Colin* and *Iris*, he advertised for sale.

Issue 5, August 1949, reported extensive weed cutting and the building of a new pair of gates for Woolhampton Lock at Aldermaston Wharf. The *Wiltshire Gazette*, always favourably disposed towards the Kennet & Avon, published an article stating that John Knill, owner of the narrow boats *Columba* and *Uranus*, was considering the trading prospects of the canal. Late in 1949 the old swing-bridge at the White House, Newbury, was replaced by the present overhead footbridge.

Issue 7, November/December 1949, told how a number of circumstantial reports had been received from both ends of the canal to the effect that maintenance was to be reduced to a minimum and that maintenance staff leaving would not be replaced. Robert Aickman had approached the Inland Waterways Executive who had assured him that the reports were greatly exaggerated and that no steps were contemplated which would result in any lowering of the standard of maintenance. The branch received similar assurances from the South Western Divisional Waterways Officer, A.C. Lisle. However, the branch hoped that instead of being lowered, the standard would be substantially raised, which they maintained could be done without any additional expenditure thereby producing extra revenue.

Also reported in *Butty* No.7 was the arrival from Birmingham of John Gould's *Colin*, with a cargo of sixteen tons of paving stones for Newbury Council. He had been assisted by George Day, who had taken the cruiser *Tudor Rose* through the canal in 1947 and repeated this feat with the narrow boats *Hesperus* and *Westminster* in 1948. John's journey from Reading to Newbury took twenty-two hours without the aid of a canal gang. Apart from some silting at the end of lock cuts, and difficulty with swing-bridges and extensive weed between Ham and Greenham Locks, the going was good despite *Colin* drawing some 3ft of water aft. This was, in all probability, the first cargo carried on this section of the Kennet & Avon Canal since 1927.

The trip was extensively reported, as was John's comment that this trial run showed that very little was required to make the waterway easily workable by loaded boats; as an interesting side comment on the cheapness of canal transport, John stated that the sixty-five-mile journey from Brentford to Reading had taken twenty hours and had used 3s 6d (35p) worth of fuel and this against the flow of the River Thames!

In February 1950, John Knill's *Columba* arrived with a cargo of twenty tons of salt from Middlewich for Newbury Laundry; this trip also received wide press coverage and John had reasonable hopes of making use of at least the Kennet section provided that the Inland

Waterways Executive co-operated, particularly in regard to the many swing-bridges, some of which were in a perilous state and difficult to operate.

Issue 8 deplored a new pontoon bridge placed across the canal at Aldermaston. There were then three such impediments – the 'floating bridge' (which seldom floated) at Honey Street, connecting the Barge Inn with the opposite bank, a bridge at Colthrop Paper Mills and this new one. These were far worse obstructions than swing-bridges since often no responsible person could be found to move them.

John Gould had negotiated a contract with T. Harrison Chapman to carry topsoil from Newbury gravel pits to Hampton Parish Wharf on the Thames. In April he wrote to the Inland Waterways Executive asking for a small job to be done in Newbury which would allow him to load. After three month's intensive effort which did not produce a result, Newbury Council kindly provided temporary wharfage by permitting the removal of some railings by St Nicholas Church, allowing the boats to lie alongside and the lorries tip straight into them. On his return from this first trip he found a letter from the Executive stating that, owing to their very bad condition, it had become necessary to close certain locks and in view of that there would be no useful purpose served in pursuing the question of wharfage. It was becoming obvious that the authorities were getting alarmed at the precedent of increased traffic making any future legal closure more difficult.

Also in April, Dr Roger Pilkington, author of the numerous *Small Boat* books, arrived in Newbury in the MY *Commodore*; she was 45ft (13.5m) long and at over 10ft (3.05m) beam was much wider than a narrow boat. Despite the maximum possible lowering of water levels and the flooding of her bilges, *Commodore* only just scraped under the Bridge Street girders after six men, including Reading's Deputy Borough Surveyor and members of his staff were taken on board as human ballast.

As part of a Whitsun rally, eight cruisers and two narrow boats left Blake's Lock at Reading on the Saturday bound for Newbury. One boat failed to get under the girders; another four, far behind their time schedule, turned back at Thatcham, leaving the remaining three cruisers and two narrow boats to reach Newbury. During the weekend, canal staff were forbidden to help and only superhuman efforts by branch members and others prevented the rally from becoming a complete failure before the visiting craft set off for home again on Tuesday. On 31 May the following notice appeared on most locks on the River Kennet section, on adjacent property and elsewhere on the navigation:

Docks and Inland Waterways Executive
Kennet & Avon Canal

Owing to the condition of Heales and other locks, the navigation will be closed from upstream of Heales Lock No.93, 13 miles, 50 chains from Reading, to downstream of Burghfield Lock No.103, 5 miles, 5 chains from Reading, until further notice. Dock Office, Gloucester. By Order 31 May 1950. AC Lisle DWO.

Predictably, both the branch and the Waterways Association protested adamantly but all to no avail and similarly the local MPs, Anthony Hurd and Christopher Hollis, could not get an answer in the House of Commons as to the likely duration of the stoppage. Some weeks later the Inland Waterways Executive stated that the affected locks would be reconditioned or repaired, but not until after mid-1951.

On 29 July John Knill's *Columba Kenelm* arrived in Reading with cargoes of salt for Newbury but, because of the stoppage, the salt had to be carried onward by road and at the same time John Gould's contract to deliver topsoil was completed by using the returning road transport to deliver the material to John Knill's boats in Reading, which then carried it on to its destination at Hampton. Meanwhile John Gould's boats remained isolated within the Newbury area.

Although the four Wootton Rivers Locks were extensively renovated in 1951 and were reported to be in first class order, the Inland Waterways Executive instruction issued in April 1951 to the engineering staff stated that maintenance on the canal should be confined to work necessary on safety grounds alone with no view to assisting navigation. A letter from the divisional engineer to the Devizes inspector requested:

> *Will you please arrange to prevent the access of any boats into the length between Bradford-on-Avon and the top lock at Devizes. This can be done by the erection of some sort of barrier or by securing the appropriate lock gates so that they cannot be opened. It is not proposed to erect stoppage notices for the length in question, but you will be quite in order to prevent craft entering the length until you receive further instructions.*

The demise of yet another swing-bridge was foreshadowed when, against the advice of the canal authority, Thames Conservancy staff attempted to move a heavy excavator across Hungerford station swing-bridge. Predictably, the bridge collapsed completely, dropping the machine into the canal from where, only with the greatest difficulty, it was extricated some days later. Initially, whilst awaiting the construction of a new bridge, a temporary footbridge was installed which had to be removed each time boat passage was required although it was later raised sufficiently to permit free boat passage.

At the IWA's headquarters the hitherto close relationship between Robert Aickman and Tom Rolt came under increasing strain due not only to the amount of work that the new organisation was creating but also on matters of policy. At the AGM held in May 1950 Tom Rolt announced that he would retire as honorary secretary as soon as a suitable replacement had completely taken over from him. However, after an exchange of heated letters between the two men, Tom resigned from the council in July. On his retirement as IWA secretary the Newbury branch passed the following resolution on 29 November 1950:

> *Expressing its appreciation of the services of Mr L.T.C. Rolt as a co-founder of the IWA and as Hon. Secretary during the first four years of its existence and regrets the necessity for him to resign.*

By classifying Rolt as a co-founder and siding with his views the branch incurred Aickman's disapproval and, after some further unpleasantness, a small meeting was held at Newbury Lock on 11 August 1951; this decided to wind up the Kennet & Avon branch of the IWA and form a new association. Those present were: Major Addington, John Lester, John Gould, K. Allen, A. Barnes, J. Rogers, W. Crocker, L. Daniels, R. Shepherd and Mr Wood.

A week later an official public meeting was held in the lecture hall of the Newbury Congregational Church to inaugurate and form the Kennet & Avon Canal Association; the speaker was Charles Hadfield and his subject, 'The Kennet & Avon, Past and Future'. This event was a bitter disappointment to Robert Aickman who had not only agreed to take the Kennet & Avon under his wing but also had constantly advocated the restoration policy of equal priorities for all waterways lest the advantage of concerted action be lost.

Although the formation of branches relieved the IWA headquarters of much of the demand for local matters, Robert was never happy over the possibility of independent action and was quite lukewarm towards the formation of additional offshoots. According to David Bolton, author of *Race Against Time*, Robert was to write many years later that 'everything depended on finding the right individuals to run the branches.' In the case of the Kennet & Avon, as subsequent events were to show, the formation of a separate association worked out quite well, but probably only because this was a major waterway detached from the main system and with all the necessary qualifications for restoration. The reader who wishes to delve more deeply into the events surrounding the campaign to save Britain's canal system will find a very full account of the formation of the IWA and the story of the ensuing battle in David Bolton's *Race Against Time*, published by Methuen (IBSN 0-413-63470-1).

4 The Kennet & Avon Canal Association 1951-1957

The objects of the Kennet & Avon Canal Association were defined as working for the greater use, maintenance and development of the inland waterways of the British Isles; in particular to promote a wider knowledge of the Kennet & Avon together with a greater use and extension of its amenities. John Lester was elected to be the first chairman and the initial membership stood at forty-seven.

During October the *Butty*, the newsletter of the former IWA branch, was replaced by *Kennet & Avon News*. The first issue reported good progress with the restoration of Burghfield and Heales Locks, with Garston Lock also being completely renovated with new top and bottom gates whilst the railway bridge at Bulls Lock was being reconstructed as a single span. There was more cheerful news as at Bulls Lock the masonry and brickwork were being repaired and the sides of Widmead Lock raised to the proper height. The flight of locks at Crofton had also been renovated and this included the fitting of several pairs of new gates. All worked well except at the bottom three locks where work had not been completed owing to unusual spring flood water; these, however, were passable with the assistance of the lengthman.

However, all was not universally well. Although the side ponds at Devizes were badly silted, dredging had been discontinued and of the dredgers formerly at work on the canal, two were removed to Gloucester and another, immobilized, lay above Burghfield Lock.

When Berkshire County Council wished to reconstruct Aldermaston and Padworth swing-

Immobilised dredger at Burghfield Lock. (David Harris)

Burghfield Lock. (K&ACT Archives)

bridges, the Inland Waterways Executive pointed out that their liability was limited to the provision of bridges capable of carrying traffic of a century ago. Should the council require that they be brought up to a standard more fitting for modern needs then, the Inland Waterways Executive insisted, the council would have to meet the additional cost. The building of the Atomic Weapons Research Establishment at Aldermaston highlighted another bridge problem as it was estimated that two thousand tons of construction traffic per day would use Thatcham swing-bridge, the replacement of which had been delayed by a shortage of steel.

In an attempt to overcome the problem, a temporary bridge was built beside the old one which was used to carry the laden contractor's vehicles whilst unladen vehicles used the old bridge with its four-ton weight limit.

As the canal here was, theoretically, open for traffic, the temporary bridge was built so that the centre span could be floated away on pontoons and was positioned to allow the old bridge to be swung. However, it is extremely unlikely that this provision was ever utilised because in May 1951 Greenham swing-bridge collapsed, thus effectively blocking the waterway completely; a replacement Thatcham swing-bridge was not installed until 1954.

Worse was to follow. In April 1952 the mitre post of Higgs Lock fractured and, despite many requests, was not repaired so the stern-wheeler *Wayfarer*, belonging to Major Addington and managed by John Gould, was craned around the unusable lock and for the rest of that year cruised as far as Devizes on more than one occasion.

The locks at Heales and Burghfield were completed by contractors in March 1952; the former was a major rebuild involving much brickwork, but the latter was a rather unsatisfactory botch. The litany of misfortune continued when a tumbling bay at Colthrop collapsed and all staff were taken off other work to deal with it. Later in the year, Fobney and Southcote Locks at Reading were declared unsafe and closed and as a final straw the bottom gates of Padworth Lock collapsed – it was to be July 1953 before the canal was usable again from Reading up to Sulhamstead Lock. In July 1952 a permanent overhead bridge of brick,

Limpley Stoke, c.1950.
(K&ACT Archives)

concrete and steel replaced the temporary Hungerford station bridge and a decision by the Inland Waterways Executive that derelict swing-bridges should be replaced wherever possible by overhead ones led to Greenham bridge being rebuilt as an overhead.

In September 1952, the *Wiltshire Gazette* published a joint letter from John Lester, Association Chairman, and Keith Allen, Association Secretary, who had recently taken over that position from John Gould. Their letter outlined the work of the association, now a year old, and explained that, although up to then its attention had been confined to the east end of the canal, it was now time to extend the membership to the west.

A meeting was called at Wilcot which resulted in the Vale of Pewsey branch being formed with Professor Steeds from the College of Military Science, Shrivenham, as chairman. At this meeting John Gould reported that he had explored the canal and found everything west of Devizes to be in a reasonable working condition but nevertheless it was decided that further branches were needed to the west with Devizes, Bradford-on-Avon, Bath and the Avon being suggested.

In November the first of the new branches was formed to cover Devizes and District with Dr Hancock, President of the Devizes Angling Association, as chairman.

With the formation of new branches, there was a need for a revised constitution to include them; this was drafted by Keith Allen and adopted at the AGM in July 1953. It set up a council on which all the branches would be represented. The branches would deal with affairs in their designated areas but in all matters concerning the wider interests of the association they should work with and through the council. The first chairman of the Kennet & Avon Canal Association was Professor Steeds with Keith Allen as secretary.

The Inland Waterways Executive ceased to exist in September 1953 following the 1952 Transport Bill which set up the British Transport Commission whose waterway interests were transferred to a new body – The British Transport Waterways (BTW).

On 30 November 1953 a deputation of MPs from Reading and Newbury and representatives from the association, together with the association's solicitor met the Transport Commission's deputy chairman, Sir John Benstead, and Sir Reginald Hill (previously the Inland Waterways Executive chairman).

The case was presented for more rapid completion of repairs so that the canal might be opened as a through route between London and Bristol with improved maintenance so that minor defects and difficulties might be remedied; the deputation was received with courtesy and consideration and probably with some mystification. It was later remarked by a canal employee that 'the bosses know nothing about canals having been brought in from road services and the Army, and as a consequence hold everything up because they haven't a clue what to do.'

In April 1954 Anthony Hurd MP was told that an official reply must await the report of a survey ordered by the Minister of Transport. It was too soon to know how long the survey of inland waterways would take; in the meanwhile restoration work between Reading and Newbury had been suspended apart from the essential repairs to sluices at Fobney and Burghfield.

The Board of Survey consisted of Lord Rusholme, Sir Rex Hedges (formerly of the Manchester Ship Canal Co.) and Mr Ives from the Gloucester office. The terms of reference were:

> To survey the use at present being made of the Commission's inland waterways and to report to the Chairman of the Commission whether all possible steps were being taken to ensure that the maximum economic advantage was being derived from the canal system under the Commission's inland waterways which could no longer be put to economic commercial use.

The association's case outlined the recent history of the canal and advanced three main arguments:

1. Abandonment by Act of Parliament had been tried by the GWR in 1926 and failed. The economics of closure were largely illusory.
2. Continuation of the present policy was a breach of at least ten statutes. By obstructing a public navigation the Transport Commission were probably liable to an automatic penalty of £5 per hour.
3. The present maintenance expenditure was not far short of the sum required to put the canal, and maintain it, in good order. However, despite the threat of work being suspended, in the latter half of 1954 various improvements did materialise. The twenty-five-year-old gates of Newbury Lock were replaced and five swing-bridges at Dundas aqueduct, Lower Foxhangers, Hisseys, (between Burghfield and Theale) and at Fobney and Southcote Locks were all rebuilt.

In October 1954, following a packed public meeting in Bath, a new branch was formed there. Lord Sidmouth who, as Major Addington was one of the initial founders of the association, was elected chairman; Cllr Smith as vice chairman; and Messrs W. Frances, J.A. Brodie and S.F. Charlton as joint secretaries and treasurers. In the same month, due to difficulties in stopping persistent leaks between Limpley Stoke bridge and Avoncliff aqueduct, the section was drained and it was apparent that there was little intention to re-water it.

On 15 December 1954 the *Daily Telegraph* published a report that the Transport Commission intended to abandon the whole of the Reading to Bath section of the Kennet & Avon, a report at first vehemently denied. John Gould was persuaded to initiate a High Court action against the British Transport Commission on the grounds that as owners they had failed to keep it open. He asked for an interim injunction to halt further deterioration.

On 13 April 1955 the report of the Rusholme Board of Survey was published; although it did contain a vast quantity of statistics now available for the very first time, the news for the Kennet & Avon was devastating.

The main recommendation divided the waterways into four groups:

1. 336 miles to be developed.
2. 994 miles, including the River Avon, to be retained.
3. 771 miles, including the Reading to Bath section of the Kennet & Avon, to be closed to navigation.
4. The Scottish Canals to be transferred to the Secretary of State for Scotland.

Both national and local press commented unfavourably, reporting that Lord Rusholme was in fact an employee of the Transport Commission.

The association objected to a change in the terms of reference, to the method of employment of the Board's members and to their ignoring the association's evidence. The IWA maintained that the retention of the 994 miles was simply the first step in abandoning them as well. Protest meetings were held all along the canal.

When John Gould's case was heard before Mr Justice Roxburgh he refused to grant the injunction but heavily criticised The British Transport Commission. The *Times* of 23 July 1955 reported:

Mr Justice Roxburgh in a reserved judgement said that the plaintiff, since 1949, had been in business as a canal carrier at Newbury, Berkshire, and he owned two canal barges on the Kennet & Avon canal. A canal carrier operating westward from Newbury came to a full stop at Higgs Lock which became impassable through want of repair in April 1952. The defendants well knew, he [his Lordship] was sure, that their failure to repair it was unlawful, but they hoped, he supposed, that no bargee would be able to find means to contest their inaction in the High Court. If this was their hope, it was frustrated when the legal aid scheme came to the rescue of this village Hampden, if Newbury would pardon that description. 'Is it right?' Sir Andrew Clark had asked during the course of the hearing 'to spend thousands of pounds merely because one man wants to sail a couple of boats on it?' [His Lordship's] answer to that tendentious proposition was: if that was the law, then it was the duty of a statutory monopoly to obey it, just as much as anyone else; indeed, if possible, even more so because its opportunities of getting the law altered would appear to be greater. That the law probably required alteration seemed clear, but that a statutory monopoly should practise and justify statute-breaking was surely pessime exempli. *This attitude, voiced by both Sir Andrew Clark and Mr Hayward, had permeated the whole of the defence in this case and gave it some measure of constitutional importance. If everybody was to settle for himself whether the law was worthy of obedience chaos would supplant the rule of law. No doubt it was hard for the defendants to be saddled at birth with a canal which was moribund, if not derelict, but such was the will of Parliament and they could never have been in doubt as to the nature or extent of the obligation imposed on them. In 1950 the defendants had wrongfully closed the section of canal between Heales and Burghfield Locks. About 1951 the locks between the top lock Devizes and Bradford inclusive were closed and the lock-keepers were unlawfully instructed not to allow traffic to pass. In April 1952 Higgs Lock became unusable and had not since been repaired. The section of the canal between Newbury and Bath had thus been unlawfully closed since summer 1951. Meanwhile what steps were The Transport Commission or its offshoots taking to regularize this statute breaking? In June 1948 The Transport Commission were advised by the Railway Executive to seek powers to close the canal to navigation between Reading and Bath. A number of investigations were carried out by the Inland Waterways Executive between*

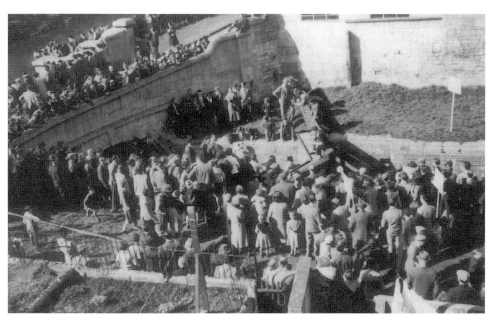

Lock 7, Bath, Easter 1955. (K&ACT Archives)

1949 and 1952 and some works of repair were executed. In November the defendants had decided to apply for powers to close the canal. Before [his Lordship] they had admitted breaches of statutory duty and by their defence they offered to submit to an enquiry as to damages but they resisted any injunctions with or without suspension. Apparently they preferred to persist in their admittedly unlawful conduct and await the action for damages which, unless Parliament intervened, any bona fide who wished to use the canal and tendered the toll would hereafter be able to bring against them with good hope of success. Whether the Court would countenance this could only be decided at the trial.

The plaintiff had overreached himself in launching this motion by which he sought to prevent further deterioration of the canal pending trial. In the first place he was too late for interlocutory relief because he had been effectively barred from the section of the canal with which [his Lordship] was concerned in 1952. He did not begin his action until 1 July 1955. Secondly, no relief which could be granted could benefit him at all because his boats could not get westward beyond Higgs Lock and no relief was asked in respect of Higgs Lock. The further deterioration of the canal between now and the trial could not affect one or the other his chance of obtaining an injunction then, with or without suspension.

The hearing was then adjourned until 20 October but the trial never took place. John Gould's case was discussed out of court and, in consideration of an immediate payment to John of £5,000 and costs, he agreed that he would not press for action until the end of 1956 when the Transport Commission would be able to see whether there was any future for the canal.

From the earliest days the association had realised that public support was of the utmost importance and so it became increasingly adept at organizing events and stage-managing occasions which would either draw the canal to the public's attention or embarrass the powers-that-be with a demonstration of their inept management of the waterway.

At Easter 1955, the Bath branch planned such an assault on the canal authority. Seven or eight cruisers from the Cabot Cruising Club would make their way from Bristol to the padlocked bottom lock in Bath. The intention to do so was communicated to British

THE BUTTY

THE OFFICIAL BULLETIN OF THE KENNET AND AVON CANAL ASSOCIATION.

No. 1 (FOLLOWING NEWBURY BULLETIN No. 9 AND BATH BULLETIN No. 2) JANUARY, 1956.

20,000
SIGNED

. . . and the crew wave as the auxiliary cutter "Foam" prepared to leave Bristol for Bath with our Petition to H.M. the Queen on Saturday, January 14th, protesting against the proposed closing of the KENNET AND AVON CANAL.

Photo by the Western Daily Press

The Butty, *January 1956.*

Transport Waterways in writing, with the Conservative MPs for Newbury, North Somerset, Devizes, Reading North and Bath also invited to attend the party.

The threat produced more activity than the canal at Bath had seen for years! On 4 April the locks were declared dangerous and, the following day, Transport Waterways staff removed paddles and paddle gear to thwart any attempt to negotiate the locks. However, if the canal authorities thought that this would alleviate the situation, they were doomed to disappointment, because on Easter Monday over a thousand people packed bridges and towpaths as, under the eye of television cameras, twenty craft approached the bottom lock.

Cllr Smith, Ted Leather, MP for North Somerset, and John Brodie of the Kennet & Avon Association proffered the requisite toll, £140 in cash, and after a short speech by Ted Leather the securing chain on the lock was ceremoniously cut to allow the first boat to pass into the inoperable lock.

When Ted Leather later stated in the House of Commons that the Transport Commission was deliberately removing important equipment from the canal to strengthen its case that it could not be kept open, Mr Boyd-Carpenter, Minister of Transport and Civil Aviation, replied that no such action was or would be contemplated!

Support grew for the association's strong opposition to the Transport Commission's proposal to abandon the Kennet & Avon with a new branch being formed at a public meeting in Reading Town Hall on 25 November 1955. The chair was taken by Cllr S.A. Smith of the association's Bath & Bristol branch, with Capt. L.R. Munk (Managing Director of Maid Line Cruisers) elected Reading Branch Chairman and Denys Hutchings as Branch Secretary.

The Transport Commission Private Bill, published in December, sought authority to prepare a scheme to abandon the canal but, because the canal was not navigable, they asked to be excused from the liability for paying compensation for the five years requested to prepare the scheme. However, Anthony Hurd, Newbury's MP, suggested that the Transport

Commission should only be excused provided that they accepted an undertaking to continue essential maintenance to prevent further deterioration: nothing would be easier, he said, than to let the banks fall in and allow the higher stretches of the canal to run dry thus claiming after five years that whatever possibilities for the canal that had existed had now disappeared.

In January 1956, the *Butty* was reinstated as the official bulletin of the association. Edited by John Brodie, it replaced the branch newsletters and the first issue was chiefly concerned with the petition against the Bill organised by the association which had secured more than twenty-two thousand signatures. Most of these signatures were from localities close to the canal and were bound in two loose-leaf albums, with a text which read:

> *We, Your Gracious Majesty's liege people, do offer unto your Majesty our humble duty and loyalty, and humbly petition your Majesty to exercise Your ancient and Royal Prerogative, as Your Majesty's ancestors have oft times done since time immemorial, of the Conservancy of Navigation, as in MAGNA CARTA provided, utterly to put down all dams and other obstructions whatsoever to the Navigation of the Kennet & Avon Canal in the Counties of Somersetshire, Wiltshire and Berkshire, which said canal is now obstructed and blocked up to the great prejudice to Your Majesty's Liege people in the neighbourhood in the exercise of their lawful occasions and rights of passage and of fishery and which Your petitioners fear will become an offence and a danger to health if not cleansed and repaired as by Parliament provided.*
>
> *And we Your loyal subjects and humble petitioners will ever pray for Your Majesty's wellbeing and for the commonwealth.*

The petition left Bristol on 14 January 1956 and was taken by cabin cruiser to Bath. From Bath to Thames Ditton it was carried by canoe, navigated by Cdr C. Wray-Bliss and Cdr J.P. Shenton, and there were frequent stops along the way to allow dignitaries and others to show their support. At Thames Ditton the canoe, complete with the petition safely stowed within, was loaded on to one of Capt. Munk's Maid Line cruisers and transported down the Thames to Westminster, a journey of 157 miles which took twelve days. Upon arrival in Westminster, the canoe was carried through the streets to the Ministry of Transport in Berkeley Square where the petition was handed over to the Minister, Harold Watkinson, with a request that it be forwarded to Her Majesty – press, film, radio and television coverage was extensive.

Continuing pressure from all sides brought results and on 1 February Harold Watkinson announced the setting up of an independent enquiry into the future of the inland waterways under the chairmanship of Leslie Bowes who was Managing Director of the Pacific Steam Navigation Co. The terms of reference of the enquiry were:

1. To consider and report on the future of the country's system of inland waterways and to make proposals for any measure to achieve:
   (i) the maximum use of the system;
   (ii) the future administration of and financial arrangements for such inland waterways as cannot be maintained economically for transport purposes, having regard in partic-ular to the requirements of public health and safety and to the facilities which these waterways can provide for purposes other than transport, such as recreation, water supply, land drainage and disposal of effluents;
   (iii) the conversion of canal sites to other purposes when this is considered desirable and practicable.
2. To consider the present law relating to the closing of waterways to navigation and to make recommendations.

At the second reading of the Transport Commission Bill in March, the House of Commons forced the removal of the clause which would have empowered the commission to prepare a scheme for the future of the Kennet & Avon. This, in effect, reprieved the canal, at least pending the report of the Bowes Commission. Later, the Select Committee on the Bill added the provision that the Transport Commission should allow no further deterioration and suspended its obligation to keep the canal open for navigation until 1960.

Continuing opposition, including that of John Gould who now ploughed back almost all of the £5,000 damages won earlier from the Transport Commission, resulted in further modifications stating that the right of navigation should remain, as far as it was navigable, in its present state and the Transport Commission were also to maintain a sufficient flow of water to preserve the amenity value.

In May, John Gould and Mr Clayton, the British Transport Waterways divisional engineer, met in Newbury when it was agreed that West Mills swing-bridge should be rebuilt and Greenham Lock repaired. However, British Transport Waterways refused to consider the repair of Bulls Lock, which was said to require new gates. When the Revd F.A. Roughton then offered to pay for the repairs to the lock, British Transport Waterways quoted him the sum of £1,000 although a firm of civil engineers gave a written opinion that the disputed gates were in fact serviceable and could be repaired for about £60 plus a few days labour. BTW stubbornly refused to allow such a repair and, about a week later, some 'unknown persons' who had 'recourse to tools', including drills, punctured the gates making them quite unusable and then, as the lock was now 'dangerous', BTW staff removed all the paddle gear.

Maintenance was, by general admission, unsatisfactory over the whole length of the canal with essential work often neglected or carried out in a thoroughly extravagant and inefficient manner. It was said that whilst purpose-designed maintenance craft lay derelict and neglected, men and materials which should have been carried on the canal itself were carried by hired road transport.

Stories also abound of skilled labour being misused and work being poorly carried out. At Burghfield Lock, rebuilt in 1952, the downstream sills had been replaced with concrete slabs which were laid without any supporting piling. The water pressure in the filled lock caused some of the gravel under the sill to be blown out thus inducing a leak which became steadily worse as time passed.

At Greenham Lock there was a sorry tale of a replacement balance beam being ordered from Gloucester. An ex-telegraph pole was found and dispatched by road to Newbury where it was unloaded one Saturday morning by a specially engaged team on overtime rates. Unfortunately, possibly for ease of transport, the pole had been cut into two and was thereby useless. Then some days later somebody remembered that there was a perfectly acceptable beam lying in the Newbury Depot; this was recovered and, in the short space of a day, the beam was replaced, but it was all to little avail as the lock remained unusable because some necessary repair work to a nearby bridge had yet to be started.

The 1957 AGM of the association found Dr Hancock elected as chairman with John Brodie as secretary. Immediately, John Brodie commenced the onerous task of co-ordinating the evidence for the Bowes Committee. He was assisted by John Gould who submitted extensive written and oral evidence which dealt with the potential traffic, both commercial and pleasure, together with fishing interests.

The association were quick to confront the Government or any of the local authorities if the need arose. To challenge these authorities on equal terms the association was able to call upon the professional services of many supporters who were highly qualified experts in many fields.

During 1957 one such supporter, Cyril Boucher, a leading canal consultant, Hon. Engineer to the IWA and the first Hon. Consulting Engineer of the Kennet & Avon Canal

Association, carried out an extensive survey of the entire length of the canal, submitting a very detailed report on conclusion. Cyril was highly qualified, being a Fellow and past President of the Society of Engineers as well as a member of both the Institution of Civil and Structural Engineers and a Fellow of the Institute of Arbitrators. His report stated that in his opinion the canal was still a sound engineering proposition suffering only from neglect; £325,000, he considered, would restore it to a state capable of carrying a million tons of cargo per year.

His summary, however, asserted that just to restore the canal to its original condition was only to perpetuate its original faults and limitations. It would be, he said, an acme of folly to repeat the designs and methods of an age when civil engineering was in its infancy. Cyril considered that it was possible to repair and modify the waterway using modern methods, techniques and materials at a capital and maintenance cost which could compete successfully with other means of transport and so form a valuable link in the nation's transport system.

But the scheme depended on the departure from the normal accepted practice prevalent at that time and, amongst the more significant suggestions, considered that only powered craft be allowed, replacement of damaged lock gates should use modern materials and designs, quicker means of operating locks must be provided and the canal must operate a twenty-four-hour day as on roads and railways. Finally some locks must be eliminated to provide a quicker and more efficient method for the transport of goods and this included a tramway to replace some locks on the Devizes Flight.

The report considered that, whereas the use of conventional boats for local carriage was reasonable, for longer journeys it may be more efficient to use 'tubs' capable of being coupled together into 'trains' which, in charge of a tug, could pass through the intervening locks and pounds.

At Devizes, however, when the 'train' arrived at the top or bottom of Caen Hill – at either Lock 28 or Lock 46 – a travelling crane would lift the tubs out of the water and place them in pairs on rail cars standing on an adjacent track. The entire train would then be conveyed, either up or down Caen Hill to the other terminal where a similar crane would return the tubs to the water to continue their journey.

The tubs with a pay load of about ten tons each needed to be tightly coupled in 'tows' of three which, with the provision of a false bow, could then either be pushed or pulled to its destination, the whole assembly being capable of safe and rapid uncoupling on arrival in a terminal dock.

For transport between the terminals a double track railway would be laid with an endless wire rope using the motive power of a normal haulage engine situated at the upper terminal. Normal wharf cranes would be suitable and two working together could lift greater loads so that some larger types of pleasure craft could also be dealt with.

It was thought that using this system a through passage from the Avon to the Thames might be made in as little as forty-four hours, allowing an average speed of 3mph and for fifteen minutes to pass each lock. The saving it was estimated would be nearly eight hours against using the Devizes Flight in a conventional manner and of course considerable economies in lockage water.

However, during 1958 there was a blow, not only to the scheme but to the vital operation of the canal when the Crofton pumping station chimney, declared to be unsafe, had approximately 30ft removed from the top; the resulting loss of draught to the boilers forced the shutdown of the steam-driven pumps and consequently, the navigation.

Reports of the time tell how British Transport Waterways were enthusiastically taking advantage of not having to maintain the navigation by building brick dams across the heads of four locks between Bedwyn Church and Dunmill rather than replace the gates. On other locks the Waterways Authorities utilized methods which included cutting off the balance

The Enterprise *at Burghfield, c.1958.* (K&ACT Archives)

beams, thus rendering them unworkable.

Later that year, instead of repairing Widmead Lock, BTW installed a timber dam. Formerly the top paddles of this lock were used to relieve flood water into the canal below and, to compensate for the loss of this facility, the river dam known as 'Dog Head Stakes' was modified, which affected the water level between Widmead and Bulls Locks lowering it by about 2ft; this was to prove an embarrassment later.

About this time Ran Meinertzhagen approached the South Western Division of British Transport Waterways to explore the possibility of running passenger trips between Reading and Burghfield, needless to say he met with obstructions and excuses to the effect that use on this scale was quite impossible. He then navigated the length in a motor launch accompanied by the association's newly elected President, Lord Methuen, together with other witnesses and, having completed the journey, he contacted BTW London Headquarters who directed Gloucester to co-operate. The boat used was the specially converted 70ft (21m) narrow boat *Enterprise*, modified to be able to pass under the Bridge Street bridge girders. The inauguration of the service took place in March 1958 when *Enterprise* was accompanied by two cargo-carrying narrow boats belonging to Willow Wren. The three boats carried about 200 passengers, including the Mayor of Reading, and this new traffic did much to raise the morale of canal staff. However, at Whitsun in 1955 the poorly repaired bottom cill of Burghfield Lock finally cracked and later, when *Enterprise* was locked through, all passengers were required to disembark. It was not until August Bank Holiday 1959 that association volunteers and BTW staff removed the defective cill and replaced it with a new wooden one, thus opening up safe navigation once again as far as Sulhamstead.

5 The Redevelopment Plan 1958–1962

The Bowes Report was published in July 1958. It divided waterways into three classes similar to those quoted in the earlier Rusholme Report. In class A were 380 miles, presently earning a surplus of about £300,000 pa and already benefiting from the Transport Commission's £5.5 million improvement scheme. This class included the River Avon.

Class B included 930 miles, mainly narrow canals, with an annual loss of £300,000. These, Bowes said, should be restored within five years to enable full loads to be carried and with a commitment that they should be maintained to that standard for twenty-five years. Instead of tolls, an annual licence of £1 per ton capacity should be paid for each boat. This would increase the loss to £500,000 pa; restoration would cost £3.5 million.

All other waterways were class C, with the remainder sections of the Kennet & Avon being the only one to merit special attention. According to Section 174:

> We have not attempted to discuss the problems of individual waterways of England and Wales. The fate of the Kennet & Avon canal, however, has aroused so much public interest that we think it right, exceptionally, to make specific reference to it. We have found no justification for restoring the section from Reading to Bath as a through navigation, and we cannot recommend that the waterway should be included in the prescribed navigable system. It is pre-eminently a case for redevelopment, in the course of which all factors would be taken fully into account, and it may well be decided that different treatments should be applied to various sections which have widely differing characteristics. The redevelopment procedure would give due weight to amenity and recreational values.

Four members of the committee, including the chairman, wanted the nationalised canals to remain under the Transport Commission while the other four thought that ownership should be transferred to a new independent Corporation. Canals, they argued, had little to do with the commission's activities. The *Times* later called the canals a 'Cinderella', deliberately neglected in favour of the ugly sisters – road and rail!

The association welcomed the report, considering that an overwhelming case had been made for the retention of the Kennet & Avon as a navigable link between the Thames & Severn for pleasure traffic and other amenities, agreeing also that the waterway should not be vested in the Transport Commission but that an independent body such as the National Trust should act in a holding and administrative capacity to its greater benefit.

Support for this proposal came when Sir Reginald Kerr, General Manager of the Transport Commission said that if the Transport Commission could restrict its activities to the main waterways and get rid of non-commercial (although beautiful) backwaters such as the Kennet & Avon, then the canals could be made to pay.

John Brodie, the association's secretary set about preparing a case to present to the National Trust, and at the same time he initiated an appeal for funds as the association's coffers were exhausted. Unfortunately a year later, at the association's AGM in 1959, John Brodie had to tender his resignation due to business pressures.

Since the founding of the Bath branch in 1954, he had worked tirelessly for the association, besides preparing the case for the Bowes Commission. He had also edited four issues of the *Butty* and prepared the dossier for the National Trust who had earlier expressed an interest in the canal, although this interest was later withdrawn.

Ran Meinertzhagen was elected honorary secretary in John Brodie's place and at the following council meeting Dr Hancock withdrew his offer for re-election and Capt. Munk was elected chairman, with Dr Ray Glaister taking over as honorary treasurer.

1959 ended with the welcome news of new gates being installed at Colthrop and Ham Locks.

The Bowes Committee had advised that all waterways should have a case-by-case review to determine to what use each could best be put and to formulate detailed schemes for putting redevelopment into effect. The full co-operation of all the interests concerned in the redevelopment should be sought and appropriate financial contributions obtained from those who would enjoy facilities or amenities provided by the redeveloped waterway.

It was also considered proper to expect appropriate financial contributions from those who, due to redevelopment, would then be relieved of continuing liabilities. Significantly, the committee had thus broken away from the previous negative concept of abandonment and were suggesting instead the new and positive approach of redevelopment. In a White Paper of 23 January 1959 the Government agreed to these recommendations and proposed an interim policy to be tried out experimentally over two years.

An Inland Waterways Redevelopment Advisory Committee was to be set up to assist in the promotion of schemes, to consider such when formulated, and to make recommendations on them to the Minister concerned. It would consist of members knowledgeable about the various interests concerned with redevelopment, including local authorities, boat owners and operators, industry, farming, land drainage and others. The cost of redevelopment would be borne by those who benefited from it, and any general legislation introduced later would be framed on this basis, taking into account, however, that in some cases a scheme might serve a diversity of functions whose costs could not be entirely matched by payments from the

Ham Lock, 1980. (K&ACT Archives)

Widmead Lock, 1988. (K&ACT Archives)

interests concerned. In that case the Government would be prepared, in principle, to bridge a small gap by a special ad hoc grant towards the capital cost of redevelopment.

Bowes recognized that canals could be redeveloped for amenity and recreation but it was important that voluntary organisations, including those who use the waterway for angling or other recreations, should take the opportunities for joint effort and contribution in the preparation of these schemes.

The question of future administration of the canals, whether by the Transport Commission or by an independent body, which would require legislation, was left open. Following the Bowes Report, the attitude of the Transport Commission changed dramatically – now they were prepared to carry out navigational improvements, provided always that the association paid for them with the Transport Commission providing a contribution.

The estimates for some of the outstanding jobs at this time are as follows and make interesting reading:

1. Bulls Lock – make and fit new pair of top gates, reset coping stones and carry out some minor repairs to the bottom gates – £500.
2. Guyers and Higgs Locks – refit complete sets of gates and clear chambers – £1,200 each.

As it was felt that the association's efforts should be concentrated on linking Reading with Newbury, the Hon. Secretary was asked to obtain a quotation for putting Widmead Lock in order. However, the association's total assets at this time only amounted to the princely sum of £24.

The association, about to undertake major capital expenditure, acknowledged that its constitution should be rewritten to allow the raising of the large sums of money and perhaps it should be formed into a company limited by guarantee. The secretary was asked to approach a solicitor with a view to obtaining a draft constitution. In March 1959 the Inland Waterway Redevelopment Advisory Committee was formed under the chairmanship of Admiral Sir Frederick Parham. Other members included Capt. Munk, Association

Chairman; Wg Cdr Grant-Ferris, MP for Nantwich; John Smith, Reading branch President; and Tom Rolt. The terms of reference were:

1. To assist as necessary in the promotion of schemes for the treatment of inland waterways which cannot economically be maintained for commercial use.
2. To consider such schemes when formulated.
3. To make recommendations to Ministers concerned.
4. To advise Ministers upon any general matter connected with the redevelopment of these waterways.

Although the Kennet & Avon would not be one of the first waterways considered, it was realised that the association should immediately consider making out its case. A sub-committee comprising Lord Methuen, Cdr Wray-Bliss, P. Hawkins of Bath branch and Tony Opperman of Newbury branch was set up, with £50 authorised for secretarial expenses. Another sub-committee was authorised to revise the constitution; Keith Allen was to be the secretary with other members representing the various branches.

The first of the current series of the *Butty* edited by Cdr Wray-Bliss appeared in June 1959.

In July of that year it was now the turn of Ran Meinertzhagen to resign as honorary secretary due to pressure of work. His place was taken by Dr Glaister who agreed to continue as treasurer *pro tem*. Dr Glaister sought volunteers as lengthmen to make regular trips along their lengths and report back any changes. The scheme was well received and the canal was divided into twenty-six lengths for this purpose.

The Transport Commission, when asked for particulars of the work they considered necessary to put the canal in order, stated that 347,000 cubic yards of dredging, seven and a half miles of puddling to stop leaks, and much bank strengthening was needed.

Between Reading and Kintbury, eleven locks required major repair or reconstruction; between Newbury and Kintbury, seven needed major works; whilst between Kintbury and Bath, seventy-one wanted attention, only eight top and nine bottom gates being in reasonable condition.

At the December 1959 council meeting, a proposal by Dr Glaister that membership of the association should be centralised to form a more closely knit body capable of acting with more authority and greater efficiency was agreed by a majority vote – there being a certain amount of friction between fishing and boating interests. To help consolidate the membership Mrs Glaister volunteered to become central membership secretary.

Dr Glaister reported to the council that following the removal of the top 30ft (10m) of the Crofton chimney for safety reasons the pumps were now unusable. A temporary diesel pump had been installed but, because of lack of maintenance and pumping, the Crofton Flight was dry in places.

Early in 1960, two sets of bottom gates from the Devizes locks were brought to Newbury, reduced in height and installed in Guyers and Higgs Locks. Guyers also had new top gates and, with Higgs cleared of silt, three boats made a triumphal run to Hamstead. However, an appeal for further Devizes gates for Bulls Lock was ignored. The new central office issued an appeal to members to write to the Inland Waterways Redevelopment Advisory Committee demanding that the waterway be retained and restored from Reading to Bristol as a through navigation. They issued a suggested text:

> *The danger is that this great trunk waterway may be reduced to the two terminal river sections with the linking section from Newbury to Bath destroyed forever. This arrangement has long been advocated by powerful interests.*
>
> *Today, thanks largely to our work, the future of the river sections is no longer in serious*

doubt; but they will be of little value as mere dead ends. The survival and rehabilitation of the whole waterway from Reading to Bristol is of fundamental importance to the entire future of the British river and canal system, and of passionate concern to thousands of people all over the country, indeed all over the world. A National Waterways Conservancy is in sight. The Transport Commission must not be permitted, before this is set up, to achieve the abandonment of the Kennet & Avon by systematically wrecking it; nor must the Redevelopment Committee be allowed to advise abandonment, largely through failure to take seriously what is at stake or to realise how many people care.

The 150th anniversary of the completion of the Kennet & Avon was celebrated by huge crowds at an Easter rally at Bathampton where, led by a horse-drawn narrow boat and watched by television cameras and crowds on the towpath, a great procession of craft cruised to Dundas and back. In his speech opening the rally, Ted Leather, MP for North Somerset, confirmed that there was pressure from MPs to transfer waterways from the Transport Commission to a special body set up to look after them.

At the other end of the canal, Berkshire County Council installed a fixed footbridge with only 3ft of headroom close to Aldermaston swing-bridge. Following a protest, Mr Clayton, the divisional engineer, stated that this could be removed at a month's notice whilst on 4-5 May, members of the Inland Waterways Redevelopment Advisory Committee carried out a detailed inspection of the entire canal.

At the 1960 AGM of the association, Lord Methuen reported that Sir Reginald Kerr, General Manager of the Transport Commission, had said that he would do everything he could to help the association within the resources and manpower available. Lord Methuen said that this change of heart should be recognised and urged co-operation instead of the continual harassment of the Transport Commission as advocated by the IWA.

In a parliamentary debate, the newly knighted Sir Anthony Hurd warned that, although a 1960 Transport Commission Bill granted powers to extend the stand-still agreement on the maintenance of the canal for a further three years, the state of the canal deteriorated month by month through disuse.

Pressure on the Transport Commission produced their estimate for the re-opening of the Bath locks – £15,000 for gates and £5,000 for other essential repairs. They, however, queried the adequacy of water supplies and wished to await the Advisory Committee's report; however, a set of top gates was fitted to Widmead Lock where sluices had earlier been used for flood relief. Serious flooding in 1960 had brought pressure from Berkshire County Council, hence the new gates and sluices; the fact that Bulls Lock was inoperative had made the transport of the gates and bank reinforcing material much more difficult.

The probable winding up of the Transport Commission and the handing over of each of its activities to separate boards was foreshadowed in a White Paper of December 1960 – *Reorganisation of the Nationalised Transport Undertakings*. The Transport Commission would be placed under an independent statutory board to be known as the Inland Waterways Authority.

This body would own and manage the nationalised waterways system and would also be responsible for proceeding with the redevelopment or disposal of waterways which no longer had a transport use. The composition, powers and duties of the new body would require further discussion, taking account, on the one hand, of the charge which the waterway system imposes on public funds and, on the other hand, the varied purposes in which waterways could be made to serve the public at large.

In the early months of 1961, the association published *The Kennet and Avon Redevelopment Scheme*, which had been prepared for the Inland Waterways Redevelopment Advisory Committee. This eighty-page printed booklet with photographs and maps was compiled by members of the association and edited by Capt. Munk. The booklet described the association, the waterway and its history with estimates of the number and variety of craft expected to use the restored waterway and, although the commercial possibilities were subordinated to its amenity value, they were by no means ruled out.

Water supplies were judged to be adequate, subject to the provision of a borehole at Great Bedwyn to augment summer supplies, coupled with the repair of Claverton and the replacement of the Crofton pumps by electric ones; it was suggested that the original Crofton pump engines could be retained as museum items.

Some of the suggestions put forward were strangely prophetic: Kennet turf-sided locks could remain where they worked successfully; standardised steel gates and balance beams might be applicable; the Devizes and Crofton Locks would need lock-keepers to conserve water; a new Aldermaston bridge should be controlled and PVC sheeting might be used in place of clay puddle.

However, the essence of the plan was contained in two sections: one entitled 'Cost of Abandonment' and the other 'Estimate of Working Income and Expenditure'. The report maintained that should the Transport Commission want to be rid of the Kennet & Avon they must pay to shed their responsibilities. The Bowes Report had considered the spending of public money in dealing with the problem of uneconomic waterways but the association, however, said it was not claiming public money for the redevelopment, rather a proper sum from the Transport Commission whose funds were not public money. The neglect had been so great that the cost of restitution was abnormal so special arrangements had to be devised and the association proposed an ingenious solution.

The association suggested that, as it was universally accepted to be more expensive to close a navigation than to put it back into working order, the Transport Commission should pay any new body taking over the canal, not only the cost of restoration, but an annual payment of the interest on the difference between the cost of restoration and the greater cost of abandonment which at that time was estimated to be in the region of £1 million. Rehabilitation they said, including an extra water supply plant, was estimated to cost in the region of £828,000 which, calculating a figure of 6% on the difference, gave an annual interest figure of £10,320.

The total revenue from all sources, including this interest, was thought to be £62,974 or £19,224 in excess of the Transport Commission's estimated annual expenditure of £43,750. It is interesting to note that all the local authorities who were consulted supported the scheme in varying degrees.

In all, 2,500 copies of the booklet were printed and widely distributed. Every Member of Parliament received one and copies were available to the public at 5s (25p) each.

Early in 1961, the Bath and Bristol branch set up a Lock Fund for the specific purpose of bringing about the necessary repairs and opening of Lock 7, which was the bottom one of the Bath Flight, thus enabling the pound above to be used as a haven from river floods, but it was to be nine long years before the Lock was finally opened.

The new constitution was adopted at the association's 1961 AGM. Apart from advocating an independent waterways authority, the only change concerned the appointment of trustees in whom the property of the association should be vested; Dr Hancock and Cdr Wray-Bliss were elected the first trustees.

At the May council meeting, Capt. Munk reported the preliminary thoughts of the Advisory Committee. It was considered very unlikely that the Government would spend £750,000 on rebuilding the canal so it was therefore suggested that, subject to the water supply position proving practical, the Transport Commission should pay to a responsible body a sum equal to that at present spent in maintaining the status quo and, if by more economical use of this sum, supplemented by appeals and by the use of volunteer labour, it should be possible to maintain the status quo and carry out restoration at either end as well as work towards the centre. Capt. Munk proposed that a trust be formed as soon as possible to supplant the association for, as he explained, an ordinary society or association is, in English law, only an unincorporated body and as such has no legal status or personality, consequently it is not recognised as a separate legal entity.

A most important consideration for members is that any creditor of the association is theoretically able to claim to the full amount of his debt against the property of any officer of the association and of its council or governing body and, indeed, sometimes against the property of an ordinary member. This situation could be quite serious if the association had to take on commitments or responsibilities and could only be put right by turning the association into a company limited by guarantee.

The result of an ordinary voluntary society becoming a company limited by guarantee is that it has a legal personality, and is capable of holding property itself and acting on its own behalf instead of through trustees. The essence of such a company is that the liability of each member is limited to a certain amount specified in the Articles of Association.

There would of course be obligations imposed on a society turning itself into a company as it would have to conform to the Companies Act in making returns to the Register of Companies and of course in the event of irregularities it would be liable to investigation and intervention by the appropriate authority. Denys Hutchings, who had been elected treasurer at this meeting, proposed that the new body be called the Kennet & Avon Canal Trust Ltd; this was accepted unanimously.

A special General Meeting was called on 19 June at Newbury to ratify the changeover and a suggestion that the IWA should have equal representation on the board of management of the new company was narrowly defeated; they were allocated two places only.

Philip Ogden's offer to serve in an honorary advisory capacity was accepted and he was elected assistant honorary consulting engineer to assist Cyril Boucher; his knowledge as chief engineer of the West Hampshire Water Co. was to prove invaluable. At the special General Meeting, Tony Opperman (Newbury) proposed and Don Collinson (Bath and Bristol) seconded a formal proposal:

> *That the Kennet & Avon Canal Association be reconstituted as a non-profit making company limited by guarantee under the name of 'The Kennet & Avon Canal Trust Ltd' and that the Council be authorised to proceed with the formation of the new company.*

This was passed unanimously and the Advisory Committee was informed of the proposal; they had already suggested that, while the canal would remain Transport Commission property, it could be jointly managed by the commission and the Trust but the commission was reluctant to co-operate in view of the uncertainty caused by the forthcoming Transport Bill. There were also differences of opinion as to the adequacy of water supply; Messrs Clayton and Ogden were to have further discussions.

The formation of the Trust was delayed by difficulty in obtaining charitable status. Mr Pollard, a solicitor representing the Trust, reported that the Charity Commissioners had rejected the application on the present constitution. This was returned to Mr Christie, another supporting solicitor, for redrafting. To satisfy a need for passenger boating at Bath, the Dundas Carrying Co. and Cdr Wray-Bliss had introduced *Lengthman*, which was a jet-propelled craft, but it proved unable to cope with weed. In place of *Lengthman*, a sunken mud hopper was rescued and converted into the paddle-wheeler *Charlotte Dundas*. In mid-1961 Cdr Wray-Bliss resigned from the association and also as *Butty* editor, the post being taken over by M.D. Butler. At the eastern end, *Enterprise* had been purchased by David Blagrove and Bill Fisher who initiated a once-weekly run to Theale as well as several daily runs to Burghfield.

The Charlotte Dundas. (Wiltshire Newspapers)

The January 1962 council meeting heard with deep regret that Dr Glaister was moving to Essex and wished to resign; Denys Hutchings was elected Hon. Secretary in his place. One other report, which was to be of tremendous importance to the future of the canal, was that General Sir Hugh Stockwell, Deputy Supreme Commander, Europe, had joined the association and offered any help in his power. His and Lady Stockwell's purchase of a cottage on the canal bank at Horton near Devizes no doubt played some part in this decision.

At the end of March, the remains of Widmead swing-bridge were demolished by volunteers to safeguard the passage of the Devizes–Westminster canoe race crews and mass meetings in support of the canal were held at Bath and Reading.

At the last AGM of the association, on 30 April, Capt. Munk reported on the general terms of the recommendations of the Advisory Committee to the Transport Commission Minister. This was that a joint committee of waterways staff and representatives of the association should redevelop the canal.

The basic funds to carry this out would be the £40,000 at present spent on the canal annually divided in half – £20,000 to maintain it in its present state, and £20,000 on rebuilding work, starting at both ends. This would be substantially augmented by massive voluntary efforts, both in fund-raising and labour. He warned, however, that the Transport Minister, Ernest Marples, was strongly opposed to redevelopment. There was concern when soil tipped on the hillside above the canal at Claverton caused a landslide. This slip, which caused great difficulties later on, so worried the Kennet & Avon Canal Trust Council that they agreed that the situation should be closely monitored.

The 1962 Transport Act set up a new independent administration to take over the waterway interests of the Transport Commission. This would start operations from 1 January 1963 and be known as the British Waterways Board.

At the end of April, the amended constitution resulted in the Trust being accorded charitable status and the Memorandum and Articles of Association were signed by Capt. Munk, Denys Hutchings, Fred Blampeid, John Gould, Dr Hancock, Brian Ambrose and Robert Aickman.

The Canal Trust was incorporated under the Companies Act 1948 on 6 June 1962. The special meeting necessary for the association formally to dissolve itself and transfer its assets and liabilities to the Canal Trust was held in Newbury on 23 October, with the other association branches later holding similar meetings.

6 The Canal Trust and British Waterways Board 1962-1967

At the first Kennet & Avon Canal Trust Council meeting, Capt. Munk was elected chairman with Denys Hutchings as secretary and treasurer. Lord Methuen was to be offered the position of President, and this he later accepted. Messrs Piper and Newman from Newbury and Reading were co-opted on to the council and Tom Burr took over the editorship of the *Butty*.

During March 1963, the newly fledged Canal Trust held a dinner at which Capt. Munk told how the Minister of Transport, Ernest Marples, had had the Advisory Committee report for over a year and had yet to come to a decision. Capt. Munk thought that the Minister probably intended to pass this responsibility on to the recently formed British Waterways Board (BWB).

He voiced the opinion that the Trust Council had waited long enough and they should now suggest that Sulhamstead, Tyle Mill and the Bath Locks should be tackled. He further proposed the setting up of a restoration fund and would write to the BWB to make friendly contact. He hoped that through this approach it would be possible to establish whether the Canal Trust would be allowed to implement a restoration scheme.

The situation was not helped when the Kennet & Avon moratorium of the 1955 Transport Commission Act, which had earlier been extended to the end of 1963, was further extended to the end of 1967 by using a section of the 1962 Transport Act. However, in December the BWB issued an interim report on its first thoughts about inland waterways. Paragraphs 160 to 166 were of particular interest to the Kennet & Avon.

160.   At present only small sections of this broad waterway (a few miles at Reading, a few miles around Newbury and about three miles at Bath) are navigable. The rest is being maintained in a state of delayed decay at an annual cost of some £50,000. Few locks are usable. At least two local authorities seem to be obstructing the canal with bridges. Parts of the canal are beset by serious engineering difficulties. In 1955 The Transport Commission proposed closure; this idea met with such opposition that it was withdrawn.

161.   The waterway connects at one end with the Thames (carrying a very large number of pleasure craft, most of which are suitable for navigating the Kennet & Avon) and at the other end with the Avon which carries a smaller but substantial number of such craft. From the pleasure boating point of view, the restoration of the waterway would clearly produce a major improvement of the entire system. Moreover the canal passes through some tracts of country which are of outstanding beauty; we understand, indeed, that the possibility of designating the entire towing path as a long-distance recreational footpath is under consideration. The Board has been impressed by the manifest enthusiasm of all those who are willing to help in the truly major task of restoring the canal and we have noted that a trust already exists with restoration as its special objective.

162.   Naturally we have thought about the alternatives to restoration. We believe the Transport Commission estimated some years ago that the cost of full elimination would be over £500,000. There are always other halfway house solutions but most of them would involve considerable cost without offering any of the prospects of

The Trust's hand dredger at work outside County Lock, Reading, 1962. (David Harris)

       revenue, particularly from pleasure craft users, which in the long term restoration would offer.

163.   There are certainly major and serious problems to be faced here. But we think, at present, that the hope of restoration merits sympathetic, careful and urgent consideration. With this hope in mind we propose soon to start discussing with the Kennet & Avon Canal Trust and other potential helpers what might be a practical and reasonable scheme.

164.   One scheme might be to divide restoration into two stages: the first from Reading to Devizes and simultaneously from Bath to Dundas; the remaining section (Dundas to Devizes) forming stage two and containing the major problems of the Devizes locks, the water supply to those locks, and the fissured section of the canal bed. If this were, on further investigation, found to be acceptable we should, during the first stage, see that the Dundas/Devizes section did not get seriously worse; the detailed consideration of the second stage could best be left to rest for the present on the general conception already stated – that the ultimate object was complete restoration in due course. Stage one, in itself, would be likely to take several years to complete.

165.   As to cost, we feel that the first source of funds must be twofold: (1) those which the Trust and other interested enthusiasts could find and (2) those which can arise from savings on maintenance. This has already been kept to a low level but the Board propose to scrutinise this with great care to see if any funds could be made available for construction work.

166.   Impressed as they were with the enthusiasm of volunteer help, the Board do not think that stage one is likely to be completed without some additional costs falling upon the undertaking. The acceptability of any proposal must depend on that extra call being kept to a very modest level. Provided it is so kept, some extra cost might be consid-

ered justified as at present the Board are spending £50,000 to no good purpose and restoration holds out the prospect of a waterway of great social value and afar from negligible financial potential. Tolls a good deal higher than the usual might possibly be levied on craft using the completed portions. If plans along this sort of line are endorsed, it might well be appropriate, both during the restoration period and after-wards, to have some kind of recognised consultative committee, containing represen-tatives all of who have assisted to restore the canal, to guide policy and exploit potential.

The report was music to the ears of the Canal Trust which, despite the Minister's lack of enthusiasm, was keen to initiate the restoration of Sulhamstead Lock. Capt. Munk first met the Board's chairman, Sir John Hawton, and the chief engineer, Mr Lisle, who confirmed that the cost would be £8,000 which could be reduced to £4,000 if army, prison and volunteer labour could be used. A meeting was then held at the lockside with Mr Clayton, the divisional engineer for the British Waterways Board, the Assistant Prison Commissioner, the governors of Winchester and Oxford prisons and David Hutchings who was, at the time, busily restoring the Stratford Canal with volunteer labour. Whilst the prison authorities were keen to help they could only allow work to be done for a non-profit making organisation such as the Trust and not for the BWB who owned the lock. Mr Clayton was not in favour of a makeshift scheme and proposed that a new lock be built within the old 122ft x 19ft (37.5m x 5.8m) chamber using steel shuttering, with Cyril Rogers, the BWB inspector at the eastern end, being seconded as the clerk of works at Sulhamstead.

A working party of Capt. Munk, Philip Ogden, Mr Clayton and David Kinnersley, BWB Assistant Manager, was set up to examine in detail sections of the waterway to be restored and to estimate costs. They surveyed the canal from Reading to Hungerford, estimating costs of £60,000 to £70,000. The Board's chairman proposed that they should contribute £30,000 of this and a further £7,000 at the western end.

The final figure rose to about £100,000 provided the work could be done by a willing contractor, and, after further negotiation, BWB's contribution was increased to £50,000. The Trust would benefit from all savings that could be made by the use of voluntary labour, the forces and prisoners. In September, the rebuilding costs of stage one had been agreed subject to the approval of the Trust, the Ministry of Transport and the Treasury.

At the other end of the canal Don Collinson, the Bath and Bristol branch chairman, asked BWB to consider opening to Bradford-on-Avon; he pointed out that it seemed odd to re-open the Bath locks just to gain access to the four miles to Dundas. Not surprisingly, this was refused as the section in question contained the fissured length at Limpley Stoke known as the 'Dry Section'.

At the second annual Trust dinner in April 1963, Charles Hadfield spoke on behalf of the Board, of which he was a member. Years later he admitted that while he had wished to encourage the Trust to increase their volunteer and money-raising efforts and to make them feel that his Board was fully behind them, he was wary of inadvertently committing the Board to anything more than had been agreed.

In preparation for a national appeal, General Stockwell was appointed chairman of an appeals committee and elected to the council. However, during October 1964, Lionel Munk became more deeply involved with the national canal scene when, following the resignation of Robert Aickman, chairman of IWA, he assumed the IWA chairman's mantle as well as remaining Canal Trust chairman.

A change of government delayed any possible early agreement with the Ministry of Transport but early in 1964 the Trust and BWB decided to press on with Sulhamstead Lock; the Trust was to be responsible for the full expense although the use of prison labour had

Above and middle: *Sulhamstead Lock, before and during restoration, 1965.* (David Harris)

Right: *Sulhamstead Lock. Work in progress by the Army, assisted by prisoners from Oxford and Winchester prisons, 1965.* (David Adams)

The Junior Division at work. (K&ACT Archives)

Moonraker clearing weed from the long pound. (K&ACT Archives)

been agreed. At the same time the Bath branch were working on the dry fissured section between Avoncliff and Limpley Stoke, clearing the undergrowth and searching for leaks.

Early in 1965 just as work at Sulhamstead was starting, disaster struck when the troublesome bottom gates of Burghfield Lock collapsed. Although Sulhamstead could now not be reached until Burghfield Lock had been rebuilt, the courageous decision was taken to carry on with the Sulhamstead work.

The Trust acquired a new treasurer when Nicholas Reynolds was elected to relieve Denys Hutchings who had carried the burden of both treasurer and hon. secretary since 1962. It was fortunate that with his interest in steam engines Nicholas was also able to report on a survey of the Crofton beam engines carried out by Messrs Plenty of Newbury, which indicated that £5,000 would be needed to get them working again, and the possibility of the Trust purchasing the engines was discussed with the BWB.

At this time an interesting organisation, the brainchild of a retired naval officer, Capt. Mansfield-Robinson, was set up to utilise the enthusiasm of youth for restoration and at the same time provide opportunities for fun and adventure. This organisation, called the 'Junior Division' of the Trust, was run by the Wiltshire branch under the supervision of the county youth officer. Using an ingenious craft, called *Moonraker*, designed by the captain, they cleared weed from sections of the Long Pound between Devizes and Wootton Rivers.

Subsequently they cleared the Devizes locks of decayed gates, vegetation and rubbish thus halting further deterioration and later, when the Trust acquired Crofton pumping station, they were to be found busily cleaning, de-rusting and polishing.

Under the spirited leadership of Capt. Mansfield-Robinson, the Junior Division, later known as the Youth Division, continued to contribute to the wellbeing of the canal until around 1978 when a nationwide dispute over pay and conditions for waterways staff caused practically all voluntary work, not only on the Kennet & Avon Canal but on other British Waterways canals as well, to come to a halt. Although the dispute was finally settled, voluntary effort on this scale was never resumed and this, sadly, soon resulted in the break-up of the Youth Division. The loss here was twofold – not only was the cessation of work on the Long Pound a blow to the Trust, but more importantly was the damage done to youthful enthusiasm with the possible loss of tomorrow's canal enthusiasts.

The Trust and the canal received much publicity from the Whitsun Boat Fairs at Newbury in 1965 and 1966 which raised over £1,200 – a considerable sum in those days. The fairs were organised, jointly, by Peter Lindley-Jones, the Newbury branch chairman, and David Harris of Reading branch who were assisted by a combined effort from all other Trust branches.

The Boat Fairs marked a shift in emphasis from political to financial activity since it was apparent that the need now was to raise substantial sums of money whilst at the same time demonstrating the amenity value of the recovered waterway and keep up the political pressure. The fairs, which attracted a Whitsun crowd estimated at between 10,000 to 12,000, proved just how effective the concerted effort of the entire organization could be.

A spin-off from the 1966 fair was that Newbury Council did not allow the grass on Northcroft, first hacked into shape for use as a fairground by the Newbury branch, to revert to its unkempt condition; it has been kept trim and is still enjoyed by the people of Newbury today. In December 1965 the BWB published *The Facts about the Waterways*, a comprehensive account of all the waterways under their jurisdiction, which pointed out their ridiculous financial position. They had to find £726,000 annually to service the capital debt of £19.3 million bequeathed to them by the 1962 Act, but their total revenue in 1964 was only £780,000.

The first Newbury Boat Fair at Victoria Park, 1965.

The dry section between Dundas aqueduct and Limpley Stoke was cleared of undergrowth and derelict boats during 1965-1966 by volunteer labour. Nearly one mile of light railway was laid and clay was transported in hoppers to re-puddle the canal bed. Unfortunately, progress was slow and this work was halted. Experiments in late 1966 using polythene sheeting and concrete to prevent leakage also ceased. (K&ACT Archives)

Until 31 December they were safeguarded against any proceedings to maintain any waterway as a navigation if it was not navigable in the six months ending November 1961. From 1967 those sections that were not actually closed were required to be put into full navigable condition, but the resources to do this were totally inadequate and so further waterways legislation was essential.

Where *The Facts About the Waterways* referred to the Kennet & Avon in particular, it mentioned the joint investigation into the possibility of restoration from Bath to Bradford-on-Avon and the rebuilding of Sulhamstead Lock and it went on to suggest that converting the central Bath to Bedwyn section to a water channel would be unrealistic owing to the various engineering difficulties whilst elimination would show no material gain.

Of the eastern section, Bedwyn to Reading, the report was quite clear – elimination would not affect any saving over conversion to a water channel, whilst for their part the Canal Trust had no doubt that, if restored, the waterway could eventually become viable. However, it needed all the possible sources of income to be energetically developed under the planned joint committee of the Board and the Trust. To support the Board's case, the Trust issued a memorandum outlining the canal's history and emphasising the importance of the work of the joint committee.

Work continued on the dry section under the direction of Don Collinson and Danny Daniels. One mile of light rail track loaned by Messrs A.E. Farr Ltd was laid to carry puddling clay for the Waterway staff to use under the direction of Stan Miles, the west end inspector; unfortunately as each section was re-watered new leaks were found. The Claverton slip repair was also in difficulties as persistent rain made it impossible to stabilise the hillside. Morale was low.

In mid-1966 BWB installed new gates, but without balance beams, at the top Wootton Rivers Lock to maintain the summit level.

In July a White Paper on Transport Policy included the following:

> *The Government accepts as a basis for the development of new policy the broad factual analysis in the British Waterways report The Facts about the Waterways.*
>
> *It proposes to discuss with the Board, the Economic Planning Council, the local authorities and other appropriate national and regional bodies, and also with the organisations representing users, what network should be kept open for pleasure boat use, the 'amenity' network.*
>
> *The commercial waterways will be reorganised in a group separate from the amenity and other waterways; all will, however, remain under the management of British Waterways. Provision will be made for the participation of suitably organised bodies in the development of waterways for recreational purposes.*

On 19 October the Ministry of Transport announced:

> *Mrs. Barbara Castle, the Transport Minister, wants to hear from everyone, individuals and organisations, interested in developing the canals and inland waterways for pleasure cruising. She wants to decide on a network of waterways which could justifiably be kept open for use by pleasure boats in the immediate future.*
>
> *A Ministry statement today considers it wrong to allow waterways of potential future value to go out of service in such a way that they could never be restored to use. The network will therefore include not only more popular waterways like the Lancaster Canal, the Langollen Canal and the Southern end of the Oxford Canal but also less used waterways to discover what opportunities exist for increasing use and revenue. British Waterways says maintaining the waterways in any condition costs £600,000 a year. But it is costing another £340,000 to maintain sufficient depth of water, locks and other works for cruising in powered boats, an increasingly popular pastime. To offset this there was a record revenue of £100,000 received from pleasure licences. The Ministry agrees that some subsidy will be necessary. The amount of the subsidy will be subject to review in the light of experience. The review will take into account the use made of the network and the increasing use and revenue. So it is up to all who use the waterways for recreation to show what facilities they wish to support.*

Towards the end of July 1966 the Canal Trust Council had suggested that to complement its expenditure on Sulhamstead, the BWB should rebuild the failed Burghfield Lock from their own resources. But it was not until October that the Board replied saying that they were not prepared to do so until the full account for Sulhamstead, completed earlier at a cost of £7,300, was settled and the Government's decision on the fate of the Kennet & Avon Canal was known.

Late in 1966, at the request of Newbury Council, BWB moved their depot, which had occupied much of the Newbury wharf frontage for some years, to Padworth. The town council intended to re-develop the amenities of the site and there was much concern over the fate of the stone building which had formed part of the Waterways depot. This handsome structure, which was probably part of the original wharf complex, stood out amid a collection of ramshackle old corrugated iron sheds.

The Newbury branch chairman convinced the Mayor of Newbury, Cllr J.W. Jones, to prevail on the council to allow the Trust to lease the building for use as a museum. This was agreed, to the chagrin of the borough surveyor who had planned to raze the entire depot to the ground to make way for a car park! It was as well that he was thwarted because today, refurbished and developed by Trust members as a tea room and souvenir shop, it is visited by tourists and sightseers who throng Newbury each summer. When negotiations for the stone building were complete, the Newbury branch made a grant to the Town Council of £50 towards the provision of a boat launching ramp at Northcroft Park to replace the loss of leisure launching facilities that had existed within the Board's depot on Newbury wharf.

The canal celebrated a real 'red letter' day on 26 November 1966 when, following legal action by a consortium which included the Trust, the notorious girders under Bridge Street, Reading, were finally removed thus allowing almost trouble-free access to the waterway.

In March 1967 Capt. Munk announced that due to the pressure of his post as IWA chairman, he wished to stand down as Canal Trust chairman, an announcement which was greeted with dismay but tempered with relief as General Sir Hugh Stockwell agreed to succeed him as chairman. In recognition of his services to the Trust Lionel Munk was elected as a vice-president. Robert Aickman and Fred Blampied also resigned, the latter due to pressure of work within the IWA.

During the summer a steam dredger, offered by the British Waterways Board, was dismantled and towed from Hillmorton to Reading by Nicholas Hill with his narrow boat *Jaguar*. The journey took eighteen working days and at times the length of tow for the seventy-ton monster was over 300ft (100m). No.14, as the dredger was known, commenced work around Reading in the Spring of 1969 after a period of refurbishment and crew training; unfortunately it suffered at times from vandalism, at one time thieves stole several pieces of brass equipment which were luckily recovered. No.14 remained in Reading until 1973 when she suffered from the inherent problem associated in operating steam-driven plant; she failed her boiler inspection and could not be used again until the boiler tubes were replaced. This expensive task coupled with a lack of volunteers and the belief that it had not come up to expectations caused Reading branch to consider her disposal. She was finally sold to the Surrey & Hants Canal Society for £200, where overhauled and repaired she was kept busy on the Basingstoke Canal.

A report on the dry section near Avoncliff suggested the use of polythene sheeting for leak stopping; this involved grading the bed of the canal and covering the polythene with 6in (150mm) of concrete. Even with volunteer labour this would cost about £1,143 per hundred yard section (92m approx.) or £2,400 if carried out by contractors. As the total length was thirty-six 100-yard lengths, this sort of expenditure was not feasible so it was thought better to transfer volunteer labour to the Bath locks.

A commercial attempt to lease Pewsey wharf prompted General Stockwell to approach Pewsey Council with a view to the Trust taking out a lease so that the wharf could remain available to all. This was eventually successful, but not until 1978 when Kennet District Council took out a twenty-one-year lease and sub-leased the wharf to the Trust who managed it, employing a permanent on-site warden. The District Council also allocated some £17,000 for work on the wharf building although it was to be some years and a great deal of effort from the Trust volunteers before the wharf and buildings became a thriving centre with facilities for walkers, boaters and the headquarters of the Pewsey Wharf Boat Club. The boat club was a thriving association which had been formed by a number of enthusiastic boat-owners in the early seventies. Unfortunately the Trust was unable to maintain this happy state of affairs when the lease, so thoughtfully negotiated by General Stockwell, ran out in 2000 and the tenancy passed into private commercial hands.

February 1967 saw yet another unhappy loss for the canal when, after one hundred years, the last three commercial working barges on any part of the waterway ceased the operation of carrying tar from Bath Gasworks to the Avonside tar works at Crews Hole Bristol.

In May the Trust became property owners when the BWB agreed to sell Crofton pumping station, complete, for the nominal sum of £75. The intriguing story of Crofton and the restoration of the two nineteenth century pumping engines is told in Appendix One – Kennet & Avon Canal Pumping Stations.

In September 1967, a Government White Paper outlined, amongst a number of subjects, the plans for the canal. Reading to Tyle Mill was designated a cruising waterway to be maintained at government expense and Don Collinson (now the link between the Canal Trust and the BWB) reported that the Board, thus authorised, would rebuild Burghfield Lock early in 1968.

The plans to be used were those of Sulhamstead where limitations brought about by building inside the old chamber shortened the new one to such an extent that a full-length narrow boat could only be accommodated diagonally.

The White Paper warned, however, that there would be no money allocated either for restoration or maintenance of restored canals not specified as cruising waterways so, apart from the section already mentioned – the River Avon and between Bulls and Hamstead Locks – the rest of the Kennet & Avon canal was excluded.

General Stockwell met Mr Allen and Mr Kinnersley, general and deputy general managers respectively of the BWB, and was advised that the Canal Trust should have a scheme for presentation to the Advisory Council which was to be set up, but were warned that it was not to be too ambitious, possibly for £50,000, which sum might re-open the Reading to Newbury section. At the same time a move should be made on the locks at Bath.

A sub-committee comprising the chairman, vice-chairman, secretary and the honorary engineer was set up to prepare such a scheme. They considered that a total of £67,000 would be needed for work between Tyle Mill and Bulls Locks, including the rebuilding of Towney and Monkey Marsh Locks at £16,000 each. Dredging would add a further £18,000 and repairs to the twelve swing-bridges estimated at £100 each.

Meanwhile, the restoration scheme as suggested by the BWB was prepared as a booklet and presented to the Advisory Council in June 1968. The illustrated booklet of forty pages described previous estimates and detailed the expenditure necessary for individual locks and other works with the total for the Reading-Newbury length being estimated as £80,450 based on 1968 costs.

Pewsey Wharf, c.1970. (K&ACT Archives)

Crofton pumping station, with the top 36ft removed from the chimney. (K&ACT Archives)

In the section governing Bath locks, the booklet described the Widcombe Road scheme first published in the *Bath and Wiltshire Evening Chronicle* the previous November which involved eliminating Lock 8 and its side pond to make room for a second A4 road bridge and then rebuilding Lock 9 to double depth and providing back pumping over this extra deep lock. This work would cost Bath City Council about £300,000 and would save the Trust the expense of restoring two locks. Repairs to the remaining Locks 10 to 13, however, were estimated at £10,000 with Lock 7 costing £2,000.

The Long Pound could be kept open by the efforts of the Junior Division and by spending £2,000 for dredging. Re-gating the four Wootton Rivers Locks would allow another three and a half miles to be re-opened, enabling boats to reach Bruce Tunnel and Crofton Top Lock which was within walking distance of the Crofton pumping station; thus for a total of £92,000 fifty-four miles of the finest cruising water in England could be acquired.

Both Mr Clayton and Mr Allen of the BWB expressed sympathy with restoration at the eastern end but they were not over keen about the Bath locks, although the Trust's Bath branch already had some £500 in their Lock 7 fund which the Trust Council doubled.

On 1 July 1968 Sir Frank Price was appointed to succeed Sir John Hawton as chairman of the BWB and Mr Harrington became chairman of the Advisory Council, which later became the Inland Waterways Amenity Advisory Council (IWAAC). On 27 July BWB organised the official opening of Burghfield and Sulhamstead Locks; Sir Frank emphasised that the BWB were in favour of sensible restoration schemes but had little or no money to offer. He hoped that more concrete support would be forthcoming from local authorities who were coming to value the waterways for the scope they offered for outdoor pursuits; his comment on cutting the Burghfield tape was 'And about time too'.

The 1968 Transport Act removed the right of navigation as applied to BWB's inland waterways but the sections of the Kennet & Avon already mentioned, namely the River Avon and between Bulls and Hamstead Locks, were included in the 'cruiseway' group. 'Remainder' waterways, however, which included the rest of the Kennet & Avon, were to be dealt with in the most economical manner possible, consistent in the case of a waterway to be retained, with the requirements of public health and the preservation of amenity and safety.

The Act also set up the IWAAC, made up of people with wide knowledge of, and deep interest in, the use of inland waterways for amenity and recreational purposes including fishing. It could include up to four BWB representatives and would advise the Waterways Board and the Minister of any proposal to add to or reduce the cruising waterways.

There was one other extremely important provision within the Act: the BWB were given powers to enter into agreements with local authorities or bodies having public or charitable objectives in maintaining or improving remainder waterways for recreational or amenity use. This very important clause was, from this point onwards, to form the whole basis for the complete restoration of the Kennet & Avon Canal.

The way was now clear for organizations such as the Kennet & Avon Canal Trust and local authorities to co-operate fully with BWB in advancing exciting plans and restoration schemes. It only needed the determination and funds to carry them out.

7 Raising the Wind
1968–1973

During June 1968 the engineering section of Bath University offered to help restore Claverton pump which had been out of action and silent since a log jammed the waterwheel and stripped the wooden teeth from an intermediate gear in November 1952. The fascinating story of the operational return of Claverton to full working order is covered in Appendix One – Kennet & Avon Canal Pumping Stations.

During August 1968, members of the newly formed IWAAC spent three days touring the Kennet & Avon from end to end and decided to back the Canal Trust's restoration scheme. Representatives of Berkshire County Council, Reading and Newbury Borough Councils and the Rural District Councils of Bradfield, Hungerford and Newbury passed a resolution declaring their willingness to initiate and enter into negotiations supporting IWAAC's decision.

All along the canal minor works were underway. At Bath, the council laid macadam along a mile of towpath; at Newbury an internal staircase was built in the stone building; at Reading the steam dredger was being overhauled and painted whilst at Crofton pumping station major renovation was underway involving not only the engines but also the fabric of the building.

Early in 1969, the restoration of the eastern end received a possible set back when the Ministry of Transport informed Berkshire County Council that they would refuse any extension of the cruiseway because, they claimed, the opening of swing-bridges would interfere with the contractors lorries who were soon to be engaged in building the M4. They further claimed that £1.5 million would need to be spent on replacing such bridges with fixed ones with sufficient headroom. A meeting of representatives of IWAAC, BWB, Berkshire County Council and the Trust was called to discuss the matter.

The Ministry of Transport had been inconsistent having allowed Theale swing-bridge, which they knew to be on the main gravel haul route, to be included in the Reading cruiseway. Berkshire County Council now wished to reinforce and permanently fix this bridge but the BWB steadfastly refused to allow this. In the end, only Aldermastson bridge, already made inoperative by the adjacent footbridge, was fixed and strengthened.

At the western end General Stockwell and Don Collinson met Bath City Council who had indicated that to promote restoration within Bath they would contribute a sum of £2,500 per year for three years if the Trust could produce one third of that amount. To enlist his general support Sir Frank Price, BWB chairman, was invited to visit the Bath locks.

In April 1969 members of Bath and Bristol branch proposed the setting up of a major appeal for restoration funds. A sub-committee met during May and recommended that provided IWAAC officially supported the restoration scheme then that should be the basis of a national appeal.

However, the Trust, realising that a degree of flexibility was an important asset, devised alternative plans in case IWAAC support was not forthcoming or the Ministry of Transport insisted Theale bridge be fixed, even temporarily. Should either of these situations arise then Bath City Council would be asked to transfer its support to the Newbury to Hungerford length, for although this length was totally contained within the Berkshire County Council's boundaries it would be a natural extension of the cruiseway with no engineering works, errant swing-bridges or water supplies to cause problems. Further, to consolidate the impetus

Claverton pumping station. (K&ACT Archives)

of restoring Sulhamstead and Burghfield Locks, it was suggested that another lock should be tackled. The next in line was Tyle Mill but, as the navigation might yet be blocked by a fixed Theale bridge, attention transferred to Hamstead Lock at a cost of £1,800.

In the event, the city council supported the Bath project and, following the grant of finance, agreement was reached with the BWB for the restoration of the Bath locks; Widcombe, Wash House and Abbey View.

An estimate of £19,000 embraced the other two locks on the Widcombe Flight, Nos 8 and 9, which might be included in the road scheme. Of the total, some £2,000 might be saved by the use of volunteer labour.

At the same time, so as not to embarrass Berkshire County Council during the building of the M4, it was decided to postpone seeking permission for the restoration of the Reading to Newbury gap and instead to concentrate on the Hamstead to Hungerford length to which the Trust was prepared to subscribe up to £5,000 whilst the IWA offered £2,500 to repair Hamstead Lock.

Besides repairing Widcombe, Wash House and Hamstead Locks in 1970, the BWB now agreed to restore three locks per year: Abbey View, Copse, and Dreweats in 1971, followed in 1972 by the top two in Bath together with one other unspecified lock.

In February 1970, the newly refurbished Newbury stone building played host to a Trust Council meeting for the first time during which Tom Burr, editor of the *Butty*, and D. Stewart, the membership secretary, retired, their places being taken by Flt Lt Tony Molland and Alan Shave.

During April, it was reported that Berkshire County Council had given £500 towards restoration west of Hamstead. Wiltshire County Council followed with a donation of £300 divided between Long Pound weed clearance and work on Caen Hill and Bradford-on-Avon.

Mid-1970 saw two new Trust branches formed, one to be called West Wiltshire located at Bradford-on-Avon where the Trust had taken a lease on the wharf, and another in the Berkshire town of Hungerford.

The BWB issued a revised estimate for Bath and Hamstead Locks up to the end of 1971; the cost would now be £22,500 or if the Widcombe Road scheme materialised this sum would be reduced to £19,000. The Trust now ordered the restoration of Hamstead, Copse and Dreweats Locks at a cost of £8,900.

On 16 May 1970, at long last, Lock 7 at Widcombe, Bath, was officially opened by Sir Frank Price. In the course of his address he praised the contribution made by volunteers. During festivities which followed the formal opening, donations from Bath City Council and the Wiltshire County Council were acknowledged as well as contributions of £200 from Devizes Borough and £100 from Devizes Rural District Councils.

In September Don Collinson reported that the Widcombe road scheme in Bath had been approved and that Wash House Lock was almost complete.

Towards the end of the year General Stockwell and Don Collinson examined the Wootton Rivers Locks and, following the BWB's estimate of £10,000, placed an order for their restoration. Wootton Rivers Lock was to be completed early in 1971, Heathy Close later that year, with the remaining Brimslade and Cadley Locks in 1972, or earlier if funds could be found. Up to 6 November 1970 £19,950 had been spent on restoration, £19,000 was planned to be spent up to August 1971 and a further £17,750 from then on until the end of 1972.

Berkshire County Council Highways Dept recommended that no money should be made available from council finances for reconstructing 'up and over bridges' but that such work could be undertaken were the money found from other sources.

When the various bridge capacities in the Reading to Newbury section had been examined it was decided that, as they only carried light traffic, those at Ufton, Padworth and Frouds could remain swing-bridges but Tyle Mill, Thatcham, Ham Marsh and Aldermaston must be 'up and over'. It was expected that as Aldermaston was on a main road this would attract a MOT grant for replacement.

Copse Lock, 1970. (K&ACT Archives)

Greenham Lock, near Newbury, early 1970s. (K&ACT Archives)

In April 1971, General Stockwell was appointed to succeed Illtyd Harrington as chairman of IWACC and he also accepted a place on the BWB. This not only paid tribute to the General but also to the Trust and its position within canal restoration circles.

1971 also saw a breakthrough in finance when Hungerford Rural District Council became the first authority to authorise the payment of regular contributions towards restoration: £500 per year for five years. Newbury Borough and Newbury District Councils followed with a grant of £1,634 per year, which was later increased to £1,866 making a total of £20,000 over five years with Whitchurch Rural District Council, whose area did not even touch the canal, made a splendid donation of £1,000 also spread over five years.

Following concerns from some authorities that such donations would be conceding responsibility for future maintenance costs, the Trust quickly informed them that they had no intention of asking them to bear such costs!

Berkshire County Council now announced that they would not seek permanently to secure Theale swing-bridge so, with that threat lifted, Reading branch set about raising funds for Tyle Mill Lock, the order for its restoration being placed in August.

At the same time contractors, financed by the BWB, started rebuilding Greenham Lock and the whole Reading to Newbury project was given a moral and financial boost when John Smith of the Manifold Trust offered £50,000, available in 1972, for work on the entire section.

On Easter Monday 1971, Lord Methuen officially re-opened Hamstead Lock and on 5 September Sir Christopher Chancellor, chairman of the Bath Preservation Trust, and Lady Chancellor re-opened Wash House Lock in Bath.

During November, Don Collinson produced *Project 75* describing the planned future work. Money from Bath, the Newbury Consortium, the IWA and other sources resulted in the Trust accruing over £30,000 in two years. This, together with the Trust's own income, enabled orders to be placed with the Waterways Board worth £63,640, allocations of £16,140 were made for the Bath locks, £8,500 for the locks between Hamstead and

Kintbury, £10,000 for the Wootton Rivers Locks, £15,300 for locks between Kintbury and Hungerford, £2,200 for Tyle Mill, £3,000 for Semington Lock and £8,500 for dredging.

When restoration started there were only nineteen locks and 24.5 miles of canal usable; in just over two years this had been increased by a further nine locks (7, 10, 11, 12, 53, 54, 79, 80, and 81) and another 2.5 miles of waterway.

On completion of Project 75, however, there would be thirty-eight locks and 62.5 miles available and the Trust could feel justifiably proud of its efforts.

This was not all, for there were negotiations in hand with two county councils, and if further finance could be raised, orders for Semington Lock (£3,000) and Bulls Lock (£3,500) with Hungerford Marsh Lock (£3,000) would be placed as agreed with the BWB.

Additionally, Crofton was now attracting some 3,000 visitors each steaming weekend and the Trust's Crofton branch was prepared to fund the restoration of locks leading up to Crofton in preparation for access to Crofton by boat from Great Bedwyn station. The good news continued with the announcement that Trust membership had reached 2,500 and was increasing at the rate of fifty a month.

In December, the Government caused a real commotion in waterway circles by announcing a plan to re-organise water and sewage services by setting up ten regional water authorities to assume responsibility for water supply, sewage disposal, river management, river and canal navigation, water amenity and recreation.

The section on waterways read:

> *Except for a few short lengths, the network of canal and river navigation managed by the BWB no longer fulfils a major transport function. On the other hand these waterways are extensively used for other purposes such as, increasingly, the supply and carriage of water supplies to water undertakings. They are of growing value for recreation and amenity, a function which the Government wishes to encourage. For these reasons, the inland waterways need to be more inte-grated into the system of river management and water supply. This can best be done at regional level. The canals today are mainly of local and regional significance. It is unnecessary and inap-propriate that they should continue to be administered by a national transport industry. The responsibilities of British Waterways for these waterways will therefore be transferred to the new Regional Water Authorities and the Board wound up. Decisions about the future of individual waterways can be taken locally by the Authorities in consultation with the various bodies inter-ested in the use of waterways including the Countryside Commission, regional Sports Councils and local authorities. Where a canal crosses Regional Water Authority boundaries, arrange-ments will need to be made for determining responsibility as between one Authority and another. Through navigation will be safeguarded as appropriate. The Government intend that the Authorities should retain the BWB's existing duties as regards maintenance of waterways with suitable statutory provision for modification of these duties if they consider it unavoidable that the costly maintenance of a waterway for navigation should be discontinued or, alterna-tively, if funds become available, for the restoration of a waterway to navigation.*

Both the BWB and the IWA reacted with some vigour to this proposition.

The BWB, having considered the serious hydrological, organisational, legal and manage-rial implications were firmly convinced that the best and most satisfactory method of achieving the Government's objective was, in the national interest, the retention of the present structure of the Board. The Secretary of State was advised that the proposal as far as the BWB was concerned would result in the collapse of the system.

The end result would, in the Board's opinion, endanger life and property and was based on apparent misconceptions of the fundamental management and canal hydrological facts of life. Sir Frank Price told a conference called by the Rt Hon. Eldon Griffiths, Parliamentary

Above: *Another step forward – the opening of the Newbury to Kintbury length by Lord Methuen.* (Hugh McKnight)

Right: *From left to right are Capt. Lionel Munk, Chairman of Kintbury UDC, Lord Methuen, General Stockwell.* (Leslie Bryce)

Under-Secretary, Dept of the Environment, that there had been no case made out for the dismemberment of the canal system, the policy was based on the report of the Central Advisory Water Committee who had not even considered the canals. Not one organisation concerned with water supply supported the policy and it was time the Government realised that canals were a national asset and should be managed as such and not to be considered a financial embarrassment to be discarded.

Needless to say, to the relief of all concerned the scheme was abandoned in January 1973, according to BWB, as 'impractical and contrary to the public interest following studies of the Board's affairs by working parties chaired by two Permanent Secretaries of the DoE.'

The Trust, wishing to accelerate restoration, asked the BWB to adopt a new programme; for 1972, the two remaining Wootton Rivers Locks with Kintbury, Tyle Mill and Buckley's Lock at Semington; and for 1973, the other Semington lock with locks at Brunsdens, Wire, Dun Mill and Hungerford and possibly Bulls Lock, Newbury, later in the year.

In March, following the inspection of the Bulls to Tyle Mill section, the chairman asked Berkshire County Council to match John Smith's offer of £50,000. This they refused to do, insisting that until the bridge problem was settled they were not interested in restoration,

Diana Kendall and Admiral Sir William O'Brien, then chairman of Devizes and Pewsey branch, at the re-opening of the four Wootton Rivers Locks, 10 June 1973. (Hugh McKnight)

offering only £100 in 1971/1972 and £50 in each of the following two years. Wiltshire County Council also refused to make any move so it was decided to use the John Smith money to rebuild at least one of the turf-sided locks west of Tyle Mill using contractors.

Volunteer work also continued apace preparing the Wootton Rivers Locks for re-gating by the BWB; the work was carried out by members of the Devizes and Pewsey branches assisted by the Conservation Corps, a band of helpers organised by Bob Chalmers from Swindon. Hungerford members were also busily clearing the wharf area and to the west, Bath and Bristol members were hard at work on the Bath locks.

At the Reading end of the canal, the trip boat *Kennet Water* began operations on the cruiseway. She was a ship's lifeboat from the liner *Iberia* with a 12ft (3.66m) beam and converted into a rather unorthodox but comfortable passenger craft. She was owned by Mr Nicklin and crewed by Reading branch members who earned commission by her operation which continued until she was sold in 1974.

The middle of May marked another step forward when Lord Methuen opened the Newbury to Kintbury length at a cost of £8,500 including the £2,500 donated by the IWA. The VIP party travelled aboard Bill Fisher's horse-drawn *Kennet Valley* accompanied by thirty craft of all shapes and sizes.

In November 1972, John Smith increased his already splendid offer to £75,000, to restore Ufton, Towney, Padworth and Aldermaston Locks subject to the work being put out to tender and his approval of the terms. There had been considerable activity on the Caen Hill

Locks with the North London Rescue Commando (NLRC), a youth organisation led by Richard Trim, working with the Trust's Junior Division clearing vegetation from the brickwork of the locks. Unfortunately serious friction developed between the parties, which was later solved by transferring the NLRC effort to Crofton Locks. By mid-1972, all the Caen Hill Locks had been cleared of the vegetation which was threatening the brickwork, three chambers had been completely cleared, half the derelict gates dismantled with four side ponds cleared and awaiting re-flooding. Both on the Devizes Flight, and at Crofton Top Lock, encampments had been set up to accommodate the youthful volunteers.

To bring the year to a successful close Miss W. Rennie, a direct descendant of John Rennie, re-opened Kintbury Lock in early December.

With the benefit of increasing income, the decision was made by the Trust to bring the restoration to Hungerford forward to 1974 and to press on with a further nine locks and the seven miles up the Crofton Flight to link up with Devizes by 1976. If this was successful, then from Newbury westwards there would be thirty-seven miles and thirty-eight locks usable and between the Thames and Devizes, only seven miles and nine locks would remain derelict. Although there was still much to do, full restoration was beginning to look a possibility at last.

Under the title 'Project 1976', the necessary new orders were placed; everything then depended on British Waterways being able to meet the agreed dates. The IWA, having previously offered £3,500 for work on Bulls Lock, was asked to make this available in 1974; on confirmation, an order would be placed.

Navigation between Dundas and Bath Top Lock was still impossible because of the Bathampton (Claverton) slip. The BWB had received £6,000 in compensation but maintained that any attempt to remove the blockage would be dangerous and insisted on a survey. Other worries at Bath were caused by the lack of funds; for instance, an estimated £8,000 was urgently required for dredging operations and recently installed lock gates began to deteriorate when pounds between them dried out.

The West Wiltshire branch complained that money had not been allocated for the restoration of Bradford-on-Avon Lock or, for that matter, anywhere else in their area, whereas at the eastern end the Tyle Mill Lock fund had exceeded its target of £2,500 by May. However, this branch, in conjunction with the Kennet & Avon Navigation Co. Ltd, a private venture based on Semington Bottom Lock, raised £3,000 under the sponsorship of Unigate, the principal event being a sponsored paddle from Bradford-on-Avon to Devizes. It was agreed that this money should be channelled through the Trust, and equally divided on projects chosen respectively by the branch and by the company.

On 10 June 1973 Diana Kendall, accompanied by Lord Methuen and Admiral Sir William O'Brien, then chairman of Devizes and Pewsey branch, re-opened the four Wootton Rivers Locks restored at a cost of only £9,000 thanks to the extensive use of volunteer labour and the generosity of Chivers & Sons and Pearce & Sons for the loan or hire of plant and equipment. Diana Kendall, who was Lord Methuen's personal secretary, had donated £1,500 in memory of her brother.

The plea from the Bath branch over the critical state of locks resulted in George Lloyd of BWB being given authority to begin dredging, the cost being covered by a BWB credit from previous work together with a loan from central Trust funds which the branch would repay. It was hoped that this would be recovered by a grant from Bath City Council the following financial year.

In July, the BWB were asked to modify the agreed restoration programme by restoring Bradford-on-Avon Lock after Tyle Mill Lock instead of that at Picketfield but they refused.

The grand re-opening to Hungerford was scheduled for 22 September 1973, but by then the last few hundred yards up to the wharf had not been dredged and the wharf itself had yet to be tidied up, so instead a small local ceremony was held above Dunmill Lock. In the same month it was learnt that the £75,000 offered for work at the eastern end had, through no fault of the donor, been reduced to £50,000. It had already been decided not to re-gate Ufton Lock with its 18in (0.46m) rise but to remove the gates and to do away with the lock altogether; however, the brick-built chamber still remains to this day.

Tenders for Padworth and Towney Locks amounted to £61,000 plus £11,000 for British Waterways manufactured gates but British Waterways would not allow Padworth Lock to be considered at this time as there was a possibility that it might be included in a scheme to lower the canal to pass under a fixed Aldermaston bridge.

The following January, the contract for rebuilding Towney Lock for the sum of £42,810 was given to Knott Brodie of Bath.

The balance of the now depleted £50,000 would pay for dredging the length between Tyle Mill and Towney Locks which had been made necessary by the deletion of Ufton Lock. The Waterway Recovery Group, a body of waterway enthusiasts led by Graham Palmer, expressed a desire to work on the Kennet & Avon and it was suggested that the two Froxfield Locks could be restored to extend the navigation beyond Picketfield which the BWB expected to complete by the end of 1974. As the original IWA offer to assist with the funding for Bulls Lock had not been taken up, they renewed the pledge with an offer of £7,500 to be set against the £10,000 estimate for the two locks.

At the western end, and smarting from BWB's refusal to restore Bradford-on-Avon Lock, there was intense pressure from the West Wiltshire branch for British Waterways to be asked to restore Buckley's Lock at Semington instead, funded with £2,500 from central funds, £1,000 from the branch and a donation of £1,500 from the Kennet & Avon Navigation Co.

Towards the end of 1973 discussions between BWB and the Berkshire County Council resulted in an agreement that the latter would meet the additional costs of maintenance between Hamstead and Hungerford and additionally a working party was set up to study the problem of Aldermaston bridge. The year ended on a high note with the news that the DoE had made a grant of £3,452 towards repairs to the buildings and sluices at Claverton.

By now the effects of inflation was starting to bite and alongside the rapid escalation of prices came the expensive need for safety awareness, all of which upset the previously reasonably secure estimates. Dun Mill had exceeded its estimate by £1,221, and Tyle Mill by £1,725; for the current financial year, costs would be in the order of £83,000 against an income of £75,000.

Nevertheless, despite this sounding like a prediction from 'Mr Wilkins Micawber', the restoration sub-committee recommended placing orders for both Semington Locks at an estimated cost of £9,700. The sum of £3,000 would also be allocated for repairs to Bradford-on-Avon wharf building. Since the original estimate for this task was £6,500 it was decided that no order would be placed until at least half the deficit had been raised. The hope was that the allocation of this £3,000 would encourage the local council to produce a grant, meanwhile any money held by the branch should now be set towards the building repairs.

The Trust Council finally decided that it would finance the rebuilding of Semington Locks helped with the £1,000 already raised by the West Wiltshire branch together with a donation from the Kennet & Avon Navigation Co. through the Unigate sponsorship.

Any remaining balance would be set against the cost of dredging between Seend and Semington. Meanwhile another private company, Wiltshire Inland Navigators, was prepared to raise the remainder as well as dredge between Semington and Bradford at an estimated cost of £16,830.

8 Changes at the Top
1974-1977

At the Canal Trust's AGM held during March 1974, General Stockwell announced his wish to resign as chairman. The resignation of 'The General', as he was affectionately known by all, was the end of an era of slow but very sure progress towards restoration.

He had led the Trust through some of the darkest hours but his steadfastness never wavered and his brilliant leadership gave courage to everyone with whom he came into contact. The Kennet & Avon Canal restoration project owes its success to quite a small band of dedicated people and truly General Sir Hugh Stockwell was one of them.

He was at once appointed President to replace Lord Methuen who had died in January. Lord Methuen's health had slowly deteriorated since an illness following a fall into the canal in 1970, despite which he had continued to attend all Trust functions.

At the following council meeting Admiral Sir William O'Brien, whose membership had been 'organised' by the General, was elected chairman. Towards the eastern end of the waterway dredging operation under Hungerford bridge was made difficult because the citizen who had purchased the adjoining towpath from the Great Western Railway refused to allow the BWB to use a dragline from the bank. This was overcome by using a floating suction dredger and on 20 July navigation was extended westward from Kintbury to beyond the restored Hungerford Lock.

An opening ceremony was performed by Cdr the Revd Rt Hon Lord Sandford, Parliamentary Under-Secretary of State at the Department of the Environment and Cdr Knapton, chairman of the Hungerford branch, who presented General Stockwell with a cheque for £1,000 towards the cost of restoring Hungerford Lock.

In mid-1974, prompted by Mr Diamond, a Trust member of the council agreed to launch an appeal for funds to be managed by Allied Communication Services Ltd. It is later recorded that the venture was not a success.

About this time, unfortunately, the relations with Mr Trim had become strained, in part because the Trust rejected his plans for radical changes within its restoration priorities and so, after much good work at Caen Hill and the Crofton Flight, the North London Rescue Commando decided to focus its efforts elsewhere. Devizes and Pewsey branch volunteers, now available following the completion of the Wootton Rivers Locks, agreed to take over the Crofton project under the auspices of Dr Simon Phillips. The Crofton Society, as the Canal Trust's Crofton branch was known, offered £1,000 to replace essential equipment. At the takeover, three lock chambers had been cleared, mainly by hand, of 3,500 tons of mud and a half-mile pound cleared of 10,000 tons of spoil.

The branch published a booklet, *The Crofton Lock Flight Project*, which told how the BWB were so impressed by what had been done that they entrusted to the branch more work than had ever been allowed to a volunteer team and stated that the BWB was anxious that the branch should not only complete mud clearance, but also undertake brick and masonry restoration, clearing old gates and other debris under their guidance, thus saving at least 30% in costs.

The booklet continued with the confident prediction that by the end of 1976 the flight would be ready for re-gating by the BWB. It ended with a list of materials together with requests for loans of machinery, site accommodation and an appeal for the £50,000 (this figure included the gates) that was needed for completion.

The project site manager was Cpl Brian Marson, Royal Electrical & Mechanical Engineers, who was employed under the terms of a Military Aid to the Civil Community exercise and was adept at securing loans of machinery and equipment.

The Managing Director of Rank Xerox was so impressed during a visit to Crofton that the firm donated £2,150 for the pair of top gates of Lock 61 as their contribution to European Architectural Year, 1975.

By now the effects of inflation were overwhelming and in February 1975, Don Collinson was told that the BWB would not in future take block orders and that the Trust must withdraw all existing orders and re-order, lock by lock; those ordered only two years before at £3,000 were now costing an average of £8,100. To continue at the present rate would require an extra £18,000 to be added to the existing allocated sum of £38,000. The resulting enhanced sum of £56,000 was more than the Trust could afford and all orders were withdrawn; only Picketfield, Froxfield Bottom and Semington were re-ordered.

At Crofton there was no shortage of machinery on loan and Brian Marson, now out of the army, was employed full-time, initially for one year at a salary of £3,000 plus expenses.

At the 1975 AGM the Canal Trust was told that the Thames Water Authority had quoted £14,000 for restoring Bulls Lock. Newbury and Reading branches were raising finance and Mike Padmore, of Costain's, volunteered to act as the Trust's engineer should BWB agree to allow it to be the contractor using volunteer labour; this they did on condition that an engineer nominated by Mike should be on site whenever any work was in progress. Work began in May and throughout the following eighteen months, the assistance and advice of the professional engineers, Inspector Rogers and Richard Dommett of BWB, was invaluable.

On 21 June Capt. Lionel Munk returned to the Kennet & Avon Canal to open the traffic light system between High Bridge and County Lock, Reading. This system was installed to prevent boats meeting head-on in the narrow winding Brewery Gut channel. The cost was defrayed, largely, from a testimonial collection from IWA members made on Captain Munk's resignation as IWA chairman and later allocated by him as a memorial to his late wife, Marion.

Restoration work by volunteers received a severe setback when, nominally owing to objections from the Waterways workforce, work on Froxfield Locks and the Crofton Lock project by the IWA and the Waterways Recovery Group (WRG) previously agreed by British Waterways had to be cancelled at the end of August. Work on Bulls Lock, however, was not affected.

The Froxfield scheme had envisaged using volunteers to drive dams and carry out lock clearance ahead of the BWB lock repair gang. However, the BWB now criticised the lack of adequate supervision to ensure satisfactory safety standards. At Crofton there had been a continuing clash of personalities which finally resulted in Brian Marson being discharged.

Later agreements with the BWB stipulated that any Trust project must be capable of supervision by a BWB Inspector who could only be expected to cover one project at a time. As an act of conciliation, British Waterways agreed to recruit a second lock repair team for the Hungerford to Crofton area provided that the Trust would finance two teams for at least two years.

During the year Dr Hancock, then eighty years old, retired from the Trust Council and was elected a vice-president and several branch chairmen changed posts, either through retirement or moving away from the area. Dr Simon Phillips replaced Admiral O'Brien at Devizes and Pewsey; Mike Stabler replaced Cdr Knapton at Hungerford; Derek Blazdell replaced Alec Ferguson at Reading and R. Garrett replaced Capt. Mansfield-Robinson who became President of the Junior Division. Flt Lt Tony Molland retired as *Butty* editor, his place being taken by Jack Dalby, the then Newbury branch chairman.

By the end of 1975, Froxfield and Oakhill Down Locks were almost complete. The estimates for the next locks westward (Little Bedwyn, Potters, Burnt Mill and Bedwyn Church) were £9,600 each.

Worries about water supplies for the restored canal was never very far from the minds of either British Waterways or the Trust Council. Prompted by the Junior Division, C.J.V. Davies of Davies & Oliver, Consulting Engineers of Ramsbury, in co-operation with Wessex Water, prepared a report which was published in 1976. It recommended providing water to compensate for seepage and evaporation losses in the Long Pound as well as usage of the Devizes Locks by an estimated twenty boat movements per day.

It also concluded that it might be necessary either to sink boreholes at Wootton Rivers at a cost of around £10,000, thereby producing some 1 million gallons per day, or to back pump around 1.06 million gallons per day up the Devizes Flight. In periods of dry weather, the report noted, the supplies from Wilton Water would hardly be enough to provide twenty boat movements through Crofton Locks, hence a back pumping scheme there and also at Wootton Rivers might be needed. However, a bore hole later sunk showed that because of existing demands on ground water in the area, boreholes could not provide anything like enough water which explains the decision in later years to implement the Devizes Locks back pumping scheme.

On 23 May 1976 Denis Howell, Minister for Sport and Recreation, formally re-opened Tyle Mill and Towney Locks, declaring the Government's moral but not financial support for the restoration of waterways, Sir Frank Price spoke of his Board's determination, with the help of the Trust, to re-open the Kennet & Avon throughout, a determination demonstrated less than two weeks later when, on 4 June, Sir Frank unveiled a plaque on Thimble Mill

Opening Bath Deep Lock, 1976.(Ken Clew)

beside Bath Lock No.7 whilst the Mayor of Bath, Councillor Mary Rawlings, declared the whole flight open. Just for the ceremony, water was lifted from the Avon by the newly restored Claverton pump and was then pumped over the Bathampton slip stop planks by an array of diesel pumps – two days later, however, these pumps were removed and the locks closed again – but it was an important step and an incentive to Bath branch.

As though to complement recent happenings at the western end, British Waterways invited the Duke of Edinburgh to visit the eastern end on 8 June. He spoke to volunteers at Bulls Lock, and visited Burghfield island as well as British Waterways' depot at Padworth. He then travelled west to watch boats using Hamstead Lock. He concluded his tour by inspecting the work at Crofton Lock and the Crofton pumps in operation.

Critics of the Trust's efforts had often doubted its ability to raise the money required to restore the more challenging locations, with re-watering the dry section and restoring the Caen Hill Flight in particular, as impossible dreams.

The appointment of Ian Walker as the new regional engineer in mid-1976 was crucial in proving the Jeremiahs wrong. For a year the Trust chairman had been trying to persuade BWB that the job creation scheme, introduced by the Government to revive unemployment, was tailor-made for canal restoration, but the general manager would not listen. At an early meeting in Gloucester his deputy, George Lloyd (a good friend to the Trust) said, 'Why don't we stop mucking about? Why don't we say we are going to restore the dry section with a job creation scheme?'

On the spot and without further discussion nor reference to his London HQ, Ian said, 'Go ahead!' This was a deciding moment in the history of the Trust, when it knew it would eventually succeed. There were to be many more occasions when the Trust would be grateful to him for not consulting Head Office; he too proved to be a friend indeed. On 23 June 1976 Ian Walker attended a special Trust Council meeting at Devizes where he and George Lloyd,

Denys Howell, Minister for Sport, opens Towney Lock, 1976. (Ken Clew)

Right (courtesy of Ken Clew) and below (courtesy of David Harris): *The inauguration of Towney Lock. Aboard the* Slough *are Denys Howell MP, General Sir Hugh Stockwell and Sir Frank Prince.*

The Duke of Edinburgh inspects Hamstead Lock, 1976. (Ken Clew)

area manager, explained the proposal for dealing with the Limpley Stoke dry section. After much discussion and consideration of the financial details, the Trust Council, without dissent, passed the following resolution:

> *That the Trust Council agrees to go ahead with the scheme in view of the great opportunity to deal with this section at a fraction of the cost, but in view of the acute water shortage problem at the western end and the time necessary for its solution, that the Crofton and Froxfield restoration be slowed down if this proved necessary.*

The scheme, accepted by the Wiltshire County Council as sponsors with the approval of the Manpower Services Commission (MSC), involved concreting a section between Dundas and Avoncliff aqueducts which had been dry since 1954.

The project was to be completed in a year with the BWB producing the plan and over-seeing its execution. The MSC would provide the labour, which being effectively free repre-sented a gift of some £100,000 whilst the Trust would pay for the materials estimated at £75,000, nevertheless the Trust's assured income was £30,000 short of the required amount so a Limpley Stoke appeal was launched.

Elsewhere there were serious water problems due to a long dry spell, raising doubts whether, for instance, even if all the locks between Hungerford and Devizes were restored would there be enough water to service them?

One victim of the drought was the Crofton Society's trip boat *Leviathan* whose hull was an old hand-dredger and which, in a vain attempt to deal with Long Pound weed, had been fitted with a steam-driven Hotchkiss cone propulsion unit. Now the shortage of water and rotting bottom planks made her disposal necessary.

On the completion of Bulls Lock in mid-1976, the BWB gave permission for volunteers to tackle the turf-sided Widmead Lock. Bulls had cost less than half the BWB's estimate, saving some £4,000 and the estimate for Widmead was considered generous at £20,000. The Froxfield Locks were also completed and work now started on Oakhill Down. The BWB installed dams westward as far as Bedwyn to maintain water levels and also started dredging, the almost dry, Wilton Water.

Major work commenced at Limpley Stoke in October by which time members and friends of the Trust had stood guarantee for £40,000, enough to convince the MSC that the money for materials could be found. Actual cash received was £25,000 with £7,000 promised for 1977. By concentrating all Trust income not already committed, including all balances held by individual branches, the shortfall was £29,000. This could be met by interest-free loans, donations or by cancelling restoration already ordered. British Waterways subscribed £28,000 and by the 1977 Trust AGM, the appeal fund had reached £38,000.

At this meeting Sir William reported that he had informed BWB that the Trust could raise, over and above that needed at Limpley Stoke, an extra £60-70,000 per annum for the next three years and because of this the BWB planned to complete restoration from Bath to the bottom of the Devizes Flight and from Newbury to the top of the flight by 1980. The re-opening of the west end would involve clearing Bathhampton slip and installing an electric pump at Claverton to supply the Bath Locks whilst there was every possibility that the next job creation scheme would be centred on the Devizes Flight.

At the other end between Reading and Newbury, turf-sided locks and many derelict bridges presented enormous problems. For perfectly good safety reasons, the BWB would not tolerate turf-sided locks; they argued that locks were always danger points and turf-siders were extremely hazardous for small craft.

The added expense of rebuilding turf-sided locks was evident when £47,000 was spent on rebuilding Towney Lock, but it also gave a very clear warning of the likely expense of

The Duke of Edinburgh at Crofton pumping station, June 1976. He was also able to see other restoration work on the eastern section of the canal, including Bulls Lock. (K&ACT Archives)

Above and left: *Work in progress on the Devizes Flight, 1976.* (K&ACT Archives)

Opposite: Ladywood *arriving at Bradford-on-Avon, 1977.* (C. Chalk)

rebuilding the remaining six. This warning proved all too true, for in the case of Widmead Lock, which was finally completed in 1990, the cost, enhanced of course by inflation, had risen to the staggering sum of £272,000. During 1976, Ham Lock on the Newbury cruiseway section was closed, being declared unsafe, but no real concern was felt because this was a lock which the BWB was statutorily required to repair.

However, because BWB funds were diverted to repair a major breach on the Monmouthshire & Brecon Canal, this rebuild, which was to have taken place during 1977, was postponed until 1978. There was no real objection to this, either locally or at Trust Council level, as the way east towards Bulls Lock was blocked by the extensive work required in rebuilding the Hambridge swing-bridge as a fixed 'up and over', a replacement much welcomed on the Newbury cruiseway for the swing-bridge had been 'only just' usable and required a small army of helpers as well as causing much traffic delay.

Volunteers were driving dams at Widmead and, at British Waterways's request, also at Monkey Marsh Lock where the top gates were in danger of collapse.

In 1977 three new passenger boats, which were used to raise funds for the Trust, arrived on the waterway: *Jubilee* at Wootton Rivers replacing The Crofton Society's *Leviathan*; *Ladywood* at Bradford-on-Avon; and *Lancing* at Reading. These boats, besides contributing valuable finance, also performed the useful function of being a centre of interest, and as such attracted many new members to the Trust.

Progress at Limpley Stoke was, disappointingly, not coming up to expectations. There was a real lack of skilled labour together with inclement weather and damage from vandalism slowed up progress. The Manpower Services Commission required BWB to submit a new scheme up to April 1978 and to guarantee completion by then. The supply of local labour was still insufficient and men had to be brought in from further afield, thus adding to the expense. The cost for plant increased and the Trust's bill threatened to be at least £20,000 more than estimated.

In spite of all these difficulties Kennet District Council and British Waterways applied successfully for a job creation scheme for the Devizes Locks. All the work required, except for the making and fitting of gates, would be included, but none of the estimated cost of £175,000, would fall on the Trust.

9 The Fraenkel Report
1978-1982

Following canal surveys in 1970, BWB advised the Department of the Environment that due to lack of funds in past years a major programme of engineering work (estimated as costing some £22 million) was required to carry out arrears of maintenance. There was a notable lack of activity for four years and then the DoE appointed independent consultants, Peter Fraenkel & Partners, to study the maintenance implications of the Board's waterways.

Their findings, the Fraenkel Report, was submitted to the Government in January 1976 but surprisingly it was not published until November 1978. It confirmed BWB's long held view in regard to cost, although Peter Fraenkel estimated that at 1978 prices the backlog of maintenance was now nearer £60 million. Paragraph 15.12.5 of the report which referred directly to the Kennet & Avon Canal is here reproduced in full:

> The Kennet & Avon Canal is unique amongst the Board's waterways in that while it originally formed part of a trunk waterway route between London and Bristol it is now divided into three Cruising lengths separated by two Remainder lengths, parts of which are quite unnavigable.
>
> Recent works, undertaken with the assistance of volunteer labour, have effectively extended the cruising facilities over parts of the Remainder lengths, but there are several major obstacles in the way of restoring through navigation over the whole length of the canal.
>
> These include the reconstruction of public highway bridges near Aldermaston, the restoration of locks and provision of adequate water supplies at Crofton, the problem of dealing with the derelict locks at Caen Hill, Devizes, and the sealing of chronic leaks in the bed of the canal between Bradford-on-Avon and Limpley Stoke. Quite clearly no amount of likely cruising and amenity revenue could justify undertaking the works needed to remove all these obstacles, and the costs shown in our tabulation for this waterway indicate, in fact, that elimination of certain sections would be the cheapest course.

Nevertheless there is a considerable amount of activity on the part of the Kennet & Avon Canal Trust and the IWA, with some encouragement from BWB and the county councils concerned, in an endeavour to continue restoration work on the unnavigable lengths. In view of the heavy expenditure involved, more particularly on the items mentioned in the preceding paragraph and in the subsequent continuing annual maintenance tasks, we consider that the future of the canal as a whole should be reviewed rather than dealing with its remainder lengths in isolation. A preliminary decision, in principle, as to whether local authorities and other bodies would be prepared to guarantee meeting costs in excess of 'most economical treatment' for defined portions of the waterway, might enable a firm policy to be agreed as to the lengths earmarked for retention. Further expenditure on the rest, to be eliminated in due course, would thus be positively discouraged.

Although the Government accepted the report in general terms, its response in terms of real help for all BWB's waterways was thought to be niggardly, allocating only £5 million for 1978-1979 and another £5 million in 1979-1980, and then this only for 'urgent maintenance works needed to protect public safety'.

One of the unforeseen consequences of the Fraenkel Report was the reaction to it from BWB employees. A spokesman for the trade union, NALGO, stated on television that BWB staff of all grades were amongst the lowest paid in the country and that they felt that some of

The Devizes HQ building before restoration. (K&ACT Archives)

the Fraenkel money should be used to improve their pay, and in an attempt to influence the Government's allocation of that money they were imposing a ban on working with volunteers.

The first the Canal Trust knew of the disagreement was when the chairman, Sir William O'Brien, received the following letter from the BWB Gloucester Area Engineer.

> *I am writing to advise you that for the time being the Board's staff have agreed not to co-operate with volunteer working parties, and to this end I would be grateful for your confirmation that all work will cease by such parties from 1 December 1978.*
>
> *It is hoped that this action will be short lived and that the amicable arrangements of the past can be restored soon.*

In order to maintain the good relations with BWB Sir William immediately asked all branches to cease work as the Gloucester office had requested but added, 'this ban is not inspired by those who work for BWB on the Kennet & Avon but comes from the more militant areas of the system'.

It was further suggested by the unions that the (then new) Health and Safety at Work Act would in any case adversely affect work by volunteers but the sad tale did not end there for, as has already been explained, the ban was the cause for disbanding the Junior Division and it also had other effects which ranged much wider than just the lost effort; it killed a lot of enthusiasm.

A great number of people, both young and old, were attracted by the prospect of being able to make a positive contribution towards restoration by donning wellies and gloves and then actually doing something about putting our canals back in business. They enjoyed whatever task they had undertaken and were happy to make the effort. They could and did, of course, take on other work within the Canal Trust branches, staffing boats, teashops and stalls, but this is hardly pioneering stuff and a lot of otherwise enthusiastic help that could have been put to good and productive use just drifted away.

There was still a further complication with Fraenkel when BWB said they would require extra staff, mainly technical, to cope with the extra work involved in the use of the money.

*Devizes shop,
1980. (K&ACT
Archives)*

The DoE, however, steadfastly refused to allow recruitment on the grounds that should there be no further money forthcoming, or that an alternative Government saw fit to cancel further work, then BWB would be left with surplus manpower.

Fortunately, as is often the way in such cases, time and diplomacy did a great deal to solve the problem but much of the original pioneering spirit seemed lost for ever.

When the Canal Trust held its AGM in 1978 it heard that a total of £107,000 had already been spent on Limpley Stoke. BWB had planned to spend £28,000, but in fact spent £130,000, this overspend being used largely in supplying transport for the workers and topping up the foreman's wages.

Additionally, they paid the cost of building the stone walling which, as part of the lining, appeared above the water line, and also they paid for the weekend overtime without which the April target date could never have been met. After this date the Manpower Services Commission allowed Wiltshire County Council, BWB and the Canal Trust to continue to employ a small workforce of about fifteen men until the limit of the original cash allowance for wages had been reached.

Water supplies again demanded attention following the failure of the borehole project. So to produce sufficient supplies BWB considered a scheme to pump water from the Avon at Claverton all the way eastward to feed Crofton and beyond at a probable cost of £1.5 million.

At the June Canal Trust Council meeting it was agreed that, subject to a reasonable financial arrangement, the Canal Trust should seek to lease the Devizes wharf building from Kennet District Council and sanctioned the setting up of a committee to negotiate suitable terms.

The restored building was the original Devizes bonded warehouse, a claim supported by the presence of thick metal straps fastened between the roof rafters, presumably there to keep the ungodly from breaking through the tiles and purloining the contents. These straps are clearly visible in the roof of the building which is now used as the Kennet & Avon Canal Museum.

When negotiations with Kennet District Council were finalised, the sum of £10,000 was allocated by the Canal Trust for repairing and fitting out the building to provide office and shop facilities, parts of which were planned to be sub-let.

This enormous task, which required input from just about every building trade, was organized and carried out with great enthusiasm by the Devizes branch and other Canal Trust members.

As Devizes is strategically placed almost at the centre point of the waterway, Admiral O'Brien proposed setting up a Canal Trust secretariat in one of the new office rooms. In March 1980 when much of the building was completed the membership office moved to Devizes, as did many of the other secretarial activities. Peter Collins, assisted by Jill Petty, took over as membership secretary from Alan Shave, Geoffrey Snelgrove became Canal Trust treasurer and the first Canal Trust Council meeting to be held there was in March 1981.

Mike Corfield, who had been the co-ordinator and driving force behind the setting up of the Wharf building, now interested the Carnegie Trust in sponsoring a Canal Interpretation Exhibition.

Such was their interest that they appointed a consultant, Andrew Pierssene, to advise on such a scheme. The Tourist Board and the Countryside Commission supported the proposal, as did the Canal Trust on condition that Mr Pierssene's plans were acceptable and that it would not bear any of the costs. The Carnegie Trust promised a grant of £7,000, which was later increased to £15,000.

Later in 1982, there came a decisive break with the past, when it was decided to bring the secretary and treasurer's functions under the Devizes umbrella.

As a result, the Canal Trust chairman asked Denys Hutchings to retire as secretary and hand over to Peter Collins. Peter's job as membership secretary passed to Jill Petty and Denys, who had been the Canal Trust's faithful secretary since January 1962, became vice chairman.

Thus after twenty years of fragmentation, with documents being stored as far apart as Reading and Avonmouth, all the Trust papers were now gathered together under one roof.

Many tributes should be paid to Denys who for over twenty years had been the very pivot around which the Canal Trust had operated. Much of the success enjoyed today stems directly from the foundations which he so patiently built. Working from Early, near Reading, and surrounded with Canal Trust papers and details, he had at all times been an accessible and conscientious contact point. From a home stacked with tea towels, pencils, post cards and all the assorted bric-a-brac so beloved by the waterway enthusiasts, Denys and his wife Margaret would sally forth to attend rallies and meetings all over the country; they even acquired a large bus type vehicle to make transportation easier.

So it was indeed a just reward when in recognition of all his efforts he was called to Buckingham Palace to be presented with the MBE by The Queen Mother.

July 1978 was a notable month with Claverton pumping station being opened to the public for the first time. The long delay since the building and pump had been restored was caused by negotiations with BWB over a licence and difficulties with access and parking. The licence finally agreed was for twenty-one years with an annual payment of £10.

Also during July, BWB suggested that only the top gates of the Devizes Locks should be ordered to allow the side pounds to be flooded and the environment improved; this arrangement would also save the expense of stop planks.

Wooden lock gates were first specified but later BWB looked into the feasibility of using galvanised steel with timber facings saving £1,000 a pair, although everyone felt that as the top lock was very much in the public view the gates should be wood; there was a strong possibility that Kennet District Council would pay for these but BWB required a down payment for all the materials before work commenced. A later tender of £70,376 for twenty-eight steel top gates for the main flight was accepted.

The BWB insisted that for safety reasons, the top balance beams must be cranked to prevent people being swept into the lock. Widespread protests that these would be downright ugly and completely non-traditional were ignored (however some years later these beams were removed and replaced with the more traditional and usual pattern). The gates were

The original Aldermaston road bridge which was replaced in 1981. (K&ACT Archives)

eventually made in one run and stored at BWB Worcester until needed at Devizes.

The restoration programme was now falling considerably behind schedule in spite of build-up of Canal Trust funds. In April 1979 it was reported that the dry Bath Locks were deteriorating and that Semington Lock and the two bottom locks at Seend were almost complete. Little Bedwyn Lock was finished but Potters had yet not started. There was some good news, however, when it was reported that Kennet District Council had agreed to pay for a new set of wooden gates for Devizes Top Lock.

Bath Locks caused a problem because being part of a remainder waterway there was no provision for maintenance costs if used for navigation. By agreement with the previous principal engineer this restriction had not been applied to locks west of Hamstead. Ian Walker, the new principal engineer, however, was not prepared to allow locks restored since his appointment to be used. Sir Frank Price backed him, insisting that hope lay only in persuading the local authority working parties earlier set up in Berkshire and Wiltshire to come up with suitable arrangements over shouldering maintenance costs.

At the start of 1980 BWB's projected restoration programme involved completing the Seend Locks, Potters and Burnt Mill Locks, three on Crofton Flight and finally the installation of the gates at Devizes Top Lock. The cost per lock, apart from Devizes, was quoted as being £15,000, making a total cost of £175,000, all of which would have to be met from investments.

There was also the expense of complying with Ian Walker's insistence that, apart from the maintenance problem, the use of Bath Locks would necessitate a new pump at Claverton. For this the Canal Trust offered £30,000. One project which did not involve Canal Trust expenditure was BWB's re-lining of Avoncliff aqueduct, started earlier in the year where a reinforced concrete channel was constructed within the original structure.

The BWB were later persuaded to start at Beech Grove Lock, near Great Bedwyn, instead of Crofton Top Lock. By working down from Beech Grove which was below the level of

The new bascule bridge at Aldermaston, which cost £300,000, was fully equipped with traffic lights with a time delay that allowed traffic to have priority during rush hours. (K&ACT Archives)

Wilton Water, navigation from Newbury could be extended without any immediate water supply problem.

The Berkshire County Council working party report was published in January 1980. The total cost of full restoration in Berkshire was estimated to be £1,275,000 with a total annual excess of £34,000 occurring in maintenance costs as used for cruising against restoring for safety reasons. The BWB, the Berkshire County Council, Newbury District Council and Reading Borough Council all agreed that the canal should be fully restored, with Berkshire County Council taking a positive step in that direction by the decision to replace Aldermaston bridge as soon as possible.

Towards the western end, the Wiltshire Working Party comprising BWB, Kennet District Council, West Wiltshire and Wiltshire County Council also agreed that the canal should be restored but had qualms about water supplies for the summit. Wilton Water was estimated to produce less than 0.75 million gallons per day and the Seend feeder only 0.25 million gallons per day. Wessex Water agreed to the extraction of eight million gallons per day from the Avon at Claverton. This amount back pumped over all locks to the summit would allow all Crofton supplies plus 1 million gallons per day from Claverton to flow eastward, the pumps costing £175,000. The total Wiltshire restoration costs would be £761,560 with £69,420 allowed for annual maintenance.

Sir Frank Price chaired the working party meetings, and advisory committees were to be set up to formulate recommendations and proposals for the future. A meeting with Avon County Council was planned.

As it now appeared possible that all locks between Newbury and the engine pound at Crofton would be completed by August 1981, the Canal Trust suggested that a major event should be held at Crofton on August Bank Holiday weekend and BWB agreed that this was possible and planning should go ahead.

Above: *Dundas aqueduct before restoration.*

Left: *The entire aqueduct was planked off following an unsuccessful attempt to seal off a leak with plastic sheeting.* (K&ACT Archives)

It was unlikely that the Padworth workforce could do more than complete Potters Lock due to pressure of other work in their section. It was therefore decided that the gang which had finished the Seend Locks should restore two Crofton Locks, and in 1980 install top gates at Crofton Crossing Lock before tackling Bedwyn Church and Burnt Mill Locks. Leonard Spray, Newbury branch chairman, became the co-ordinator of 'Crofton Unlocked 1981'.

Canal Trust finances soon came under severe strain. Following BWB's work at Sheffield Lock where the original brickwork had been extended above full water level, the finance and restoration committee wished to order the restoration of Padworth in 1981 and Aldermaston in 1982 at a cost, based on Sheffield, of £45,000 each. A further £64,000 would be needed for locks up to Crofton, another £54,000 was owed and £30,000 pledged for the Claverton pump. To meet the expected costs some, if not all of the Canal Trust's investments would have to be liquidated and yet another appeal launched. Nevertheless work continued.

An attempt to seal off a leak in Dundas aqueduct with plastic sheeting proved to be unsuccessful so the entire aqueduct remained planked off. But there was, however, some success when a number of Bath Lock sills were replaced.

Negotiations with Wiltshire County Council continued and Avon County Council considered granting £20,000 per annum between 1982 and 1983. Only Wansdyke District Council refused to take any interest.

Following constant pressure BWB, for the first time, entered into a legal maintenance agreement with a voluntary body – the Canal Trust – by allowing the use of Bath Locks and the canal as far as Dundas. The period of lock opening would be from Good Friday to the end of September.

The agreement would come into operation on the day the new Claverton pump became operational with the Canal Trust providing £30,000 towards the cost of the pump, three quarters of the wages of a lock-keeper and any additional costs. There would be joint inspections of the length before and after each season to establish these costs. The agreement would run for five years unless some alternative arrangement with local authorities was achieved, in which case the agreement would terminate automatically.

At the east end Berkshire County Council granted £4,900 which, together with £10,000 from Newbury District Council, would go towards Padworth Lock; Kennet District Council allocated £5,000 for a slipway at Devizes Wharf. Admiral O'Brien, however, warned against over-optimism; in addition to the estimated £300,000 needed for the back pumping scheme, £100,000 would be required for Crofton Locks, at least £150,000 for the missing Devizes bottom gates, £100,000 for locks at Padworth and Aldermaston, and a frightening £600,000 for Woolhampton, Heales, Monkey Marsh and Widmead Locks. This came to a grand total of £1.25 million.

At the meeting of the Finance and Restoration Committee in June 1981, Admiral O'Brien reported that the Canal Trust would offer £90,000 spread over three years for back pumps at Bradford, Semington and Seend. He said that Padworth would cost at least £60,000 but could not be started until 1982 and the Claverton pump would not be ready for Bath Locks to be used in 1981. At the same meeting the treasurer reported that the current income was £75,000 per annum and that all reserves would be used up for the completion of the two Crofton Locks, while Church and Burnt Mill Locks at Great Bedwyn would be charged at £22,000, £4,000 more than first quoted.

There was regret when it was announced that Don Collinson was to resign from the council and the Restoration Committee. The Canal Trust owes a great debt of gratitude to Don for being one of the principal architects of restoration for well over twenty years. Robin Bradbury agreed to take over Don's liaison work with BWB at Gloucester.

'Crofton Unlocked' was a tremendous success with fine weather and the engine pound packed with boats. The Admiral in his opening speech confirmed that the remaining Crofton Locks would not be restored in the near future because of difficulties over water supplies and that restoration would now shift to the east. Following a BWB inspection of Dundas aqueduct the BWB considered that the major works needed should be funded by the Canal Trust. The council demurred; Dundas was a scheduled ancient monument and the responsibility for its repair rested firmly on the BWB's shoulders. BWB replied that higher priorities had greater claim on their limited finance.

A major obstacle to progress westwards was removed in October 1981; Lewis Moss, chairman of Berkshire County Council, opened the new bascule bridge at Aldermaston which had cost £300,000. Fully equipped with traffic lights and a time delay, which allowed traffic to have priority in rush hours, the bridge was a most impressive sight as it slowly lifted to permit the passage of boats. With the bridge complete, effort shifted just along the tow path to nearby Padworth Lock where work began in earnest clearing away the debris and vegetation.

Following a discussion on trip boats for fund-raising, the Devizes & Pewsey branch was granted £18,000 (£6,000 was already available from interest-free loans) to replace the elderly *Charlotte Dundas*, whilst up to £20,000 was allocated to the Hungerford branch, under its new chairman Bob Charlton, to purchase a boat.

This craft, *Rose of Hungerford*, built by Peter Nichols, was launched in 1983 at which an amusing incident occurred; the bottle of champagne with which Lady O'Brien was destined to christen the vessel missed its target and to this day remains in the bottom of the canal. *Rose of Hungerford* is a wide boat having a beam of some 10ft 6in (3.2m) and a length of 55ft (16m) thus allowing her to be a very comfortable trip boat indeed. From her base on Hungerford wharf she has cruised the Kennet & Avon taking many thousands of happy people for rides ever since. Her most famous role was when she carried Her Majesty the Queen to the Grand Re-opening in 1990.

At the end of 1981 Berkshire County Council and Newbury County Council agreed to contribute £5,000 each for the year 1982-1983 towards maintaining the sections from Tyle

Rose of Hungerford *was launched in 1983.* (Author)

Mill to Aldermaston and Hamstead to Kintbury. Later this was increased to a five-year agreement; Newbury also granted another £20,000 for restoration. There was, however, no support from Wiltshire County Council, Avon County Council or Wansdyke District Council, although early in 1982 Wiltshire County Council sent a paper to all councillors suggesting that councils should take on the maintenance cost of the Dundas to Bradford length when BWB had dealt with Dundas aqueduct. Although Kennet and West Wiltshire District Council's accepted the recommendation, Wiltshire County Council Policy Committee turned it down flat.

A political change in Avon County Council now meant that canal maintenance had less priority although the Advisory Group remained. On 9 April 1982, Bath Locks were re-opened once again and on the following day a vast flotilla of boats cruised to Dundas and back.

At the AGM in 1982 the chairman reported that the work at Padworth was progressing reasonably well, although Padworth swing-bridge was still inoperable and without any firm plans for its repair or replacement. The BWB had refused to accept an order for the Bradford-on-Avon back pump until Dundas aqueduct had been repaired; no date for this could be forecast.

In July Sir Frank Price visited Devizes and was shown around the canal centre and the bottom locks where a Community Enterprise Project was completing the work left unfinished at the end of the 1978-1979 job creation scheme. On the same day, Lock 49 was named 'Maton Lock', after the late Eustace Bertram Maton, a local farmer, thereby acknowledging a donation of £20,000, and Lock 50 was named 'Kennet Lock' by Mrs Wookey, the Kennet District Council chairman, in recognition of that council's great contributions.

BWB announced that the Devizes gates would cost £15,000 more than the £20,000 estimated. As they had already overspent for 1982 the extra money was required immediately if fitting the gates was to continue.

10 The Manpower Services Commission to the Rescue 1983-1988

The 1982 Government Community Programme, successor to the Community Enterprise Programme, sought to provide work for some 200,000 people whose ages ranged from eighteen to twenty-four years and who had been out of work for six months or more, or those twenty-five years and older who had not worked for a year. The jobs to be undertaken were those of value to the community which needed doing but were not being done, a description clearly embracing canal restoration, and the Berkshire County Council was quick to propose a major project on the canal.

They called a meeting with the BWB, Newbury District Council, the chairman and vice chairman of the Canal Trust and the chairman of Newbury branch to consider a project, later agreed by the Manpower Services Commission (MSC), to employ fifty men to tackle a number of outstanding tasks.

They comprised Aldermaston Lock at an estimated cost of £35,000, Aldermaston Wharf and adjacent area at £12,000, Widmead Lock at £70,000 and two further minor jobs which could proceed without estimates. These were, firstly, to carry out some exploratory work on the restoration of Monkey Marsh Lock which was to be retained as an example of a Kennet turf-sided lock and, secondly, to carry out some towpath improvements.

Berkshire County Council had £35,000 remaining in the 1982 Community budget which would be transferred to the Canal Trust; Newbury District Council agreed that the £20,000 already budgeted for work on the canal in 1983 could also be transferred to the project and

Aldermaston Lock nearing completion. (Leslie Bryce)

*Aldermaston Lock,
July 1983.*
(K&ACT Archives)

*Sulhamstead Lock under
restoration, 1983.*
(David Harris)

*Dundas aqueduct under
repair.* (M. Jones)

Above and right: *By Easter 1983, Ham Lock had
been rebuilt by contractors who used steel piles to line the
walls.* (K&ACT Archives)

the Trust offered the £50,000 allocated to Aldermaston Lock. Additionally all the wages
would be paid by the MSC. It was hoped that this injection of money, together with the
£300,000 Berkshire County Council had spent on Aldermaston bridge, would put pressure
on the DoE to solve the problems of the other swing-bridges on the Berkshire length.

By Easter 1983 Ham Lock had been rebuilt by contractors who used steel piles to line the
walls; this allowed Bulls Lock, which had been completed in 1976, to be used for the first time.

The really exciting event was on 26 April when the Berkshire Manpower Services
Commission project was launched by Sir Frank Price, BWB chairman, and Mr Timperley,
chairman of the Berkshire County Council. In his speech, Sir Frank announced that he had
persuaded his Board to alter their priorities to include the repair of Dundas aqueduct as no
major structural faults were revealed by their detailed inspection. This was a gracious gesture
to the Trust since Dundas aqueduct was low on the BWB's list of canal structures demanding
capital expenditure.

On the following day ACE, an association of river and canal commercial enterprises,
presented a case for maintenance agreements. Using figures published in an Inland Waterways
Amenity Advisory Council report of 1980, ACE suggested that if the local authorities
invested some £1.2 million over the next ten years for canal maintenance this would attract
three times that sum in private sector investment and ten times that sum in additional local
spending. They also thought it would double the amount in BWB income and considered it
would produce three times the invested sum in returns to the exchequer together with 200
to 300 new jobs and the provision of a fantastic amenity to visitors and locals alike.

It is noticeable that ACE themselves did not volunteer any financial help but it seemed to
have had some effect as almost immediately Avon County Council granted £10,000 towards
western end maintenance.

Other grants and donations followed: £2,000 from the Slough Canal Association on its
dissolution, £1,000 bequeathed to the Canal Trust by Dr Hancock and £7,000 donated by
the Avon and Wiltshire branch of the IWA to be used towards the Devizes Locks.

The official opening of Dundas aqueduct on 1 July 1984 by Sir Frank Price, who had retired as BWB chairman the previous day. (Robin Bradbury)

There were two important anniversaries celebrated in 1983: first, the 21st birthday of the Canal Trust; and second, the 80th birthday of General Sir Hugh Stockwell for which a birthday fund was initiated with a view to raising enough money to sponsor the naming of a Devizes Lock in General Stockwell's honour.

September saw the completion of the Interpretation Scheme in the Devizes Wharf building which was declared opened by canal author Anthony Burton. This superb exhibition of canal history, the brainchild of Mike Corfield and assisted by the Carnegie Trust, is appreciated by hundreds of tourists and canal enthusiasts who visit Devizes every year. It is now a musuem registered with the Museums & Galleries Commission (No.1058) and, although small, has won many awards and commendations; it is not content to rest on its laurels so the museum's exhibits are always being reviewed and improved.

During 1998, an interactive viewing system was added; popular with visitors this system is constantly up-dated with the latest canal news.

Besides the museum an archive has been established within the canal centre in which to preserve documents and pictorial canal matter for the future. The Trust archivists, the first of which was Michael Smith, have been greatly supported by the Wiltshire Museum and Library Service which has given much valued assistance and advice. The archives, which have grown over the years, are open by appointment to scholars, research students and other interested parties and are thoroughly protected within the provisions of the Museums & Galleries Commission registration so there is little danger of the comprehensive collection ever being lost.

The wharf building also contains a canal shop where a comprehensive collection of canal books, canal ware and gift items are on sale.

Towards the end of 1983 Wiltshire County Council and the West Wiltshire District Council agreed to sign a five-year maintenance agreement covering the length from the Avon/Wiltshire border to Foxhangers, provided the BWB was satisfied that in normal conditions there would be sufficient water available for navigation. This would require installing backpumping equipment around Bradford-on-Avon Lock to be financed by the Canal Trust. The agreement was signed in April 1985 and other local authorities, attracted by this practical approach, added their approval. This joint initiative was an important watershed which, although not fully appreciated at the time, paid handsome dividends for the waterway in later years.

Meanwhile, for 1983-1984 the shortfall of some £5,892 was paid by the Trust and, because of the refusal of Wansdyke to contribute, the Trust also undertook to pay 20% of the Bath to Dundas maintenance costs.

After some preliminary work on the provision of an access road at Widmead Lock carried out under the MSC scheme, the BWB proposed that the 1984-1985 effort should be transferred to the rebuilding of Woolhampton Lock thus focusing the pressure on the DoE to renovate Froudes and Woolhampton swing-bridges, which were the next two barriers west of Aldermaston.

An offer by the Newbury branch working party to restore Midgham Lock was turned down by the BWB who had given an undertaking to the Unions that if they would accept the MSC scheme such volunteer work would be forbidden.

On 1 July 1984 Sir Frank Price, who had the previous day retired as the BWB chairman, declared open Dundas aqueduct. This had been renovated and concrete-lined at no expense to the Canal Trust. After the opening, the official party cruised to Bradford Wharf over the re-lined Dundas and Avoncliff aqueducts, passing along the former dry section and through Bradford-on-Avon Lock which had just been re-opened only a few hours previously. Following this tremendous parting gift, Sir Frank was invited to become a Kennet & Avon Canal Trust Vice President.

Veteran volunteers hate to see good money paid to anyone for doing the work that they have for so many years done for free but the Trust's activities had become too various and complicated to be properly overseen by part-time officers so consequently, after much heart searching, the council agreed that a grant should be sought from the DoE towards the salary of a full time administrator. Approval for a grant for a limited period, together with support

Lock 48 became 'Trust Lock' to commemorate the Kennet & Avon Canal Trust's 21st birthday in 1983. Left to right: General Stockwell, Admiral O'Brien and John Smith. (K&ACT Archives)

Left and below: *Padworth Lock before and after restoration. The lock was opened on 12 June 1984.*
(K&ACT Archives)

from local authorities, was forthcoming and in September 1984, Cdr Nick Wright was appointed the Canal Trust's first full-time general secretary.

The decision, although inevitable, was still a courageous one for once the post had been filled and the matter settled there really was no easy way of going back on it because, as will be appreciated, employing paid staff not only changes the character of a small charitable volunteer organization but will also put a strain on resources, which up until this time had all been funneled directly into restoring the canal and that, after all, was the Trust's *raison d'être*.

Although the Canal Trust was protected, for a limited period at least, from the financial burden of providing salaries, when the grant ceased the membership subscriptions would then have to underwrite the administration costs on a permanent basis without any guarantee that it would remain financially possible. Fortunately finances have allowed the Head Office at Devizes to continue and it now serves as a canal information centre as well as the Kennet & Avon Canal Trust administrative headquarters.

There was further reorganisation within head office when two ladies, one dealing with membership matters and another as finance assistant, were appointed as salaried part-time staff. Peter Collins became 'secretary to the council'. His duties included calling and recording meetings, handling all Canal Trust legal business and making the annual Canal Trust returns. All other management matters excepting those local to branches became the duty of the new general secretary.

However, this divided administrative arrangement was not entirely satisfactory so towards the end of 1986 the post of 'Secretary to the Council' was abolished with the new general secretary, assisted by the treasurer, accepting all duties with the exception of minute secretary which was undertaken by Jill Petty. Peter Collins and Alan Shave, the former minute secretary, became Vice-Presidents and later Peter Collins played a major part in the organisation of the Canal Trust's Silver Jubilee AGM.

Meanwhile, the new general secretary soon settled into his new position at the canal centre and, coupled with working a long day, could be found on many evenings travelling the length of the waterway either visiting branches or giving lectures.

The BWB's ban on volunteer effort was relaxed when it became obvious that footbridges for the Caen Hill Locks were needed. Volunteers from Devizes and Pewsey branches, along with the Newbury working party, commenced work on two whilst a third was built by a Melksham school. The project was to be self-supporting, each bridge costing £200 for materials.

On 29 September 1984 great activity took place on the Devizes Locks when, in the absence through illness of the new BWB chairman Sir Leslie Young, Vice Chairman Dr Robertson named five locks on the flight. Lock 48 became 'Trust Lock' to commemorate the Kennet & Avon Canal Trust's 21st birthday whilst Lock 47 became 'Manifold Lock' in honour of John Smith's Manifold Trust, a most generous supporter.

With a donation of £10,000 from IWA branches, Lock 46 became 'A.P. Herbert Lock' in memory of A.P. Herbert, the first President of the IWA, and Lock 45 was named 'Cave Lock' in appreciation of the Cave Foundation's generosity. Finally, Lock 44 became 'General Sir Hugh Stockwell Lock' in honour of the Trust President, then in his eighty-second year.

Smaller MSC schemes were now set up along the canal, one of which prepared a landing stage and an approved walkway between Crofton pump house and the canal. Unfortunately a larger scheme to prepare the upper Crofton locks for new gates suffered from lack of adequate supervision but other work successfully completed consisted of towpath improvements and the provision of facilities for disabled anglers at Devizes.

On 12 June Admiral O'Brien re-opened Padworth Lock in the presence of Martin Japes, then BWB's director of engineering, together with the chairmen of both Berkshire County and Newbury District Councils; also present were members of the Clark family who placed a commemorative plaque on one of the balance beams in memory of their late son. Padworth

Lock had been unapproachable by boat because the nearby Padworth swing-bridge was derelict and unusable so to celebrate the occasion the vice chairman's immaculate 100-year-old skiff was launched over the bank and ceremoniously locked through the newly re-opened lock. The Admiral complimented the small BWB gang who, under Inspector Cyril Rogers, had built the new lock from scratch.

The Canal Trust was always looking for novel ways in which to raise money so, when John Petty hit upon the idea of organising a series of sponsored inflatable boat races across the side ponds on Caen Hill, everyone joined in with gusto. The first races, which rejoiced under the title of Boto-X, were held in June and despite the atrocious weather raised the handsome sum of £8,600 which was then divided between the Bath Cancer Appeal and the Trust. They eventually were to raise some £100,000, becoming a hugely popular event much enjoyed by competitors and spectators alike, although today, no doubt, they would be deeply frowned on by environmentalists who would not approve of the damage to the banks of the ponds!

When the two Bradford back pumps had been installed and tested in mid-1985, the section between Bradford and Avoncliff was de-watered and the process of leak stopping then occupied the rest of the summer and autumn; this was followed by re-puddling the length enabling the section to be completed in time for a 1986 Easter opening.

The pumps had a capacity of some 5.6 million gallons; one working alone could fill a lock in twenty minutes and if both were used this could be accomplished in twelve.

In March 1986, the BWB announced that the anticipated restoration completion, scheduled for 1988-1989, could only be met if lock gates could be provided from a source other than their own workshops which were incapable of producing the required thirty-five sets of bottom gates and six sets of top gates in time. A proposed MSC-funded gate-making workshop could produce all these and save some £391,000. The National Association for the Care and Rehabilitation of Offenders (NACRO) agreed to sponsor such a workshop to manufacture the Crofton and Devizes gates, the remainder would be produced by the BWB at a cost of £117,000.

Other Canal Trust commitments at this time were a contribution of £200,000 over four years to the Berkshire Consortium's rebuild of Monkey Marsh, Heales, Widmead and Colthrop Locks, and the sum of £180,00 for pumps at Semington and Seend, only one pump being installed at each site but with provision for a second.

A very welcome financial injection came in April when the Policy and Resources Committee of the Newbury District Council found a nest egg of £120,000 surplus to immediate requirements and granted this to the Canal Trust for restoration work, thereby crowning that council's wonderful support given over many years.

In September 1986, the restoration of Aldermaston Lock and surrounding wharf was finished and the remaining workforce moving on to Woolhampton Lock where a complete rebuild was approaching the finishing stages. The completion at Aldermaston was celebrated when Bryan Nicholson, chairman of the MSC scheme that had contributed so much effort, unveiled a commemorative plaque. Since the start of the Manpower Services Commission scheme in February 1983, some 200 people had taken part, most of whom had progressed on to permanent jobs.

In anticipation of the next outstanding task, an approach road from the A4 to Heales Lock was laid using materials excavated from the site of the derelict turf-sided lock. Also at this time the towpath between Froudes and Wickham Knights bridges was restored.

Early in 1986, Cyril Rogers and Stan Miles retired as Section Inspectors at Padworth and Devizes respectively. Cyril was awarded an MBE in the New Years Honours List and both were elected honorary Canal Trust members. Cyril was replaced by David Berezynskyj and Stan by Nick Dodds whilst, higher up the chain, Ian White succeeded Roger House as SW area manager in Gloucester.

Boto-X, 1988.
(Hugh Tilley)

Once again the question of water supplies, which was never very far away, surfaced when the decision was taken not to install back pumps at Devizes and Wootton Rivers but instead to consider raising the level of the Long Pound to act as a larger reservoir at an estimated cost of £600,000. This proposal was not carried through, and in any case would not have been a practical solution as massive leaks were later discovered along this stretch during the 1998 restoration.

During 1986, fund-raising continued apace. There was another successful Boto-X; Timothy West and Prunella Scales, both keen canal boaters and Trust members, presented a show with David Bamber at Devizes Wharf Theatre which raised over £1,000; later a successful appeal on HTV by Timothy produced a further £8,000, whilst TV presenter Richard Stilgoe also presented a show which helped swell the funds.

The good news continued when a donation from Kleinwort Benson for the restoration of Midgham Lock enabled the schedule for that lock to be brought forward to January 1987. To help matters along, the gates which were planned for Heales Lock, which was still just an enormous hole in the ground, would be transferred to Midgham and the Heales Lock gates refitted in the 1987-1988 programme; however, in the event this was not necessary as the TVS Charitable Trust donated £10,000 specifically for the Midgham gates.

Early in 1987 progress on the Crofton Locks MSC scheme was falling well behind schedule so it was decided to put the two locks near the Crofton pumping station out to contract.

The replacement of Padworth swing-bridge, for years a barrier to progress westwards from Reading, was scheduled to be completed by July 1987 – and, most acceptably, at no cost to the Canal Trust.

To assist the NACRO-sponsored gate-building scheme, some old railway premises at Shrivenham were leased and made ready as a workshop. Almost a year had passed since the scheme had been agreed but it had taken all that time for suitable premises to be found.

The 1987 chairman's report stated that the financial target of £750,000 needed for complete restoration was assured, but hinted that to keep to the completion target of 1988-1989 it might be necessary to put one of the Berkshire locks out to contract and, if so, an extra fund-raising effort would be needed.

The Canal Trust's Silver Jubilee AGM was held at Crofton on 6 June 1987. Goodwill messages, including one from the Duke of Edinburgh, were carried to Crofton by water where a packed meeting was first addressed by the new Trust President, Lord Jellicoe. Admiral

O'Brien then welcomed the host of dignitaries, including some of the former officers from the earliest days, and introduced Sir Leslie Young, Guest of Honour and chairman of BWB, who announced that restoration, including all necessary bridge works, dredging etc. could and would be completed by the end of December 1989.

Boto-X 1987, raised a splendid total of £16,500: £7,750 was donated to the RNLI for a new D-class inshore rescue craft. A further £7,500 provided funds towards the Caen Hill gates and £1,000 was given to the Rotary Club of Devizes, partial organisers of the event, for their Rotary International Polio Plus appeal. The Silver Jubilee Draw, organised by Newbury branch members under their chairman, Bill Nicholson, reached a record £9,000 towards the Completion Appeal launched early in 1985 and this had, by the end of 1987, raised a remarkable £417,268.

As 1987 was drawing to a close, the sad news came that General Sir Hugh Stockwell, the Canal Trust's president and former chairman, had died in November. His oft-stated ambition of navigating the restored canal from end to end unfulfilled, yet by now he knew that the progress towards complete restoration was unstoppable and that the task which he had master-minded for so many years would be completed successfully.

Referring to his command of the Anglo-French task force during the 1955-1956 Suez canal crisis, he jovially once remarked, 'I lost one canal so I have no intention of losing another'. That he did not is evident to all who, in life's hustle and bustle, may pause for a moment and enjoy the peace of the tranquil waters.

The following May, the position as president passed to the Rt Hon. Earl Jellicoe KBE, DSO, MC, who having been a vice president since 1962, kindly agreed to don the mantle.

With the possible re-opening date rapidly approaching, the recurring debate concerning the role of the Kennet & Avon Canal Trust after completion resulted in the appointment of Penrose Associates of Bristol to undertake a study of the Trust's material assets, to consider their future operation or disposal and to draw up proposals for their promotion, phased development and future management. This was indeed a 'first' for the Trust which was now the subject of a report, albeit at their own request rather than being an interested party in a report on some other organization!

The report was somewhat un-enthusiastically accepted by the Canal Trust Council although there were a number of quite useful recommendations contained within its pages. That the report was commissioned at all indicated that within the minds of some councillors there was the notion that with the canal opened the Canal Trust could be disbanded, its task complete. This was strengthened by the report making two important assumptions which now, with the benefit of hindsight, we know were overambitious. Firstly, they gave the impression that the local authorities would, quite easily, be persuaded to enter into long-term agreements to cover maintenance; secondly, that within five years the canal would be automatically upgraded to 'Cruiseway' thus lifting the financial burden of repair from voluntary shoulders.

Although both these aims would finally be met they would not be achieved, either as easily, or quite in the form that Penrose had anticipated. In the case of the long-term maintenance agreements it was due to a great deal of protracted negotiations with the partnership and, of course, the fortunate Lottery grant which at that time no one could possibly have envisaged.

The Lottery grant in its turn triggered the twenty-one-year agreement with British Waterways and this will, in the fullness of time, set the stage for some sort of re-classification.

However, it is extremely unlikely that the canal will ever be re-classified a 'Cruiseway', as defined by the 1968 Act, as this would require the Act to be modified. What is more likely is that the waterway will be re-classified as a 'Cruiseway in all but name' until such time that it is thought appropriate to advance its status legally.

Although the Canal Trust Council did not take full advantage of the Penrose Report, they did, however, issue a set of medium and long-term objectives derived mainly but not wholly from it, and submitted them to the membership for general discussion. They suggested that so long as all major obstructions had been cleared away from the waterway and provided that there was sufficient experienced staff, together with a reasonable level of Trust membership to be able to continue involvement with development, then the long-term objectives should be:

1. Complete the restoration from Reading to Bristol.
2. Develop, in conjunction with the BWB, a water supply plan.
3. Work towards 'Cruiseway' status for the entire canal.
4. Monitor planning applications which impinge on the canal.
5. Monitor and liaise with the BWB on canal operation & maintenance.
6. Operate and exhibit Crofton and Claverton pumping stations.
7. Operate trip boats that could produce a useful return.
8. Operate shops etc, principally selling souvenirs.
9. Obtain, preserve & exhibit canal artifacts & information.
10. Provide public information.
11. Ensure Canal Trust's participation in all canal usage.

Considering all the endeavour involved it seemed a pity the entire subject evoked little interest from Trust members. However, before the Penrose Report is forgotten and returned to the dusty shelf of history, it should be noted that later events were to show that Penrose Associates did correctly identify two areas of concern.

Firstly they suggested that Crofton pumping station was not being operated with an eye to profitability and secondly they were more than a little concerned that 'there are clearly profitable trading activities taking place by the Kennet & Avon Canal Trust and that the Canal Trust should ensure that this does not infringe its charitable status'.

These remarks should have rung warning bells for, particularly in the case of Crofton pumping station, they were harbingers of problems which was to cause the Canal Trust some concern at a later date. Perhaps they either failed to spot the significance of these remarks or chose to ignore the importance of them simply because by now eyes were very firmly fixed on the major job of completing the task of re-opening the waterway.

On 9 September 1988 the project took a great step forward in Berkshire when the first boats passed through the replacement Padworth swing-bridge and locks at Padworth and Aldermaston.

The bridge was declared open by Sir William O'Brien who was delighted to be asked to open a bridge which had cost the Canal Trust not one penny of the £187,000 involved. Following a lunch hosted and addressed by Dr Alan Robertson, acting BWB chairman, Woolhampton Lock was declared open by Councillor Gimblett, the Berkshire County Council chairman, who unexpectedly announced that Thatcham swing-bridge, a constant source of worry due to the adjacent railway level crossing and steadily increasing traffic, would be replaced by a high-level fixed bridge by July 1989.

Because Woolhampton Lock was unapproachable by water for all except portable craft, Frouds bridge being fixed on one side and the unusable Midgham Lock on the other, once again, Denys Hutching's beautiful skiff was launched over the bank and ceremoniously locked through to celebrate the opening. This blockage was soon to be eliminated. Frouds swing-bridge was due for replacement with a fixed high bridge by the end of 1988 and Midgham Lock, although kept waterless to aid the reconstruction of the adjacent Midgham bridge, was later opened by Mr Henderson of Kleinwort Benson and Lord Faversham of TVS Charitable Trust.

The construction of lock gates at Shrivenham got off to a very slow start. To speed up production and give more confidence to the NACRO team, 'knock down' gates were

Sam Farmer Lock. (K&ACT Archives)

prepared by BWB yards or MSC sites with spare capacity; these gates, cut, planed, shaped and jointed were then assembled at Shrivenham, only twelve sets being wholly made there.

This scheme increased labour costs by £51,520 above the December 1987 estimate of £170,000 but the manufacture of forty sets of made-to-measure gates in two and a half years was seen as the Achilles heel of the whole restoration project. Later, sponsored by the Canal Trust, the return of Stan Miles, the former BWB Inspector of Devizes, to oversee production was very successful.

Early in 1988, BWB decided to replace the acutely cranked balance beams of the top gates of the Devizes Locks with beams that were less cranked. But to allow safety clearance between the beams and the bridges that crossed over the tail of each lock, the proposed beams on the bottom gates were angled as before. The bridges were very much a safety requirement and those bridges already completed were modified and more constructed by the Newbury Working Party Group led by Bill Nicholson. The beams were fabricated at Shrivenham.

During this year short-term maintenance agreements covering the whole canal except in the Wansdyke area were agreed. In June, the BWB planned to restore the two Crofton pumping station locks by direct labour with the help of subcontractors, a decision made after receiving tenders from contractors who obviously did not want the job, quoting high prices or unreasonable completion dates. The BWB would also finish Crofton Top Lock, the inadequate MSC team on site being transferred to towpath work.

In June, the Minister of Sport, the Hon. Colin Moyniham MP, accompanied by the chairman of both BWB and the Trust toured the canal, visiting the Widcombe Flight, Dundas, Caen Hill, Crofton Locks and pumping station, Monkey Marsh and Aldermaston Locks. Luckily, unlike previous Ministerial visitors, he retained his post in the Government reshuffle announced almost simultaneously.

At the Canal Trust 1988 AGM Brian Dice, BWB's Chief Executive, confirmed that the completion date was still attainable. He commented on the fact that at last Wansdyke Council had agreed to contribute towards maintenance, the last local authority to do so, but that they were not prepared to extend the contribution beyond the life of the present council. This time was far too short to secure the upgrading of the waterway to cruiseway status by the Secretary of State.

By the week before the August Bank Holiday the BWB, using direct labour, had restored Crofton Top Lock and the two at the pumping station and the intervening pounds had been cleared of debris and growth. Using extra pumps the flight was flooded for the first time since the mid-1950s and, on Sunday 26 August, a limited number of boats were allowed to ascend and descend; it took a delicate balancing act keeping the engine pound, the flight and the summit pound adequately supplied with water, but only just. By the following day most of the water had drained away, not all finding its way back to Wilton Water, and it was clear that the leaking pounds would have to be repaired before the flight could be kept permanently in water.

In spite of this, the official opening scheduled for 6 October went ahead on the insistence of BWB. Only the pound between Locks 59 and 60 directly west of the Crofton pumping station on the Crofton Flight was flooded.

At Lock 58 Henry Rendell, a trustee of the Samuel William Farmer Trust, unveiled a plaque naming it 'Sam Farmer Lock'. Sam Farmer was an agriculturist and philanthropist who lived at Little Bedwyn Manor from 1874 to 1926. The guests then walked down to Crofton Lock 59, some boarding *Rose of Hungerford* to cruise down to Lock 60 where Sir Charles Morrison and Sir Michael McNair Wilson, the MPs for Devizes and Newbury, whose territories included the Crofton Flight, unveiled a plaque commemorating the event.

At the subsequent reception, Dr Alan Robertson, BWB vice chairman, stated that rather than endanger present and future water supplies to the canal, the flight had been de-watered and that during the winter the necessary sealing work would be undertaken. He was confident that the flight would be in water in the spring. He confirmed that BWB engineers believed that they could still achieve mechanical completion of the restoration of the entire canal by late 1989 or early 1990. He acknowledged the contributions of the Kennet & Avon, Cave and Farmer Trusts and the skill and perseverance of the MSC schemes, contractors and BWB staff. It did, however, at a later date, fund the cost of making and fitting of lock gates.

On 28 August the official opening of the three miles from Hungerford to Little Bedwyn was held at Oakhill Down Lock. R.W. Holledge, vice chairman of Kennet District Council, performed the ceremony by cutting the tape which marked the entry of the restored canal into Wiltshire.

Not all news was good news. At the end of 1977, volunteer effort received a setback when the BWB stated that Widmead and Monkey Marsh Locks were in such a dangerous condition that volunteers must withdraw. This was, to those who had worked there, palpably untrue but had to be accepted; the decision did, however, foreshadow coming events. Meanwhile, the volunteers, who had proved their abilities at Bulls Lock, were offered Midgham and Colthrop which were both brick-structured locks.

Early in 1978, the BWB agreed a four-year completion date for the twenty locks (not including Devizes) between Bath and Little Bedwyn, each set of gates costing £11,000 and, provided the money was forthcoming, they considered that they could re-gate ten Devizes locks per year in between 1979 and 1981.

To cover the estimated £1.5 million needed over the following four years an appeal for donations and an interest-free loan was initiated, although the income from the Allied Communication Services Ltd appeal of 1974 had been disappointing.

Two other events now took place: firstly, George Lloyd, BWB Area Engineer, Gloucester, retired and his place was taken by Roger House; secondly, Kennet District Council again showed its support for the canal when it set up a job creation scheme for refurbishing the Devizes Wharf buildings.

11
Closing the Berkshire Gap
1989-1990

Restoration attention now turned towards the east with the spotlight falling squarely on Widmead and Monkey Marsh Locks both of which, over the years, had been the focus of varying attempts to repair. Despite the obvious success of the Berkshire Manpower Services scheme, recruitment – always a problem – had by mid-1988 fallen so low that the possibility of the restoration of Monkey Marsh Lock by the end of 1989 appeared doubtful.

The change from Community Programme to Employment Training also reduced the availability of labour for both lock restoration and gate building at Shrivenham. This problem was resolved by the Consortium and the Canal Trust employing and paying the wages of all the supervisory grades together with some of the labour. This extra expense was the only alternative to abandoning both schemes.

It became clear that to complete work within the desired time-scale, it would be necessary to raise funds for the rebuild of Widmead Lock and the completion of Monkey Marsh Lock. During September 1988 it was decided to launch a 'Last Lock' appeal which would enable the task to be completed by contractors. The appeal sought to raise at least £45,000 from Canal Trust members with a parallel public appeal aimed chiefly at the Reading, Newbury and Hungerford districts. By July, an earlier Completion appeal had raised £534,143 of which Trust members had contributed some £45,810. However, all was not straightforward because there was considerable pressure on building facilities in the south, already emphasised by excessive costs shown in the tender responses for Locks 59 and 60 at Crofton, and this made estimation of the probable cost of the rebuild of Widmead Lock by outside contractors difficult.

The sum of £200,000 was forecast and considering that the partially completed approach road had already cost £22,000, this figure had to be accepted as realistic. Provided, therefore, that the figure of £200,000 could be met, and that the money promised by the Manifold Trust was taken up, the projected shortfall on completion of restoration would be £66,000.

In late 1988, the BWB changed its title to plain British Waterways (BW) and announced a major reorganisation, breaking up the earlier functional divisions of engineering, accounts, estates etc. and setting up six regions enabling decisions on local problems to be taken locally but still within the general framework of the BW organization.

This prompted a number of management changes with Ian White, until then the Gloucester area engineer and an enthusiastic supporter of restoration, moving to the post of Regional Manager North East. The manager of the newly formed South West Region, which included the Kennet & Avon as well as Welsh and Somerset canals, would be Brian Rodgers, formerly manager of the Wigan area. The regional engineer would be Roger House, making a welcome and popular return.

Terry Kemp, only recently appointed as the eastern end project officer, became the waterway manager directly responsible to the regional manager for the day-to-day operation of the Kennet & Avon including all engineering and commercial aspects, although Roger House would retain the areas undergoing restoration. One of Terry's earliest duties would be producing and costing a scheme for marketing the canal.

The reorganisation was completed early in 1989. One of Roger House's first concerns was the problem of the lowered water levels on the river section between Bulls and Widmead

Locks following the removal of Dog Head Stakes, which was a rudimentary eighteenth-century weir located above Widmead and removed by canal staff in or about 1955 on the eve of the expected abandonment of the canal. This action was taken to avoid any obligation on the canal company to maintain the canal between Widmead and Monkey Marsh Locks as a floodwater channel by allowing all the floodwater to flow down the original river channel.

Until a satisfactory plan for Bulls Lock could be produced, the restored design of Widmead Lock was in doubt. Thames Water, who were the river and drainage authority, would not permit the replacement of the weir and much discussion was to take place before it was decided to lower the bed of the canal and the bottom gate cill at Bulls Lock to provide adequate depth at all seasons.

During March 1989 the re-puddling of the Crofton pounds began; this involved the procurement, transportation and laying of vast quantities of clay by a Swindon-based firm who nevertheless completed the task in time to allow limited use of the flight by 29 May. Also in March, work at last commenced on rebuilding Midgham bridge and replacing Thatcham swing-bridge by the promised up and over brick-built construction. Work had still yet to start on rebuilding Froude bridge, the delay being due to difficulties with British Telecom over the resiting of a fibre optic cable. Woolhampton bridge was still in the hands of the consultants, but the contract for Widmead Lock was expected to be placed at the end of August.

By the middle of August rebuilding preparations at Monkey Marsh Lock were well advanced with some fifty per cent of the dismantling work completed. Unfortunately English Heritage had laid down quite stringent restrictive requirements on the rebuilding of Monkey Marsh, which had been listed many years beforehand as an Ancient Monument. As has been noted previously, BW always objected to turf-sided locks stressing how dangerous they could be not only for the boating fraternity but also for the general public who more frequently would be using the canal towpaths for leisure activities.

Turf-sided locks, which were only to be found on the Kennet Navigation section of the Kennet & Avon, differed from the normally accepted lock pattern which had a regular rectangular chamber lined with brick or steel piling. A turf-sided lock, as its name implies, had a turf-lined chamber of which the sides sloped gently outwards above the lower water level at an angle of about forty-five degrees. This resulted in there being a very wide expanse of water in the filled lock and although there was often a steel rail to mark the boundaries of the inner chamber the potential for disaster can easily be imagined, particularly where small boats, small children and animals were concerned.

The turf-type lock, which had been inexpensive to build, had another obvious modern drawback – it used vast quantities of water to operate, much of which would soak into the surrounding area each time it was filled. Although not originally a problem in the eighteenth century when the River Kennet could deliver copious amounts of water all year round, present-day water conservation could not measure up to such a wasteful practice.

There were a number of problems in rebuilding Monkey Marsh which prompted BW (in conjunction with the Canal Trust) to approach English Heritage with a view to transferring the Ancient Monument listing to Garston Lock, which was actually a very much better example of an original Kennet lock.

This would allow Monkey Marsh to be rebuilt in a more economical manner. This proposal was refused and after much negotiation it was not until May 1989 that permission was finally given for work to proceed on Monkey Marsh Lock – little of which remained to be preserved anyway.

During the work a large amount of important historical information was obtained and evidence uncovered, much of which now lies buried under the modern materials. The final result pleased no one, having only the slightest resemblance to an original turf lock on the

Left and below:
Before and during
reconstruction work on
Monkey Marsh Lock.
(K&ACT Archives)

Monkey Marsh rebuilt.
(K&ACT Archives)

1. An example of a typical lock before restoration.

2. Before work commenced, all fish were removed to other parts of the canal.

3. The temporary bridge at Victoria Park, Newbury, which nearly caused the canal to be closed for ever.

4. Work begins on the Devizes back pumping scheme in July 1994 with a stone laid by Trust Chairman Brian Stark, watched by the Town Mayor and Waterway Manager Michael Goodenough.

5. Instability is apparent in the Foxhangers footbridge.

6. The completed back pumping house with the restored Lower Foxhangers lock in 1998.

7 & 8. The repairs and new pumphouse at Wootton Rivers lock.

9. New lock gates arrive. Many gates were supplied from the Dutch firm of Wisma Kampen BV.

10. The contractors provided paved paths beneath the lock beams.

11 & 12. Bank piling in Winter 1997/1998.

13. Aldermaston bridge looking west.

14. Bascule bridge looking east at Aldermaston. Opened in October 1981, the bridge cost £300,000.

15 & 16. Canal pumping station at Claverton.

17 & 18. Canal pumping station at Crofton.

19 & 20. Bath Valley in July 1999 after relining in the previous winter.

21, 22 & 23.
The waterway
gives pleasure to
a wide range of
different interests.

24. The Canal Trust won many awards. Here Terry Kemp of British Waterways and David Lamb, Trust Chairman, hold the Millennium Marque Award for Environmental Excellence.

25. Michael Goodenough, Waterway Manager, opens the new swing-bridge at West Mills, Newbury.

26. Newbury Wharf.

27. Bernard Henderson, BW Chairman, gives a television interview in Hungerford.

28. Kennet & Avon Canal Trust Headquarters at Devizes Wharf.

29. The wharf at Bradford-upon-Avon.

30. The George Inn, Bathampton.

31. The tranquil canal, Bath.

32. A boat at rest on the Long Pound.

one hand, whilst being a poor example of a modern one on the other. There was a report that an attempt was made at the time to create some of the original atmosphere in the new lock by turfing what remained of the sloping sides, but to the chagrin of all concerned the turves just floated away the first time the lock was filled!

The task of rebuilding Monkey Marsh was formidable indeed; even before work on the lock could begin in earnest, a major item was the completion of the approach road. This involved culverting a stream and filling in part of the canal beside the towpath bridge to increase the width of the path. An overflow weir was then built above the earth embankment isolating the lock and replacing the piling driven by volunteers in 1976.

The rebuilding of Monkey Marsh Lock highlights a dilemma in respect to canal restoration. The interest and inflexibility which English Heritage had shown in attempting to preserve the lock were completely incompatible with the safety concerns that BW had expressed over using it. This poses an interesting question – is it possible to preserve the historical integrity of a waterway and at the same time ensure the safety of modern day operation?

No doubt the debate will swing back and forth between the various interested parties as to what degree is it reasonable to retain the original canal features and equipment before replacing them with modern alternatives. If funds had been available, and as turf-sided locks are so unique, perhaps at Monkey Marsh the ideal solution might have been to have built a new modern lock alongside the old one and then preserved the original turf-sided lock as an historical example.

During May 1989 the BW resources engineer, John Taylor, produced the long awaited report on water supplies which expanded an earlier review published in 1982. It stated that almost all the water west of the top of Crofton Locks would have to be obtained from the River Avon at Claverton and Bath by back pumping over all lock flights. Wilton Water would supply the eastern end; any surplus water could augment supplies to the summit and the west. The pumps at Seend, Semington and Bradford would need regrading and new ones should be installed at Crofton, Wootton Rivers, Devizes and Widcombe. BW would pay the cost of regrading.

The Canal Trust was somewhat unhappy with the report so set up a water sub-committee which suggested that BW's estimate of demand, based on a report by Liverpool University, was excessive. BW agreed that lock movements west of Crofton were already well monitored and that similar studies east of Crofton where the 'cheapest' water could be obtained should be carried out. It was suggested that with the aid of volunteers an annual survey should be conducted with the following aims:

1. To help forecast the likely pattern of usage by boaters.
2. To decide what usage present water resources will permit.
3. How much extra each additional level of usage will cost.
4. To establish a factual record for the future on water levels and how they interact with usage, weather, etc.

At the May Canal Trust Annual General Meeting, Martin Japes, BW director of engineering, stated that on the best advice forthcoming, the back pumping and dredging estimated to be necessary would cost approximately £2.5 million, all of which would not necessarily fall on the Canal Trust.

In the interim, the use of locks would have to be restricted and under BW control. Admiral O'Brien, Canal Trust chairman, emphasised that because of water shortage even though completion of mechanical restoration was on schedule for mid-1990, the canal would not immediately be a perfect leisure waterway upon which every boater would be able to move as and when he wished. Martin Japes also commented on the unsolved problem of maintenance agreements. Even after many years of negotiation no long-term agreements had been signed. Local authorities proposed short-term ones, he thought, in the hope that when the completed and improved canal had been elevated to Cruiseway status the cost of maintenance would automatically fall on BW.

This was not true, he said – at no time would maintenance be paid for from central Government funds; only waterways classified as Cruiseways under the 1968 Act were so covered. Most of the agreements BW had with interested parties for other restored canals were for at least twenty-one years and similar conditions would apply to the Kennet & Avon Canal, with the exception, of course, to those sections which already held Cruiseway status. Clearly, here was the key to the future of the Kennet & Avon canal; some way had to be found to convince the local authorities that therein lay great potential for leisure activities, local tourism and employment that was worthy of investment over a lengthy period. As will be demonstrated later, it was the solution to this problem which eventually led to the formation of the Kennet & Avon Canal Partnership in 1994.

Before the AGM closed, the chairman thanked Paul Ensor for his efforts in running the very successful '500 Club' which over the years had raised some £20,000 for the Canal Trust.

The lease on the Shrivenham workshop was due to run out in July 1989 but BW agreed to co-operate with the Canal Trust in extending this until the end of the year. The gate-building team could then build all the steel balance beams for the Devizes Locks including those to replace the unpopular cranked beams on the top gates. Besides completing the remaining bottom gates for Devizes, they could also build the new gates for the rebuilt Widmead and Bulls Locks. When the workshop finally closed on 5 January 1990, the team had completed all but five of the eighty-four gates for Crofton and Caen Hill. Those remaining would be completed by BW without any extra cost being incurred by the Canal Trust.

On the Spring Bank Holiday 1989, boats from Newbury arrived in Devizes and others from Pewsey travelled to Hungerford. The transit of the Crofton Locks operated by BW staff took well over an hour. On the return journey a consignment of gift-ware for Newbury branch sales was carried, the first commercial traffic for many years. Prior to this the last boat able to use Crofton Flight had been *Wayfarer* which the Gould family had brought from Honeystreet to Newbury in late 1951.

The capacity of the electric pump at Crofton and the supplies at Wilton Water were now insufficient to satisfy all the demands placed upon them.

Not only were supplies needed for the summit and the operation of Wootton Rivers Locks, but abnormal amounts were used to swell up the dry Crofton gates as well as to compensate for the loss of water which the new clay puddle was absorbing. Consequently some of the pounds soon dried out and the flight was closed again to allow supplies to build up.

The pounds started to refill when water losses were reduced by racking the gates when closed (pouring fine ash into the gate joints) so only limited use of the locks could be expected in 1989. By August, through draining down water and back pumping over some locks all pounds were once again full with the top gates, at least, holding water.

Later in August some of the bottom gates of the Crofton Locks were fitted with wooden battens to cover the gaps which had opened in the dried out planking and, taking advantage of the steaming of the Crofton pumps, limited use of the locks under BW control allowed three boats to use them.

Water levels in the lower pounds were low but, provided that sufficient water was available, the locks could be similarly used each Wednesday from September onwards, with the Wootton Rivers Locks continuing to be operated by boaters as before. However, a gloomy letter from the BW regional manager foresaw virtually no use of the Crofton, Wootton Rivers or Devizes Locks until the back pumping scheme was implemented.

Up-and-over bridges at Thatcham (above) and Midgham (right) were opened in mid-August 1989. (K&ACT Archives)

Boto-X 1989 raised £21,500 mainly on behalf of the Canal Trust and the International Rescue Corps, with funds also going to the Royal Naval Benevolent Trust and Devizes Lions Club. In 1990 all sponsor money for this and the Devizes to Westminster race would go to the 'Last Lock' appeal. Newbury Waterways Weekend raised £1,000 for that appeal in June.

For four days at the beginning of June volunteers operated the 1813 Claverton pump following a failure of the modern electric one. However, leaks in the pound from Bradford to Avoncliff necessitated an August stoppage.

At another abortive meeting with local authorities, BW rejected two of their demands, firstly that any additional money accruing as a result of the canal re-opening should be returned to them and secondly, that assurance be given that at the end of five years the canal would be upgraded. The lack of will to complete reasonable maintenance agreements was at this time becoming extremely serious.

By mid-August 1989, both the new overhead bridges at Thatcham and Midgham were open to road traffic although work was still continuing at the latter, where attempts to pile between the lock and bridge were frustrated by the presence of large elm beams below water level. Favourite foundations for the earlier builders, these beams had to be dug out before piling could continue.

In late November 1989, Timothy West and Prunella Scales put on another show, *Battle of the Sexes*, at the Watermill Theatre, Newbury, raising over £7,250 for the 'Last Lock' Appeal.

Towards the end of the year, the perennial problem of unsigned maintenance agreements now reached a truly critical stage when BW stated, 'We do not have sufficient confidence to proceed further unless the agreements are signed.'

Above and left:
*Midgham Lock before
(1987) and after
restoration (1990).*
(K&ACT Archives)

A meeting of the local authorities on 1 December made sufficient progress towards signing to ensure that the individual councils would support the proposals but until they did so and the full budgetary progress had been followed, BW would not agree to either planning a re-opening ceremony with the Canal Trust or carrying on the work of removing the remaining obstacles. Newbury District Council agreed to set aside £250,000 over five years for their share of the maintenance costs and also to pay half of the emergency work costs.

Although the situation remained critical, it did appear, to the relief of all concerned, as if the immediate crisis had passed but it showed quite clearly that BW would, despite adverse publicity, call a halt to ongoing restoration if they felt it necessary.

A contract for the rebuilding of Widmead Lock on similar lines to Padworth had been placed with Rees Hough, with work to start early in December for completion in twenty-six weeks at a cost of £246,980, some £50,000 more than budgeted.

To the great delight of all concerned it was announced on 4 January 1990 that Her Majesty Queen Elizabeth II would perform an opening ceremony at Devizes on 8 August. It was an important target to meet and nothing so concentrates the mind as effectively as a deadline.

The first considerations were to take stock of the current restoration situation and examine the progress of work still required to be completed by August. The tasks were:

1. The completion of the Devizes Flight.
2. Reconstruction of Widmead Lock.
3. Reconstruction of swing-bridges at Monkey Marsh, Cranwells, Oxlease and Woolhampton.
4. Reconstruction of Wickham Knights footbridge.
5. Building Frouds up and over road bridge.
6. Completion of Monkey Marsh Lock.
7. Complete rebuild of Widmead Lock.
8. Substantial dredging work.

This was a very tight timescale commitment by BW and the Canal Trust, the fulfilment of which seemed at times to be impossible. Some works continued after the deadline but the major unblocking works were completed on time.

There were great celebrations when Reading and Newbury were at last reunited by water on 17 July. The ceremony took place at Monkey Marsh Lock when Tony Wise, chairman of Berkshire County Council, and Canal Trust chairman, Admiral Sir William O'Brien unveiled a mile post. The lock was still a work site, being somewhat untidy with scaffold poles still in place, but it was usable and a scramble of boats took place for the honour of being first through.

The next task was an in-depth scrutiny of all the procedures which would be required in connection with the royal visit, together with a proposed rolling programme of celebrations.

The event, it had been agreed, was to take place on the Devizes Flight; apart from being not only a fair approximation of the centre of the canal, it was also one of its most spectacular features.

BW were to play an increasingly vital part in the arrangements and the all-important security implications. The importance of timing the various features of the royal progress was of some concern not least when it was agreed that part of the journey would consist of a short boat passage, including passing through a lock, all of which needed to be timed precisely.

The shortage of water was to be a problem, so much so that the Canal Trust's trip boat *Rose of Hungerford* had to be ferried to Devizes by road and any rehearsals using water were carried out with a good deal of economy.

It was hoped that the *Rose of Hungerford* from the east and the other Canal Trust boat, *Ladywood*, from the west would, therefore, be the first boats to officially use the restored Devizes Flight, but it all depended on the water supply. This, it has to be said was jealously guarded by Terry Kemp, the BW manager. In the event all was well and an expectant crowd now waited for their monarch to declare the canal re-opened.

The sun gleamed down as the Queen arrived on Devizes Wharf to be greeted by the Kennet & Avon Canal Trust's President, Earl Jellicoe and Lady Jellicoe, the Chairman, Admiral Sir William O'Brien and Lady O'Brien together with David Ingman and Brian Dice, chairman and chief executive of BW.

The Queen, accompanied by the two chairmen, then enjoyed a brief walkabout stopping to talk to some of the elderly patients from the local hospital. Her Majesty gave a smile of approval to the flotilla of small boats gathered at the wharf and could not resist showing her appreciation of the two, impeccably groomed, Wadworth dray horses before entering the Canal Centre.

At the Canal Centre, the Queen was presented to the Canal Trust's general secretary, Cdr Wright, and to the team of helpers and Canal Trust staff. Her Majesty then toured the

Left and opposite: *Her Majesty The Queen in the Devizes Museum.*

museum where she showed great interest in the exhibition after having been presented to Mike Corfield, the museum's founder, and to Jack Fulker, the curator. The Queen had a special word with John Gould before returning to her car and proceeding to the next phase of the celebrations.

The Queen now travelled through Devizes to the BW depot on Caen Hill where, as the sun shone from a cloudless sky, the excited crowd began to cheer. Everyone was in good humour and enjoying the day enormously, even the rank-and-file Canal Trust members, who had received, as they thought, tickets which entitled them to an advantageous position, managed to hide their disappointment when they found themselves huddled together and imprisoned on a spit of land from which they could hear or see only a little of the festivities.

While the *Rose of Hungerford* waited for her royal passenger at the lock named after General Sir Hugh Stockwell, Her Majesty, escorted by BW chairman David Ingman, chatted to a group of children from Monkton Primary School in Chippenham who arrived complete with an imitation barge. Then, stepping on board the *Rose of Hungerford*, the Queen was presented with a scroll from the Mayor of Hungerford and a single red rose; the red rose is said to be traditionally presented to a monarch when visiting Hungerford.

Aboard the *Rose of Hungerford*, Her Majesty met a number of Canal Trust and BW officials and chatted to them whilst the level of the lock slowly dropped and, at precisely 11.55 a.m. as planned, the lower gates opened to reveal Her Majesty standing in the bows of the craft flanked either side by the chairmen of the Canal Trust and BW. The boat slowly edged forward to the tape stretched across the canal and as it broke there was a fly-past of three Hercules from RAF Lyneham.

The *Rose of Hungerford* moved slowly into 'plain' Lock 43 – now to be named Queen Elizabeth II Lock – and stepping ashore, Her Majesty unveiled a plaque which bore the lock's new name.

Admiral Sir William thanked the Queen on behalf of all the Kennet & Avon Canal Trust members and presented the Queen with a magnificent commemorative glass bowl engraved by Laurence Whistler who, until recently, had lived near the canal at Honey Street.

The Queen was then introduced to a long line of people, a number of whom had put many years of effort into achieving the present result of which many had dreamed but few thought possible. With a final look over the impressive view and a wave to the crowd Her Majesty took her place in the glass-topped Rolls-Royce which glided away to the next appointment.

With the departure of the Queen celebrations began to mark the successful completion of so many years of effort.

Although this grand event may have marked the completion of the restoration in many minds, few realised that what had actually been achieved was only to revive the waterway to the standards of the late 1930s. There still remained the serious in-built defects of a canal now over 180 years old in the 'youngest' sections.

Therefore, to the older, wiser and informed members of the Kennet & Avon Canal Trust and BW, this was not to be the last chapter in the Kennet & Avon story; far from it, as Sir Winston Churchill, no doubt, would have remarked, this was certainly not the end nor even the beginning of the end but, may be, just may be, the end of the beginning.

Sir William O'Brien summed the situation up during his AGM speech in 1990 when he quoted from a letter sent to Sir Francis Walsingham from Sir Francis Drake in 1587.

There must be a beginning to any great matter, but the continuing unto the end until it be thoroughly finished yields the true glory.

The unveiling of the plaque.

The lower gates opened to reveal Her Majesty standing in the bows of the craft, flanked either side by the chairmen of the Canal Trust and British Waterways. (K&ACT Archives)

12 After the Party
1991-1994

The joy of the re-opening was to be tinged with sadness when in April came the news of the untimely death of Jack Dalby – Canal Trust Council member and Newbury branch chairman from 1972 until 1980. Jack, however, will best be remembered for his stalwart editorship of the *Butty*, a position which he held for over fourteen years until ill-health forced his retirement in January 1990.

He was a prodigious writer on canal affairs and the prime mover behind this restoration story, a task which unfortunately he was not destined to see finished. Jack was to be missed by all those associated both with the Kennet & Avon Canal as well as the Wiltshire & Berkshire Canal to which he also gave freely of his time. It was fitting indeed when it was announced that Lock 38 on the Devizes Flight would be re-named Jack Dalby Lock in his memory. Jack's position as *Butty* editor was taken over by Alan Jux.

As the euphoria of the Queen's visit and all the excitement and bustle in re-opening the canal began to evaporate, the Canal Trust had to look inward and devote some time to its own internal affairs, beginning with the disappointing news that Admiral Sir William O`Brien was to resign as Trust chairman at the coming annual general meeting. He had announced his retirement to the council during April 1990, suggesting that they should appoint a deputy who could then progressively assume the chairman's responsibilities thus ensuring that the day-to-day Trust activities would continue without disruption.

The council deliberated for some months over electing a new chairman, before deciding that 'The Canal Trust should now look hard at its future organization in the light of a change of emphasis from restoration to overseeing usage and leisure facilities' and consider 'future aims and objectives of the organization to create a new profile for the canal in its open state'. The council, or a significant majority of it at least, appeared to think the restoration task was complete. Having the canal opened to through traffic by no lesser person than Her Majesty the Queen was without question a tremendous boost to morale and a vital high point, tending as it did to establish a position from which BW might find future retreat difficult, but as far as the structure and the future wellbeing of the canal was concerned, however, very little had materially changed.

The waterway, though nominally open, was still in a most perilous state. Parts of the bed, particulaly towards Bath, were known to be unstable and many of the repairs that had been carried out in the past, quite often with an eye to economy, were now requiring further attention.

Additionally, uncertain water supplies complicated the position for the BW manager, Terry Kemp, for although the canal was now navigable from one end to the other the water shortages and general lack of facilities along the way would certainly create a less than favourable impression with potential visitors. There also existed the alarming possibility that extra traffic could weaken or expose some of the known critical areas and, worse still, expose others as yet un-suspected.

The very real danger was that should a substantial investment be required to effect any major repairs then BW, consistent with all the warnings they had given over the years, would be unable to depart from the conditions of the 1968 Transport Act in supplying financial aid, neither could the Trust reasonably expect to raise the sizeable funds which would likely to be needed.

With so many vital repair tasks still requiring attention it was clearly not yet the time for the Canal Trust to simply sit back and merely 'oversee usage and leisure'.

Concerned as the council was with the future ongoing management structure, it was by no means a certainty that the Trust had a future unless it continued to be supported by its rank-and-file members who had originally been drawn to the organization in response to the restoration call – would they continue to support the organization which now seemed to suggest that this had been all but accomplished?

Yet still the Canal Trust Council deliberated over the position of chairman, now wishing 'to diminish the role' to enable 'more participative management by council'. Although this was no doubt laudably democratic, and as necessary as the council was, the Canal Trust's overall successes up to this time could largely be attributed to discussions and contacts, usually at top level, by whoever was the Canal Trust chairman at the time.

Capt. Munk, for example, chaired the IWA and General Sir Hugh Stockwell was appointed to the Board of British Waterways whilst the hand of Sir William O'Brien clearly showed with the presence of Her Majesty the Queen gracing the re-opening proceedings.

Understandably, the council's reluctance to appoint a new chairman prompted a worried Sir William to write a letter to all the councillors expressing his concern over the delay and emphasizing strongly that he did not relish presiding at the coming AGM, vacating the chair and leaving it empty. At last the council arrived at a decision electing Brian Stark, a recent addition to the council, to be the new chairman on 23 April 1991. He had, he said, hopes for early retirement from his present position and then, being able to give almost full time to the task, hoped to steer the Trust forward through the imminent changes over the next few months.

At a council meeting held during July 1991 Admiral O'Brien, together with Messrs D. Collis, D. Blazdell and B. Oram, resigned from the council and a vote of thanks was made to them and to the Admiral in recognition of his long and valued service.

The retirement of Sir William effectively closed the book on the important early years in the history of the Kennet & Avon Canal restoration. Sir Hugh Stockwell had fought and won the battle of acceptance but it was Sir William O'Brien who, taking the helm at a most critical hour, had carried the campaign forwards towards the target of re-establishing that vital Reading to Bristol through passage and the psychological victory which that represented. Within a short time there was another departure from the council; K.I. Mackintosh, the Canal Trust's treasurer, felt he was unable to continue his stewardship and resigned. Ian had been most successful in finally centralising Trust funds which, when he took office, were scattered over dozens of separate current and deposit bank accounts – all earning minimal interest. Each branch considered that any cash raised was 'their money', to be handed over to the central organization at the next AGM with due ceremony and amid much applause.

Ian Mackintosh successfully completed the accounting overhaul started under Geff Snelgrove by reducing the number of bank accounts, banking centrally and placing restrictions on the size of cheques which each branch could authorise. Although unpopular, the sound reasoning behind this action was demonstrated when under the new treasurer, John Petty, the Trust became embroiled with a critical problem concerning the management of accounts by the Crofton pumping station.

The trouble was heralded by a request from the Crofton committee to reserve the sum of £4,000 within the central financial budget to cover an outstanding account which was the cause of some confusion between the Crofton Society and a firm of consulting engineers.

The complication arose over the cost of a qualified structural engineer's survey on the strength of the boiler house floor. This followed the dismantling by the Crofton Society of the last remaining original GWR Lancashire boiler and the desire to site a replacement, not back in the original position but on the other side of the boiler house alongside the present serviceable boiler (which was itself a replacement obtained from W.D. & H.O. Wills Bristol tobacco factory in 1987).

The scrapping of this last remaining GWR boiler was deeply controversial; it was not needed operationally and historically it should have been left in place, particularly as a promise of a grant towards the repair of the boiler house roof specifically to protect it had been obtained from English Heritage. When the demise of the boiler had become known the Canal Trust was black-listed by English Heritage and the grant withdrawn, leaving the Trust to fund the roof repairs which had already started.

Being very conscious of the limitation and demands of charity laws it is of little wonder, therefore, that a request for a further large sum of money in relation to almost the same subject caused enough concern for chairman, Brian Stark, to call for a written report in an attempt to resolve the situation.

The Crofton Society Committee, however, appeared completely unrepentant, resisting a request for their resignation and vigorously defending their position with a flurry of letters containing accusations and criticisms of the Canal Trust and the way that it operated.

Despite lengthy correspondence by both the general secretary, Commander Wright, and chairman, Brian Stark, the difficulty of uncovering the actual true situation finally led Brian Stark to request a special meeting of the entire Crofton Society workforce.

The meeting held at Pewsey wharf attracted an audience of some eighty people; it was both unpleasant and acrimonious with members of the Crofton Society challenging the controlling authority of the Canal Trust. After enduring some ten minutes of uproar Brian Stark suspended the meeting briefly whilst the Canal Trust Council met in an emergency session.

When the meeting resumed Brian Stark courageouly declared the council's decision to formally suspend, with immediate effect, all activities of the Crofton Society and announced that a further council meeting was arranged to be held on 21 November, its sole purpose being 'in view of the conduct of the Crofton Society Committee and in accordance with Articles of Association' to remove some nine members of the ex-Crofton Committee from membership of the Kennet & Avon Canal Trust. Later, at this council meeting, all nine Crofton committee members were interviewed separately and subsequently all nine resigned from the Crofton committee; additionally six of the nine members were expelled from the Canal Trust.

Brian Stark expressed his sadness at having to take disciplinary action against Trust members but expressed his grave concern over the management of affairs at Crofton. Clearly, the unauthorised expenditure of a considerable amount of money indicated that the financial and business competence of a committee controlling one of the Canal Trust's most valuable assets was very much in question.

What was so sad about this whole affair was not only the damage that all this brought on the hitherto high reputation of the original Crofton Society but the disregard shown for the constitution and management of the Canal Trust. This was possibly prompted by the mistaken belief that the Society's members occupied a position of strength in that it was they, and only they, who were qualified and able to maintain and operate the machinery.

With the demise of the Crofton Society the process of assembling a new Crofton team began when Brian Oram was formally appointed Chairman of the new Crofton branch and re-elected to the Trust Council. Assisted by Cdr Wright he quickly put together a powerful squad including two certified steam engineers, a number of mechanical engineers together with volunteers from varying trades and professions including many local residents, but most welcome were two of the original restoration team, Ian Broome and Roy Simmons, who were able to provide essential help and information. The team were also joined by a few of the people who had been working with the now-deposed Crofton Society.

Above: *The memorial to Denys Hutchings was unveiled by his wife Margaret (left) on Easter Sunday 1993.*

Right: *The canal company clock that had been salvaged from the wharf at Honey Street.* (K&ACT Archives)

Denys Hutchings (David Harris)

During that winter the engines and buildings were cosseted and cleaned so that the following spring they hissed and gurgled their way back into operation in a far healthier, happier and cleaner condition than they had been for some years.

With the unhappy Crofton episode now resolved, further misfortune was to follow with yet another resignation as Denys Hutchings MBE let it be known that, with the dawning of a new era, he felt it was time to draw to a close his long love affair with the Kennet & Avon Canal. During fifty-seven years of involvement and supported by his wife, Margaret, Denys had spent over forty years as a council member and travelled some 40,000 miles on canal business. The Canal Trust was to feel the loss of Denys's wise council and his in-depth knowledge gained over the years. There was unanimous accord when it was proposed that 'Hutch', as he was affectionately known, should be asked to become a vice-president of the Canal Trust.

Sadly, only a few months later Denys died and to honour his memory the canal company clock that had been salvaged from the wharf at Honey Street was repaired and erected within the boiler house at Crofton. Denys had, in the past, been deeply involved with the pumping station so it was fitting that, in the presence of many of his friends, this memorial should be unveiled by Margaret Hutchings on Easter Sunday 1993.

The Trust Council, with five new council members – Messrs T. Bond, T. Brookman, M. Lee, K. Shave and Mrs J. Poulton – returned to the task of defining both a new management structure and the future aims of the Canal Trust. They set up a Review Working Party to continue the investigation but, whilst the Trust Council members were busily cogitating the future structure of the Canal Trust and the local authorities looked forward to the end of the maintenance payments, the dry summer drained sections of the canal dry.

With the lock pounds at Crofton emptied, the long pound water supply effectively failed and the porous nature of parts of the Caen Hill Flight were revealed whilst further west the problems of leaking and slippage in the Bath valley also began to reveal themselves.

The working party report, when it appeared, ran to some eight pages, but hardly addressed the essential question of further maintenance or continuing repair, concentrating instead on internal arrangements. The working party, however, did investigate problems associated with the ever present water supply, together with the protection of the canal environment and wildlife. Further, they examined the task of maintaining the pumping stations and preserving and exhibiting the many canal artifacts which the Canal Trust were collecting. Finally, in a long overdue response to the Penrose Report on the future of the Canal Trust, the working party considered the establishment of a trading company to oversee the Trust's commercial business interests.

The council adopted the report but Brian Stark, now fully established as chairman, could see that, although some reorganization was no doubt desirable, the main thrust must concentrate instead on the continuing repair and long-term future of the canal.

There was a morsel of good news for him with the announcement that the DoE was to carry on the grant of some £14,500 towards the Trust's administration costs thus continuing, in part, to relieve the Trust of a sizeable financial responsibility.

But of immediate concern to Brian Stark was an announcement from the general secretary, Cdr Wright, voicing disquiet over the new council arrangements. He now dealt a grievous blow to the management structure as, regretfully, he tendered his resignation, having no wish, as he saw it, to act only as an administration manager. Thus it was that within a very short space of time Denys Hutchings and three of the principal architects of the successful re-opening had left the stage.

The triumvirate of Sir William, Nick Wright and Ian Mackintosh had over the last six or seven years worked very successfully together using their accounting efficiency, naval organisational and social skills to bring a level of dedication and ability which would be difficult to replace.

Later, after Cdr Wright left, it was decided to advertise the position as an administration appointment and during May 1992, from some forty or so applicants, a small sub-committee selected Fleur de Rhe-Philipe to fill the post.

Having settled into the position of Canal Trust treasurer and ever mindful of the recent problems at Crofton, John Petty, having contacted the Charity Commissioners, recommended to the Canal Trust Council that it was now imperative to hasten the setting up of a trading company. It would be necessary, he said, to make suitable amendments to the constitution but above all it would require all concerned to improve the Canal Trust's financial reporting and accounting ability which would be essential when the trading company came into existence.

Notwithstanding the urgent need, there was a great deal of work required to establish the venture, many Charity Commission rules with which to comply, and much patience demanded. It was to be July 1992 before the trading company, Kennet & Avon Canal Trust (Enterprise) Ltd, as it was to be known, was established with a loan from the parent body of £45,000. Together with trip boats valued at some £30,000, the whole future Canal Trust trading operations were duly handed over to a board of directors.

Legally there was now a clear distinction between the charitable operations of the Kennet & Avon Trust and the trading for profit operations of the Kennet & Avon Trust (Enterprise) Ltd; but for the volunteers working in the Canal Trust shops, boats and pumping stations the clarity was much less sharply defined and the Trust was a little backward in ensuring that they understood the situation thoroughly. Some failed completely to understand the technicalities of why, for example, at the Crofton pumping station the visitor entrance fee accrued to the Canal Trust while the proceeds of selling the same visitor an ice cream was directed towards the Kennet & Avon Canal Trust (Enterprise) Ltd.

With the subject of the trading position resolved council members expressed concern when it was revealed that during 1992 administration costs had exceeded the basic membership receipts by almost 100 per cent. This, they felt was a substantial burden for such a small organization to carry. Ever conscious of the intense efforts required to raise funds councillors were naturally keen to submit administration costs to close scrutiny but, covering so many spheres, it proved difficult to identify exactly just where any possible overspending may have occurred.

Therefore, with cost very much in mind, when it was proposed to install a £6,000 computer system there were the expected protests. Although the decision to install the system was eventually carried, many felt it excessive spending and looked around for ways to reduce further expense. One suggestion was to reduce administration costs by reformatting the Canal Trust's *Butty* magazine or to replace the *Butty* with a system of local newsletters.

The problems associated with the *Butty* were to become pronounced when, in July 1992, Alan Jux resigned as editor and the search commenced for a replacement. Following much discussion and investigation Brian Stark summarized the situation in a paper issued in October 1992 which came to the conclusion that a professionally produced and attractive *Butty*, while costing more in gross terms, may attract a wider circulation which, coupled with greater advertising potential, would offset much of the production costs.

There remained only the problem of an editor, which was solved when an offer to produce a number of issues on a trial basis was received from David Harris, a professional editor and Canal Trust member of long standing. This proposal was accepted by council with the chairman authorised to arrange fees and make any executive decisions.

The improved *Butty* was welcomed; it had a complete range of new features and articles catering to a wide appeal which eventually won it the prestigious Tom Rolt Award for Canal Society Magazines in 1993. Unfortunately the distribution arrangements and sales did not match up to the quality of the contents so although technically sound, financially it was not the success it should have been. So with the trial completed, it was decided to return the *Butty* to the original format with David Harris handing the editorship over to Hugh Tilley.

A bright note came when a Trust Council Meeting in July 1992 released the splendid news that John Gould, Founder and Vice President, had been awarded a very well deserved MBE.

BW in Devizes showed the way forward with the publication in April 1992 of *A Plan for the Environment, Tourism and Leisure*. This plan, known colloquially as PETAL, was a positive attempt by BW to provide a vision for the Kennet & Avon Canal and its management as a functional, living link, providing benefits for all, with harmony between the environment, tourism and leisure. It showed in some detail the many advantages and attractions of the revived waterway and recognised the need for a future plan involving co-operation with local authorities, together with the need for extensive expenditure, but it did not give many clues as to where those funds might originate.

The Canal Trust, under the guidance of chairman Brian Stark, realised that a major effort was required to visibly improve the conditions on the canal. Not only would this be good for the waterway but it would demonstrate to the local authorities and also to Trust members the resolve of the organization; improving the water levels which, apart from being very acceptable to the canal users, would also be obvious evidence of progress which everyone could see, there only remained the question of what to do and where to do it.

The choice fell quite easily on the Caen Hill Flight of locks. Ever since the re-opening of the navigation in 1990, drought conditions and limited water supplies had meant that the flight had been closed for more days than it had been open. Boaters had been disappointed and the local authorities had expressed concern regarding local economic returns. Bad publicity was, unfortunately, the name of the game.

Providing extra supplies of water was not possible – they did not exist – but re-using what was available in the form of a back pumping scheme up Caen Hill was an attractive alternative.

The project needed finance: BW liked the idea but the 1968 Transport Act required them to maintain expenditure at a level necessary only to preserve public safety. Back pumps would, therefore, be considered a new feature and thus could not be supported directly by BW.

The size of the task was enormous, as was the required sum of around £1 million which would have to come from sources other than BW, and that in essence meant the Canal Trust plus any assistance they could raise from the local authorities.

BW were keen to assist in any way they properly could so they seconded Waterway Manager Terry Kemp to the Canal Trust to assist as appeal co-ordinator for three years; the post of waterway manager passed first to John Weston before being awarded to a BW newcomer, Michael Goodenough. There was further help for the project with the second-ment of Canal Trust Chairman Brian Stark from his job at the Royal Mail.

The vital step, however, was to re-involve the local authorities who were, by now, very conscious that the end of the original maintenance agreements was in sight.

The doubtful possibility of extending the existing five-year maintenance agreements between BW and local authorities beyond the expiry date of March 1995 had prompted the Wiltshire County Council to call a meeting in January 1994.

Under the chairmanship of Peter Chalke, the Wiltshire County Council and the Canal Trust invited all eight riparian authorities to attend, the object being to find a method of securing future funding which would be generally acceptable not only to those present but also to BW. This initial meeting resulted in the formation of the steering group with the Canal Trust chairman, Brian Stark, being elected chairman and the Canal Trust providing the secretarial support.

Within a month a further meeting was held, but this time it was attended by BW members – such was the success that at a later gathering when the subject of the major back pumping exercise was proposed the local authorities agreed, very reluctantly, to extend the five-year agreement by a further two years to provide continued maintenance and specifi-cally to build the back pumping scheme.

A small focus group was formed to carry the project forward, appeal objectives and expec-tations were formulated, documents prepared and the appeal launched during March 1993. By May the appeal had raised over £80,000, with many events planned and prepared including a prize draw and an explanatory road show travelling along the length of the waterway.

The Canal Trust agreed to fund the pump house at Lower Foxhangers and purchase the pumps, whilst the Kennet District Council, greatly assisted by Mike Lee, the Canal Trust's honorary civil engineer, provided the services of its engineering department to design and supervise the project. The scheme was designed, costed and carried through, overseen by the Steering Committee group, on budget and completed within the three-year target.

The statistics for the completed project are impressive; the pumps are capable of lifting 300,000 gallons of water every hour to a height of 235ft through a pipe two and a quarter miles long. This equates roughly to a lock full of water (some 55,000 gallons) every eleven minutes with the two electric pumps, housed in the pump house at Lower Foxhangers, working together.

The total cost of the scheme came to £1.1 million pounds, raised by the Canal Trust with the eight local authorities – Avon, Wiltshire and Berkshire County Councils, Wansdyke, West Wiltshire, Kennet and Newbury District Councils and Bath City Council.

The back pumps were formally commissioned at a ceremony performed by Sir Anthony Durrant MP on Friday 6 September 1996.

For the first time in over forty years, the longest flight of broad locks in the country would be open to boats every day of the week and, at long last, it could be truly said that the Kennet & Avon Canal was coming back to life.

With the successful completion of the first stage of the scheme Brian Stark, who had masterminded the whole concept, decided that he would now step down from the very arduous position of Canal Trust chairman, handing over the reigns to David Lamb, a member of the Devizes branch. To Brian Stark goes the credit for guiding the Canal Trust along the difficult road which followed the re-opening and instilling, within the organization, a return to the pioneering spirit which had been so successful in past years.

The next step would be to install further back pumping systems at Bath and at the far end of the Long Pound at Wootton Rivers. But before any of this could be implemented there came a decision that was to change everything when BW and the Kennet & Avon Canal Trust, under the patronage of the Kennet & Avon Partnership, made a submission to the Heritage Lottery Funds for assistance in restoring and securing the future of this beautiful waterway for many years to come.

13 The Lottery Bid
1995-1996

To help appreciate the quite inspirational notion of applying for a Lottery grant one needs to look back at how financial support and individual co-operation was established between BW, the Canal Trust and the local authorities, and how this led them to the eventual development of an ad hoc working relationship. This alliance provided the basis of mutual trust which was so essential for the presentation of such a large and imaginative scheme.

As has been shown in the earlier chapters, John Gould's inspired challenge against the closure of the canal was soon faced head on with the lack of funds and the reluctance of the Transport Commission to maintain the waterway in anywhere near operating condition.

The Transport Act of 1968, which gave the authorities the legal right to differential main-tenance standards, further complicated the situation to the detriment of the Kennet & Avon. Clearly the owners of the canal were never voluntarily going to put matters right so canal enthusiasts bent on restoration needed to look to other alternatives. They could support BW schemes by providing financial assistance or support the local authorities that had specific projects which coincided with the needs and amenity desires of the waterway.

A prime example of this was the co-operation displayed by the Bath City Council in connection with the Widcombe project at Bath and the Claverton electric pumps. The Bath inner ring road design dictated the need to merge two locks and as part of this scheme the rest of the flight received financial assistance and this allowed the whole flight to be repaired.

As well as this initiative, Bath City Council was keen to ensure that its section of the canal remained 'in water' as a public amenity so support was given in the form of annual payments to fund the electrical supply to the Claverton pumps, and this is now incorporated into the long-term financial agreement.

The ad hoc financial agreements were crystallized by 1985 when most of the riparian local authorities entered into a common form of five-year agreement with BW to finance the maintenance of the canal.

A total annual payment of £500,000 was committed to by Avon, Bath, West Wiltshire District Council, Kennet District Council, Wiltshire County Council, Berkshire County Council and Newbury Council – with the benefit of hindsight one can see that this 1985 agreement and the formation of the ad hoc committee foreshadowed the Kennet & Avon Partnership upon which the Lottery bid developed.

After a period of working the 1985 agreement and with the increasing momentum for the completion of restoration, a number of authorities began to question the direction of the maintenance expenditure. It emerged from these enquiries that the maintenance funds were being spent on both capital and repair items on the canal. In retrospect, it is difficult to see how this could be otherwise but this realisation prompted a move by the local author-ities to divide their contributions equally between maintenance and capital expenditure. They then began to show an interest in restoration, where up to this time the Canal Trust had been alone in raising and spending, through the agency of BW, all the funds it could raise to achieve this end.

The growing awareness of the local authorities to the direction of the five-year funds and their need for an independent and informed view on the scope and direction of the capital expenditure funds led the local authorities to seek closer co-operation with the Canal Trust. The guidance and the informal one-to-one consultations which now resulted paved the way for the first ad hoc 'steering committee' meeting.

These events paralleled the events leading up to the Queen re-opening the canal in August 1990, but as has already been pointed out in the previous chapter, although this was a great achievement the canal required very much more attention which, as has been shown, prompted building the Caen Hill back pumping scheme. This was a new landmark in what can be called phase two of the restoration but it did not bring a solution to the looming problems in the Bath valley – the magnitude of which were, only later, to be too well appreciated.

It was suspected, and work now completed has vindicated that suspicion, that at almost any point within the Bath valley between the section west of Dundas aqueduct, past Bathampton, and into Bath itself, a substantial breach could have occurred at any time with catastrophic consequences for the canal. These lengths were designated remainder lengths and had they failed then BW would have been barred by statute from spending their funds on repairs

This gloom and doom scenario coincided with the approaching end of the agreements which had now been extended to seven years. The quite clear policy views of the local authorities were that, whilst some continuing funds might be made available, certain conditions would have to be satisfied.

These conditions were, firstly, that payments should be more fairly shared out between the local authorities, and that there must be a tapering down to the payment which would lead to a definite point when they would cease altogether. When this point was reached, they insisted, it needed to be clearly understood that any continuing operational costs would be funded without any recourse to the local authorities – effectively saying that the canal now needed to become a 'cruiseway' with all the benefits that this would attract.

Serendipity has many faces; the fact that these apparently intractable problems coincided with the launch of the National Lottery and the creation of one of its arms, the Heritage Lottery Fund (HLF), was something none of the protagonists in the restoration saga could ever have foreseen, much less banked upon! It is not known exactly from whose fertile mind the idea of an application to the Lottery fund originated but the initiative was encouraged by the steering committee.

As the idea developed it became clear that some fundamental decisions had to be made. The most obvious was how much should be asked for, what support funds (called match funding in Lottery jargon) would be required of the partnership, how much it could raise and, of vital importance, what administrative mechanism would be used to receive and control any grant it obtained.

As the bid was investigated another requirement emerged: any Lottery-supported scheme has to be financially viable after the grant has been spent. A sensible enough requirement that ensured that if a village hall, for example, was built with a grant, then permanent income would be available in the future to heat, light and maintain it and pay for taxes and running costs. That standard, applied to a British canal, however, was itself a matter for deep thought and commitment.

The question of 'how much' was initially addressed against the background of the looming problems in the Bath valley. The figure for this work was estimated to be over £10 million.

However, the many discussions which took place highlighted the anomaly of securing the structural integrity of five miles of the canal for the next hundred years whilst leaving the rest in the state of Victorian decay. This in itself raised the question of how the 'financial sustainability' of the Bath valley section could rely on the unrepaired eighty-two miles which remained.

Broadening the scope of the bid to do all the necessary and desirable work produced a figure of £21 million. This seemed to BW and the Canal Trust an enormous amount of money to be asking for, and clearly it was. The arguments raised for or against the larger or smaller sum were followed the 'we have nothing to lose' school of thought or the 'proceed with caution' approach.

The Canal Trust believed that the request should be for the larger amount, for they reasoned that there was always a fighting chance that the bid would be successful. If, on the other hand it failed, but serious consideration had been given to the application, then there was always the possibility of a scaled down grant.

The 'proceed with caution' faction, however, considered how much would be demanded by the Lottery fund by way of match funding as this could govern the practicability of the entire scheme. No guidance was given as to the possible level that may be requested although, anecdotal evidence indicated that twenty-five per cent of the grant was normally looked for.

Enquiries of the supporting authorities on what funds they may provide, whilst encouraging, were not guarantees – none would, indeed none could, promise anything until all the parties, including the HLF, had made a commitment. The amount which could be provided for 'match funding' was in reality the 'tail that wagged the dog' of grant applications. The size relationship of the two was unknown and in the final analysis depended wholly on the HLF trustees' decision.

This would be made entirely at their discretion and would take into account the long-term sustainability test which required projection of income generation and maintenance costs over a twenty-one-year period, and this to a standard, and amount, which would satisfy the investigation HLF officers.

The resolution of these questions was complex and the enormous amount of work required, although helped by the Canal Trust, was almost all carried out by BW at Devizes.

Professional studies of usage, economic prospects, employment and revenue generation were commissioned. A great deal of the work was carried out by Coopers & Lybrand and whilst some of their conclusions caused raised eyebrows amongst both Canal Trust and BW officers, nonetheless they were used on the basis that it was no use keeping a dog and barking yourself.

With the cost of these studies and other works funded in part by the Canal Trust, but largely by BW, the elements of the bid was eventually brought together.

In its initial form the bid to the Heritage fund was for £21,568,000 to be supported by match funding of £3,202,000. There was an indicated value of fifteen per cent non-cash contribution by way of labour and materials 'donated' by BW, with the Canal Trust and the private sector adding another £610,000 of value to the match funding contribution.

The view taken by the steering group, guided by BW and the Canal Trust, was to 'go for' the big scheme. This decision was influenced by the announcements of a number of largish Lottery-funded grants to benefit comparatively narrow-based interests. Grants to refurbish the Royal Opera House and for the retention of Sir Winston Churchill's papers are two that produced adverse press comment, but there were many more.

It was felt that the Kennet & Avon Canal application afforded the opportunity to make a grant that would be spread over a wide geographical location to an amenity demonstrably used and enjoyed by some millions of people each year.

The match funding element at fifteen per cent was all that the group could possibly manage to raise and it was felt that this amount might just scrape through. BW committed all revenue raised on the Kennet & Avon to be ploughed back into the canal over the life of the scheme which was scheduled to last six years.

This six-year timing decision was a compromise, as the best method of spending any grant given would doubtless have been to close the canal completely for two years and carry out the work in one go. However, to placate the commercial interests already established on the canal, the decision was made to carry out any work over six winter shutdown periods.

The one unresolved decision was the question of the administrative mechanism to make and run the bid. In the event, the bidding process itself clarified the issue as it emerged that only the owners of the asset being improved could apply for a grant. So although it would have been excellent publicity to make the bid in the name of the Kennet & Avon Canal Partnership (a style of address agreed by the steering group to identify itself) as a nominated group, they could not take any part in the process as the grant would have to flow to BW as owners of the canal and to the Canal Trust as owners of the Crofton pumping station.

The bid documents were formally submitted on 3 October 1995, comprising an A4-sized book over 50mm thick; it contained schedules specifying all the works proposed in considerable detail.

The engineering works specified forty-nine separate contracts totalling over £11 million. Dredging involved 99km in sixteen identified areas requiring 292,756 cubic metres of spoil to be moved at a cost of £2.5 million. Also with this work there was a list of some 885 minor tasks at a cost of some £6.5 million which included allocations for lock refurbishment, bridges and landing stages, water control, bank protection, access environment and interpretation. Finally there was a cost allocation of £3.8 million to cover management and fees which then produced a total round sum of £25 million in total, plus the match funding.

This very brief summary does not, in any way, do justice to the work involved. Each job or group of jobs was identified in its position on the canal, and each was priced according to a necessary brief specification of the work to be undertaken. This allowed the overall sum necessary to complete the job including the design and supervising costs per job and overall project management to be calculated. The completion of this task remains a monument to the dedication of the BW team who put it together; Admiral O'Brien, the former chairman, after reading the application from cover to cover, commented that 'it was as good a piece of staff work as he had ever seen'. The other elements of the bid document comprised eight further appendices covering:

1. Design fees and supervision.
2. Overview of the Heritage and Environment.
3. Heritage database.
4. Socio-Economic Benefit Report.
5. The Kennet & Avon Partnership.
6. Project Finance.
7. Canal length by length analysis.
8. Testimonials from supporters (totalling nearly sixty organizations, MPs, councils and clubs contributed letters).
9. Documentary sources.
10. Heritage Philosophy and British Waterways Environmental Policy.

Supporting these working documents was a glossy booklet called *The Kennet & Avon Canal Partnership Project – A Business Plan for a Bid to the Heritage Lottery Fund*, which was a public relation-based summary of the salient points of the bid together with some attractive pictures of the waterway. The booklet was intended to be read by the Lottery trustees and other interested parties who wanted the basic picture set out succinctly, leaving the Lottery managers to absorb and master the pages of minutiae. Amazingly enough, the six-page form which was the actual application was hand-written (very neatly) by Michael Goodenough, the Kennet & Avon Canal waterway manager, and signed by Bernard Henderson, the British Waterway chairman.

Once the bid was committed to the Lottery Fund managers the awful period of waiting commenced.

The Partnership was later to discover that the HLF had been inundated with applications and being in start-up mode themselves were undermanned, inexperienced and literally making up the rules of procedure as they went along, indeed the Kennet & Avon bid was to prove the template for some of these rules and influenced the HLF in their handling of subsequent bids.

At one stage it was said that the corridors of the HLF office were filled with plastic dustbin bags containing unopened Lottery applications awaiting attention. In fact the Partnership bid was receiving attention, and after an anguished debate as to whether prospects would be jeopardized by enquiring as to the progress, contact was made and the identity of the partnership supervising officer established.

There was a promise of an answer to be given either in March or July but both of these dates passed without any confirmation of success and it was to be an agonizing thirteen months wait before an announcement was finally made on 31 October 1996.

At times there were periods of frenzied activity to answer particular points raised and then resounding silences whilst the HLF absorbed the information, or, for all the Partnership knew, forgot about the whole thing. Although BW officials were called to the HLF on a number of occasions to explain certain aspects, there was a high point when the HLF team of two or three trustees with their consultants and accompanied by the case officer paid a visit to Bath. They were given a whistle-stop tour of the Bath valley, with coffee taken onboard the Bath trip boat. A visit was arranged to view the bottom of the Caen Hill Flight at Foxhangers and after lunch, provided by Canal Trust volunteers at the wharf in Devizes, they were given a slide presentation and address by the BW team. As the HLF Team made their way to the local railway stations en route to Lottery headquarters there was great local satisfaction at the reception the HLF representatives appeared to have for the project, but alas, no commitments!

Meanwhile, at BW offices in Devizes there was growing concern regarding the outcome of the bid; the end of the local authority funding stared BW in the face and with further deterioration in the Bath valley it now seemed inevitable that a major breach would occur in this length and that would have the potential to wreck the canal before the bid was agreed, indeed there was debate whether it would be safe to keep the canal open at all.

As the year moved on to the autumn it became clear that the start date of the programme of work as outlined in the bid was no longer feasible because insufficient time was now left for the first winter's work to be planned, specified and quoted for. Urgent work on a modest scale for the winter of 1996 was identified and the main programme was moved back to allow for the time slippage.

Within the partnership itself, other unresolved questions were being addressed in order to satisfy direct and anticipated questions from HLF. As stated earlier, the application clarified the fact that only the two groups, BW or Canal Trust, could receive any grant. The question of the mechanism for handling and spending the money loomed large. The facts of life, or rather the fact of VAT, committed the group to the reality that not only did BW have to be the spender of any grant but more particulaly it was required that no other agency controlled that spending. This also dictated the requirement that the partnership constitution, which was still ad hoc, could only be in the loosest form and it could not be permitted to exercise any control or direction over expenditure.

Equally within the steering group the legal beavers of the local authorities pointed out that they could not enter into a 'partnership' in the legal sense of the word. Fortunately this was resolved by the chairman of the steering group proposing a layman's draft of a partnership which said, in effect, let's all be chums together and meet from time to time to guide BW in what we would like them to do with any bid money.

This innocent draft then passed through the hands of the legal departments of the local authorities, led by the Wiltshire County Council, and finally emerged, although in a different form, saying just that.

An altogether more intractable problem also had to be addressed head-on when appeals to the local authority partners to prepare a new and more equable form of sharing the funding found no direct response. There required to be a formula which would provide some relationship between canal length, population and the rateable value within any particular authority, but the task proved to be a near impossibility especially having regard to the overlap between District and County Councils. The bid had been constructed on the basis of maintaining the local authority contribution at the time the bid was put together, and holding this amount for five years, then gradually tapering it away so that at the end of a further sixteen years it disappeared completely.

This formula gave the local authorities a twenty-one-year involvement and was built against the revenue projection of BW which, even though they provided for all the revenue from the Kennet & Avon to be ploughed back (a unique situation in national BW financing arrangements), more or less left a shortfall of projected maintenance costs over projected revenue of £240,000 per annum. Rather than re-open the draft financial negotiations within the partnership, BW locally were able to persuade their 'powers that be' to guarantee the payment of any such shortfall from central BW funds.

These arrangements, which were extraordinarily far sighted and even generous in their context, still rested on the basis that when schemes were proposed they would be submitted to all the partners for individual ratification; it is obvious that all would have to agree, and yet there were those who were finding this difficult. The debate at the steering group floundered through the rather unsatisfactory ideas of the Canal Trust officers to find a solution without success. Fortunately the situation was salvaged by Philip Owen, chief executive of the Kennet District Council and their representative of long standing on the committee.

The Kennet District Council was one of the larger payers – their burden was clearly unfair and, unless it was addressed, they would not proceed so Philip Owen brought his director of finance, Frank Marshall, to the discussion table and after deliberation the problem was submitted to Frank Marshall to propose a solution.

By the next meeting his proposals emerged as an official paper with a schedule of payments per authority, plus the sixteen-year taper which produced the numbers required by the BW bid, but redistributed the amounts. These calculations were agreed with very little difficulty, still on the basis of final ratification, and passed into the long-term arrangements of the partnership.

No serious attempt was made either to establish Frank Marshall's formula or even test it; it was in all probability a 'suck it and see' calculation based, perhaps, on what Kennet District Council felt was fair for them and empirical judgments on what the other authorities would also feel fair for themselves.

Thus the partnership owes a great deal to Philip Owen for his sustained support over many years and particularly to Frank Marshall for blazing a trail through the jungle of past contributions and proposing an escape route that all the partners could accept.

The components for completion of the partnership were now all in place as far as the progress of the bid allowed and a (nearly) final meeting was held at the HLF Headquarters attended by Peter Coyne, BW area manager, Michael Goodenough, Kennet & Avon BW manager, and Brian Oram, Canal Trust Council member and chairman of the partnership.

Attending for the HLF was the senior case officer, Sue Bowers, as well as HLF's independent financial economic adviser. The subsequent discussions spread over a wide spectrum of questions and answers concerning the practical aspects raised by the bid; there was emphasis on the breadth of local support and benefit which a grant would produce.

The Canal Trust/British Waterways team was quick to point out to the HLF the publicity of a Lottery-funded scheme with such wide-ranging benefits for the ordinary person, hoping this may help to allay some of the recent elitist adverse criticism of Lottery grants.

As far as the British Waterways/Canal Trust team were able to judge, the meeting was a success but at the very end a casual enquiry from the British Waterways/Canal Trust team to the effect that they assumed that standard inflation increases would be applied to the grant and expenditure throughout the term of the work brought the totally unexpected reply that it did not. The team had now to return to the figures and add a 'best guess' estimated inflation factor to the costs for the six-year term. This exercise in crystal ball gazing produced a final bid figure of a grant request of £21,568,000 with match-funding of £7,421,000 to produce a total spend of £28,989,000. The figures were proffered with prayers that the judgments in inflation would prove to be sufficient.

The final period of waiting was almost too nerve-racking to endure until on 3 October 1996 Sue Bowers wrote to Michael Goodenough, purely for his information and for that of the partnership chairman, Brian Oram, with the news that the trustees had approved the bid. However, there was a final, yet more pleasant, twist of the screw when they were both placed, on the pain of cancellation, under an absolute embargo not to release this information until the formal announcement by the chairman of the HLF, Lord Rothchild, to be made on 31 October. There followed four weeks of the most difficult lip buttoning that could be asked of anyone – and they did not say a word but, as a colleague remarked afterwards, they both suddenly appeared to be so much more cheerful!

There were initial hopes that the grant decision would be forthcoming during the spring of 1996. The delay until the autumn of that year meant, unfortunately, the winter of 1996-1997 was lost to the repair programme. The only work that could be carried out was the rebuilding of the Crofton chimney which the Canal Trust had already put in hand with the help of Sir John Smith, together with two small but urgent tasks which could be designed and put in hand in the short period available.

Nevertheless, the euphoria within the various partnership members was enormous, but before a real start could be made all the local authorities now formally had to agree to the twenty-one-year agreement and present it through their various committee structures for ratification.

During this process the waterway manager, Michael Goodenough, and the chairman of the partnership committee, Brian Oram, made three presentations to council groupings – the Bath City Council, the West Wiltshire District Council and the Wiltshire County Council. The presentation to the county council was given to council members followed by a formal meeting of the council where Michael Goodenough and Brian Oram had the satisfaction of having the proposal adopted by the authority there and then.

The meetings at Bath and West Wiltshire were of a differing level of formality and sought to inform the councillors in advance of their formal meetings.

By early 1997 all the authorities concerned had ratified their commitments and it only required the agreement between each local authority and BW to be legally formed.

These agreements depended on, and were an integral part of, the legal grant agreement between the Heritage Lottery Fund, BW and the Kennet & Avon Canal Trust. The fact that the Kennet & Avon Canal project grant was the largest ever given by the HLF was starkly revealed by the tortuous progress of the basic agreement.

The HLF had set themselves up with fundamental documentation designed to deal with one-off grants centred on the construction of a single object – best explained by using the 'village hall' analogy as an example.

The complications, not just of size but also the number of individual components in the Kennet & Avon scheme, strained this documentation beyond its limits.

Further, the almost inevitable delay factor which appears to accompany almost any arrangement involving lawyers was magnified by the HLF's London solicitors who, although with an international reputation, just could not physically cope with the overwhelming flow of HLF work. Now the original frustration due to the lack of decision over the grant was multiplied by the frustration of not being able to get to the proceeds as a result of HLF internal legal delays.

It was not until late in 1997 that all the agreements were finally brought together to allow the money to flow. Contrary to popular belief, no grant funds are ever handed to the recipient so neither BW nor the Kennet & Avon Canal Trust saw anything approaching £25 million enhancing their bank account. Sensibly and necessarily HLF guard assiduously against fraud and overcharging. Thus every contract has to conform to EU standards of tendering and five prices have to be obtained, although as the work on the project progressed the knowledge gained through working with experienced contractors allowed this requirement to become slightly relaxed.

Each section of the work is agreed with the HLF's professional advisers during the preceding summer planning sessions and then worked on a normal monthly contract programme based on measured work done. As each instalment is claimed, the project manager has to demonstrate that the fifteen per cent match funding is in the bank before HLF pay the grant contribution of eighty-five per cent for that instalment. This system works efficiently with the lead monitor, Ove Arup, a firm of international engineers, and assisted by the associate monitors – English Nature, English Heritage and the Countryside Commission – performing a professional task of monitoring the works in a balanced and efficient manner.

With the benefit of 20/20 vision that hindsight brings, the partnership was very lucky with its timing even though the timing owed nothing to any deliberate choice. Very lucky for three main reasons: the first has to do with the political changes which took place in the year following the granting of the bid, for there were changes in the structure of some of the local authorities which affected the handling of their part in the financing agreement. It is accepted that had the twenty-one-year financing agreements been presented to the local authorities twelve months later, then these changes in the national and local political tempers would have meant that some, if not all, would have refused to commit to this funding. As the funding depended very much on an 'all or nothing' approach, just one dissenter would have destroyed the scheme.

The second reason was a development at HLF itself under a combination of internal reconsideration and, one has to assume, new government 'guidance' on what was appropriate for continuing grant funding. It has been bluntly stated by HLF that the Kennet & Avon Canal project is not only the largest it has granted but also it is doubtful if it will ever again award a grant of such a size. Future grants will be smaller – figures of £3 million are mooted. No doubt the argument for more smaller grants was to spread the benefits of the Lottery over a wider group of communities and participants, but clearly part of the motive was to silence the criticism of large value grants which benefit a minority interest, although this sentiment hardly squares with the enormous sums of Lottery money spent, only a few years later, on the notorious Millennium Dome. The Kennet & Avon project avoided that minority interest criticism by covering a length of eighty-seven miles and with well over ten million people using the amenity each year, but nevertheless would fail on the 'large value' criteria.

The final reason and also the hurdle which would have broken the back of the project, even if the timing of the two preceding matters would not have intervened, was the Conservation Plan, which, of all the problems and difficulties that had so far been encountered, none was so unexpected and so demanding.

The need for a Conservation Plan grew out of an acceptance in the bid application by BW to 'carefully consider nature conservation during any restoration'; this was then specified by the HLF in the original grant approval list of 'special conditions'. It stated that:

A Conservation Plan should be drawn up by appropriate consultants to an agreed brief with English Heritage, English Nature and the Countryside Commission. This should encompass a full historical, architectural and environmental assessment of the canal, its structure and eco system.

All this to be approved by the HLF before work could commence! Preparation of the plan was an overwhelming task and a period of some twelve months was allowed but, although preparation began in October 1996, it was not completed until March 1999 and then it took until the autumn of 2000 before it was published in its final form – nearly four years!

Because of the time and argument experiences caused by the Kennet & Avon Conservation Plan, the HLF ruled that no further bids would be considered without a conservation plan having been produced as a prior consideration, which they say they might fund whether or not the bid is eventually agreed, but one has to have very grave doubts as to whether the ad hoc partnership group which existed in 1995-1996 would have produced the required fifteen per cent share of that cost without any guarantee of success.

With the grant in place, initial work – only urgent contracts were carried out pending the completion of the conservation report – began seriously over winter 1997-1998 and the progress of the work and the problems that were yet to be uncovered are recorded in later chapters.

The vital nature of the work for the long-term security of the canal was underlined several times during the early years of the project. A major slip near Bathhampton would have, in time, produced a tremendous breach. Again at Bathampton the creeping movement outwards on the large bend near Hampton Cottage, if not detected and secured by embankment toe piling, would have resulted in the entire section of canal embankment slipping away down to the railway and river below. Massive leaks at Martinslade embankment and All Cannings also pointed to the potential for catastrophic failure; the Kennet & Avon Canal has been very lucky!

14 Preparing to use the Lottery Funding
1997

Thanks to the efforts of BW and the Canal Trust team led by Brian Oram, the right Lottery numbers had certainly come up for the Kennet & Avon Canal. Seasoned campaigners might well be forgiven if they pinched themselves to confirm this was not a dream.

The exciting news was revealed to a packed press conference held outside the BW headquarters at Devizes. Surrounded by representatives from BW, the Canal Trust, County Councils, and the Association of Canal Enterprises, Prof. Palmer Newbold (Heritage Lottery Trustee) announced the good tidings, which flashed quickly along the canal towpath telegraph to reach canal enthusiasts everywhere. At long last it would be possible not only to repair the ravages of time and neglect but, with the modern machinery and techniques available, correct the inherent faults that had so plagued the waterway during its entire existence.

Although first and foremost a navigation, the increasing use of the canal as a leisure facility and the granting of, what were in essence, public funds to repair it did tend to suggest that no one group could claim to monopolize the waterway. There was hope that a spirit of tolerance would prevail among all the potential users. With so many differing interests, it was important to ensure that the canal was as safe and as user-friendly as possible – Section Inspector Cyril Rodgers, in the late 1960s and early 1970s, doubted the wisdom of restoring a waterway that people would have, as he said, 'to walk about with stones in their shoes' to use.

Quite apart from the necessary structural repairs, hopefully there would be improvements to hernia-inducing lock gear and back-breaking swing-bridges, provision of landing stages, ladders and other safety features at locks which, coupled with the provision of water and refuse disposal points, would contribute not just to safe, but to more enjoyable pleasure craft operation. For the walkers, cyclists and fishermen the important considerations would be easy access and the safe condition of the towpath, while the casual visitor would certainly look for car parks, notice and information boards. There were also other improvements that were less obvious to the layman. The saving of water resources by building bye-washes or weirs on most of the non-river locks being an important example.

All this required to be backed up by the official encouragement of commercial interest in providing, at fair and equitable prices, all the varying facilities which the visitor would look for, from tea rooms and shops, to boat hire, marine repair and support services.

The 'professional' boatmen and boatwomen of yesteryear, whose livelihood depended on maintaining the canal in working order, ensured that every good care was taken to conserve precious water supplies and avoid flooding. The need for bye-washes and weirs was not then as demanding as on a waterway mainly devoted to the leisure industry where a bye-wash does provide a measure of flood protection against carelessness and mindless vandalism.

The prospect was exciting and with BW preparing to start operations, the Kennet & Avon Canal Trust had to knuckle down to fulfil the obligation in providing its agreed share of the match funding. The amount promised to the partnership was estimated to be in the region of £50,000 per annum (this expressed somewhat dramatically, was at least ten pence per minute day and night, week in week out, for the entire period of the task!) plus an unknown annual inflationary addition which would unquestionably increase the longer the work progressed. Additionally, there were still the administrative overheads of the Canal Trust to pay and this, with government support now long since withdrawn, had by 1997 become quite a sizeable sum.

The priority was the need to raise funds and fund-raising is at best a most uncertain business, particularly if it does not have a 'heart string tugging' life or death essence to the appeal. The Canal Trust Council were fortunate, initially, in having sufficient cash reserves to meet immediate needs, but substantial amounts of the much needed revenue would have to be generated by the Canal Trust's trading arm – Canal Trust (Enterprises) Ltd.

During 1996, the post of Managing Director of the Enterprise arm passed from Hugh Maitland-Jones to David Saady, who immediately started to build up and rationalize the organization to cope with the hoped-for extra business.

The Canal Trust's tea shops at Newbury and Bradford-on-Avon were renovated and enlarged, with two new shops opened, one at Woolhampton and the other in the old lock-keepers cottage at the top of the Caen Hill Flight in Devizes. This latter tea room, The Firs, proved popular and made over £6,500 in its first year of trading, helped by the provision of a nearby car park constructed for use by visitors to the impressive flight of locks.

Attention was also given to the trip boats which plied their trade from bases in Hungerford, Bath and Bradford-on-Avon. These boats provided a ready source of income to Canal Trust Enterprise as well as being a great source of pleasure to the visiting public. To generate the maximum benefit from the boat operations, Peter Crawford was appointed as Enterprise Boat Director to assist the boat crews by co-ordinating procedures and methods. Although actual boat operation was still left to the individual branches to arrange, it was thought that there was a positive need for a correlating hand in the field of advertising, crew training, maintenance and attention to health and safety requirements.

The Kennet & Avon Canal Trust (Enterprise) Ltd's fleet in 1997 comprised four boats: the *Rose of Hungerford*, an all-weather purpose-built wide-beamed vessel operating from Hungerford; *Ladywood*, another comfortable all-weather narrow-beamed craft which was completely refurbished by Bradford branch and brought into service in the late 1970s – she had been operating from Bradford-on-Avon for over twenty years; *Jubilee*, also a narrow-beamed trip boat, but with roll-down weather protection, fitted out by Canal Trust volunteers at Wootton Rivers and originally used as an attraction at Crofton Pumping station, but in 1997 was operating from the Bath area; and finally there was *Dragonfly*, a small craft operating from Pewsey Wharf.

During the following years *Dragonfly* was retired and during 1999 it was considered desirable to replace Bradford-on-Avon's ageing *Ladywood*, which needed renovation and was disadvantaged by being unable to accommodate the entire complement of a modern touring coach. Although many people were sad to see the *Ladywood* go, even more so considering its long association with the area, the search commenced to find a suitable replacement.

A team led by Peter Crawford found a craft they thought ideal – *Aquarius*, a wide-beamed, 65ft (20m) long, ex-restaurant boat which came complete with all facilities. This craft was swiftly purchased and transported to Bradford-on-Avon.

There was some apprehension as to whether the commercial viability of albeit such a handsome acquisition could possibly justify the cost, which was in excess of £50,000. There were those who thought that the capital return, even with sustained efforts by the Bradford-on-Avon branch was at best a long-term venture, when the immediate requirement was for instant proceeds to fund the ongoing Heritage Lottery Project.

However, such criticisms were silenced when, in what must rank as an amazing turn of good fortune, a charitable trust whose work is with the infirm and disadvantaged offered to purchase the *Aquarius* for the Canal Trust in reward, they said, for all the help given to the disadvantaged over the years by Canal Trust volunteers. In recognition of this truly magnificent gesture by the McLellan Trust, *Aquarius* was renamed *Barbara McLellan* and was ready to carry out her first 'Santa' trips during the 1999 Christmas season.

As well as the Canal Trust Enterprise trading operations there were other fund-raising

There were a number of schemes to raise funds towards match-funding contributions.

opportunities which did not transgress the strict charity laws and could, therefore, be quite properly organized by the Canal Trust itself. These included raffles, jazz nights and locally arranged events, which together with boat rallies and gatherings, were held at varying locations along the length of the canal.

There were productive corporate steamings arranged by the Crofton branch, successful real ale festivals held at Devizes and occasionally some slightly more sophisticated entertainments, organized centrally, of which the opera evening at Coombe Manor was always a notable and well- attended event raising annually more than £2,000. BW also played its part by organizing 'Fun Days' on the Caen Hill during the summers of 1998 and 1999 which were much enjoyed by the local inhabitants of Devizes and district.

But as much fun and success as all these events were, they required many volunteer hours of labour just to produce comparatively small returns. Presenting events that will attract the public and produce funds is never easy – the public now look increasingly for new and interesting ways to be entertained and it requires a great deal of courage and foresight to venture into hitherto untried ventures. Trust members do occasionally produce some new and exciting ideas which deserve trying and a number of schemes were promoted during the HLF project, all designed to raise funds to go towards the match-funding contributions.

One such idea was the Canal Adoption Scheme which raised just short of £40,000 over a comparatively short period of time. The stratagem was based on the well-tried 'Buy a Brick' concept but with a variation allowing the participant to select a favourite stretch or feature of the canal. The 'Adopter' has his or her name recorded in the Canal museum at Devizes and all receive a certificate showing the precise location of their choice. Of course, the 'Adoption' does not attract any responsibilities or rights but it does seem to establish a

Above (courtesy of Terry Kemp) and left: *David Lamb, Canal Trust Chairman, and Michael Goodenough, British Waterways Canal Manager, unveil the plaque for Adopters Lock in August 2001.*

lasting affinity between the Adopter and the waterway. This was reinforced by BW when in the summer of 2001 they named Crofton Lock 57 'Adopters Lock'.

The Canal Trust has always been fortunate in attracting sizeable donations and legacies and so had every confidence in raising the Canal Trust's agreed match-funding allocation, as past experience had so often dictated, the money would be forthcoming.

The early months of 1997 saw much activity in the BW office as they geared up to start the six-year stint. Despite the excitement there was still the day-to-day task of keeping the canal open and work totalling some £3 million was already in hand; this included Allington swing-bridge which was by then nearing completion. But, of course, no major tasks could proceed until the ever-present problem of the conservation plan had been agreed as this would form the framework for the future work programme.

This process began in the early spring with Waterways Environmental Services, the BW specialist department at Hillmorton, preparing a draft document for submission to the HLF towards the end of 1997. It was expected there would be a period of consultation to produce a final draft in 1998 but, as we now know, this was an optimistic forecast which proved to be wildly inaccurate.

There was, however, work which needed to be put in hand urgently so an arrangement was sought with the HLF to allow the more pressing requirements to be attended to. This was agreed provided that at all times the spirit, if not the letter of the developing conservation plan was adhered to in principle. This understanding approved plans for the winter of 1997–1998 to go ahead as follows:.

1. Complete rebuilding of Lower Foxhangers Lock and major repairs to the adjoining bridge at the bottom of the Devizes Flight.
2. Gates to be replaced or part replaced at the three Seend Locks as well as at Crofton, Towney and Tyle Mill.
3. Channel lining works at Claverton in the Bath valley.
4. Embankment repairs at Martinslade.
5. Replacement of the Claverton pumping station discharge pipeline.
6. Dredging operations at seven locations where there were plans to spend £700,000 (although in actual fact less was spent).

For ecological reasons dredging work was restricted to lengths no longer than 3km and then a gap of 3km had to be left before work on another length could commence, with work on the intermediate sections being planned at a minimum of two years hence. Also on the programme were various inspections and repairs to pipelines and culverts with, in addition, work detailed under BW's statutory obligations involving repairs or replacements to Hissey's bridge at Burghfield and the bridge near Towney Lock.

This was an impressive and ambitious programme of quite frightening proportions for the limited resources of the BW team on the Kennet & Avon which, keen as they were, just could not undertake this enormous work load. Then to complicate matters further, July 1997 saw the commencement of 'Fibreway', a project to use the tow-path to accommodate underground ducts to carry fibre optic cables.

It came as no surprise, therefore, when BW and the partnership decided that the actual restoration operations would best be conducted and supervised by a specially recruited squad of qualified engineers, to be employed and paid through the partnership by the HLF.

The first requirement was to appoint a team leader. The post was advertised nationally and Michael Goodenough then patiently sifted through the many applications before selecting a short list of prospective candidates for interviews, held in Devizes and conducted jointly by the partnership and BW.

During the later part of 1996, John Laverick CEng., FICE, FIMgt, MIStructE, an experienced maritime civil engineer then working at the Broads Authority in Norfolk, was chosen from well over 150 applicants to be manager of the HLF project. John had started his career in the Port of Bristol Authority, moving to a consulting engineering practice and then later to the Navy Works Department, a post which took him to see service in all the main UK naval bases in the western Mediterranean and NWD Headquarters, retiring from the post of Director of Operations based at HM Dockyard Plymouth.

As later events were to prove John was an inspired and happy choice – both John and his wife Valerie had previously lived in the west country and John, having been educated in Bristol, knew the area well and both were keen to return. They were also, curiously enough, long-time members of the Kennet & Avon Canal Trust which added a further element of personal interest. It was understandable, therefore, that when John saw the position advertised in the pages of the professional journal *The New Civil Engineer* the appeal was instant.

As John settled in during April 1997, the connection that the name John had for the Kennet & Avon canal did not go unnoticed; first there were John Hore and John Rennie who were responsible for the original construction, then John Gould who saved it from dereliction and now John Laverick with his bucket of Lottery money to breath back substantial life to the waterway – he was very welcome. John moved into temporary offices which had been set up alongside the BW headquarters in Devizes and began building up a team of engineers and other specialists.

To complement the work of the permanent team, designs and various studies relating to the conservation plan were also commissioned from a range of consultants and other BW offices, whilst throughout the period of the project Mike Lee, the Canal Trust's honorary civil engineer, was on hand to provide useful input at all design team and site progress meetings. Mike Lee also performed the most essential task of liaison contact between BW and the Canal Trust.

Essentially the actual work was to be undertaken by a series of contractors, who having been selected for each task by the strict HLF standards of tendering, would work under the direction of the project team.

The project team in their turn were to be monitored by the international engineers, Ove Arup, who would act as lead monitors assisted by the associate project monitors, English Nature, English Heritage and the Countryside Commission, all four appointed by the HLF.

Before the operations could begin in earnest and the contract between the HLF, BW and the Canal Trust signed, wording on the contract had to be revised to cover a requirement that the HLF had insisted upon right from the outset that, on completion of the restoration work, BW would upgrade the Kennet & Avon Canal to 'Cruiseway', which would underline the sustainability clause in the original bid documents.

As has been explained so many times to Kennet & Avon enthusiasts, BW were unable to concede this demand even if they felt it justified because an Act of Parliament, passed during the later part of the 1960s, had graded parts of the Kennet & Avon as remainder canal. It would, therefore, necessarily require a similar Act of Parliament to amend that classification.

BW and the HLF did, however, solve this seemingly intractable problem by coming to an agreement that BW would 'use its best endeavours' to seek to have the canal re-classified. This agreement was wrapped up in legalistic jargon which satisfied the Lottery authorities and gave BW a generous time-scale in which to operate.

All was now set in place to begin operations. Slowly at first, as the team settled in, the HLF project began to gather momentum – in the offices all the computer-aided design equipment was assembled and plugged in whilst outside John Laverick, clad in wellington boots and waterproofs, led the team in trudging the canal banks to thoroughly familiarize themselves with the waterway and the problems which loomed ahead.

15 Completing the Restoration 1997–2002

Contracts for the 1997-1998 winter work were all in place before the autumn leaves started to fall. The first tasks to be tackled were those that had been agreed by the HLF as being in urgent need of attention, principally within the Bath Valley, Martinslade embankment and Lower Foxhangers Lock and bridge.

There was also the task of rebuilding the Crofton chimney; returning the chimney to its full original height had been for many years the ultimate ambition of many devoted pumping engine supporters and this hugely important task, helped financially by Sir John Smith, took almost a year to complete.

The work in the Bath Valley required the reconstruction of 1.7km of canal at Claverton, together with the replacement of the pipeline connecting the River Avon to the canal. The canal length at Claverton had a history of problems with land instability, slippage and water loss. Much repair had been carried out in the past but the geology of the area is such that land slippage within the valley had always been a constant threat, so work to secure the canal structure was urgently required.

The first length to be tackled was from Millbrook swing-bridge to Hardings bridge, a distance of about 1.7km. The contract, totalling £1,619,719, was awarded to Johnstone Construction of Somerset.

Constructional access to this section from the A36 road into Bath was extremely difficult so the first task was to contrive a suitable approach to the canal bed for the construction machinery and to remove the silt and other soft material, together with some of the redundant drainage system. This was done after de-watering and rescuing the fish; such was the extent of the soft areas encountered that eventually some 3,000 extra tons of stone fill was required.

The method of constructing the new channel was to lay a PVC liner protected by a layer of concrete. Once the channel had been profiled a layer of stone was compacted over the surface. This layer was increased in thickness to 125mm (6in) at the bottom of the canal which served as a construction haul road and the sub-base of a future access road. Beneath this sub-base a new longitudinal drain kept the haul road dry during construction and provided a permanent cut off relief drain for spring water from higher ground above the canal which for decades previously had caused damage to the clay puddle lining.

Laid upon the completed stone was the lining sandwich of two layers of geotextile fabric encapsulating a 1.6mm thick PVC waterproof membrane. On top of the sandwich for final protection from mechanical damage of boat impact and fishing hooks was placed 125mm (6in) of concrete. The weight of this concrete also resisted the residual upward pressure from spring water at times when the canal might be drained for future maintenance.

Once the PVC liner had been laid it was bonded to a concrete wall on the towpath side, while on the opposite side it was taken to above water level. A great deal of effort went into designing the non-towpath side of the channel edge to allow for re-establishing and sustaining the abundant flora and fauna of the area. Care was taken to preserve top soil taken from the towpath as well as removing canal reed to a temporary storage pond before work commenced, all of which guaranteed that with the work finished the canal would soon regain its green and natural appearance.

With the preparation work completed the bed was profiled at a rate of about 100m a day; this was followed by constructing the towpath wall and the installation of the watertight membrane. As each section was completed it was covered by placing a layer of concrete over it on the following day. The work commenced from the middle section with extra sections being laid at either end on alternate days – this ensured that placing concrete followed laying the liner, and also that neither the team working on the liner or the team placing the concrete got in each others way. There was a lack of frost during that period which made the task simpler, although perhaps muddier! This lining contract, over a mile long, was already one of the longest continuous lengths ever attempted on the canal system in one winter season so, although the work had proceeded with surprisingly little hold up, any extra work in the vicinity was not welcome.

When a major slip occurred on an embankment at nearby Bathampton it was essential that remedial work should be carried out immediately. Following a survey of the slip, the Johnstone Construction contract was extended and as well as the work at Claverton they were asked to undertake repairs to the Bathampton embankment at Hampton Cottage.

When the temporary repairs were finished it was thought prudent to install some instrumentation in the form of piezometers and inclinometers to measure any continuing movement of the canal bank and underlying hillside. This proved to be a wise decision as, during the following months, further movement occurred and tenders were sought from specialist contractors to carry out permanent remedial work during the following summer.

Towards Devizes another contractor, Dew Construction, was hard at work on the other large task of the 1997-1998 season, piling a 650m length of the Martinslade embankment and repairing Lower Foxhangers Lock and bridge, the contract being priced at approximately £603,780. This price, however, did not include the cost of the piles, valued at some £377,000, which were purchased through BW whose buying power saved some £34,000 over the best price offered by the contractors.

The first task was to repair the section of the embankment which carries the canal across the shallow valley of Summerham Brook to the west of Foxhangers and the bottom of the Devizes Flight. This length had a long history of leaks and repairs that were now urgent: over the years, material had been washed away from under the embankment with the result that the whole structure was slowly sinking.

The remedial design is known as 'piled cut-off' which requires the installation of piles either side of the channel, forming a watertight barrier by being driven into an underlying clay strata, thus preventing further leakage and destabilisation.

Steel sheet 'Larssen LX12' piles of between 4.5m and 9m long were driven through the towpath and offside embankment within a trench. This allowed the tops to be buried so that none of the work except at boat moorings, where the piles were placed at the water's edge, were visible on completion. In addition, the canal remained in water with minimal effect on the water fringe vegetation.

The length included three culverts which allowed Summerham Brook and two other water courses to run under the canal. Because piles could not be driven across these structures, a different lining design, which was very similar to that used at Claverton, was called for.

Piles were driven across the canal below the channel bed to form a connecting beam which allowed the PVC lining to be terminated in a watertight seal. As all the work was within the embankment crest the soft edges of the canal remained, thus there was little effect or change to the wildlife habitat; during the work some 1,200 linear metres of piles were driven with a total weight of 800 tons.

Canal access was always a problem. An indication of the kind of nasty little surprises that fate had in store for the engineers came when one of the lorries delivering piles destined for Martinslade slipped from the narrow farm track and became bogged down, blocking the road completely. Unfortunately the track was frequently used so the chaos has only to be imagined.

Road bridge,
Bathampton.
(British
Waterways)

Work was also carried out on Lower Foxhangers Lock and footbridge as both were showing signs of instability. In the lock chamber the walls had moved inwards, narrowing the chamber so that two narrow boats side-by-side could no longer be accommodated. This had caused considerable water wastage when operating the lower section of the Caen Hill Flight.

The footbridge over the tail of Lower Foxhangers had also developed substantial cracks and apart from the inconvenience of the narrow lock there was always the suspicion that greater dangers lurked within the structure, all of which hastened the need for repairs. A fabric dam was placed at the down stream end of the lock and work started to demolish the lock chamber and bridge approach walls to lower masonry level. The walls were then rebuilt with ties to a mass concrete backfill which provided stability. On the bridge, the wing wall and bridge bed over the arch were removed so that a reinforced concrete saddle could be constructed across it.

During this first winter's operations, Seend Flight was re-gated, repairs were undertaken at Crofton Crossing Lock with new gates installed and stop plank grooves provided. Gates were also replaced at Towney and Tyle Mill Locks, whilst dredging operations were carried out at seven locations between Tyle Mill and Great Bedwyn.

During this period BW supplemented the work by the Heritage Lottery Fund team by installing new footbridges in the Newbury area at Bulls and Copse Locks. These bridges, of a teak-type hardwood, although imported, have the advantage that they were 'kit built' so any future damage is relatively easy to repair, all the components being standardised.

Much of the lock gear was checked and overhauled; the hydraulic lock mechanisms were being replaced as they did not fit in with Heritage restoration requirements nor were they as robust, vandal-proof or as ecologically satisfactory as was once believed.

Details of the first year's work would not be complete without a mention of the dredging programme. Although not strictly an emergency requirement, Ove Arup allowed some work to proceed ahead of the conservation plan because the loss of the original Year One programme, together with conservation limitations, severely handicapped the ability to dredge the whole of the remainder length within the six year term of the project.

Re-lining in progress at Trowbridge. (British Waterways)

The lengths dredged to a minimum depth of 4ft 6in (1.37m) were:

3km   Tyle Mill to Aldermaston Wharf.
2.25km   Woolhampton swing-bridge to Midgham Lock.
3km   Monkey Marsh Lock to Bulls Lock.
1.25km   Hamstead Lock to Dreweat's Lock.
3.25km   Kintbury Lock to Dunmill Lock.
3km   Hungerford Marsh Lock to Froxfield Upper Lock.
2.5km   Burnt Mill Lock to Crofton Lock.

This dredging programme proceeded apace thanks to the careful selection of contractors. From the companies who expressed interest in the project, nine were shortlisted and two were finally selected to carry out the work. The successful contractors, Land & Water Services and Loates Brothers Ltd, duly completed their work well before the contract completion date of late February, a date set to avoid work being undertaken during the bird nesting season, as required by the Conservation Plan.

There was one final task completed within the 1997-1998 programme which involved work on the Aldermaston Mill sluices judged to be well past their design life and close to collapse. Work, however, had to be extended well into the summer of 1998 due to design modifications being required when excavations revealed the historical remains of earlier sluices. This work was managed by the Environment Agency (EA) but jointly funded by the Kennet & Avon Partnership, the mill owner and the EA, the object being to ensure that water levels would be maintained within the navigation.

As the waterway re-opened for use at Easter 1998 everybody involved felt that all in all it had been a most successful start to the project. John Laverick expressed his delight at the progress, adding that it was an honour to add his contribution to the long-term sustainability of John Rennie's creation.

Amid the great satisfaction that at long last major restoration was really under way came sadness with the passing of Sir John Knill in April. Sir John was one of the early pioneers who, alongside John Gould and Tom Rolt, led the campaign to restore the Kennet & Avon Canal. He was active in the Commercial Narrow Boat Operators Association and managed his own company which he formed after active service as a Lieutenant RNVR during the Second World War. Being advised to seek outdoor employment he bought two narrow boats on the Grand Union Canal and carried salt from Middlewich to Newbury for use in the Newbury Laundry. It was the problems which he encountered in this pursuit that spurred his restoration crusade. Sir John later took to farming but lived his remaining years in the old canal lengthman's cottage by the Bathampton swing-bridge.

With the canal re-opened for the 1998 tourist season, plans were being prepared in the restoration project offices for the 1998-1999 winter's work. At a Canal Trust Council meeting held during June of 1998 the Canal Trust's honorary engineer, Mike Lee, gave a broad outline of what was proposed and although the conservation plan had still not materialised in its final form the monitors had agreed to allow some non-emergency work to proceed. The design for these works took into account the principles laid down in the working draft of the Conservation Plan.

During October 1998, Mike Lee was able to announce that all design work had proceeded to programme with valid tenders returned for all the civil engineering works, much of which was still of an emergency nature and centred largely on the Bath valley. At Bathampton, Stent Foundations Ltd were given a 'design and construct' contract to stabilise the embankment where the slip had occurred. During August a row of large diameter cast in-situ concrete-bored piles were placed in the field along the toe of the canal embankment. The piles, which were over 12m long, formed an underground reinforced concrete wall, its top being just below ground level, thus ensuring that after the field had been restored little evidence remained of any work being carried out. This method allowed the navigation to be unaffected and the towpath to remain open throughout.

Operations on other sites got underway according to plan, but what a winter! January was the wettest since records began, producing some of the worst working conditions imaginable, but as work progressed they were spared blankets of snow which would have called a halt to the entire proceedings.

In the Bath Valley a contract for 2.3km of channel lining from Hardings bridge to Bathampton bridge was awarded to Alun Griffiths Ltd of Abergavenny with a start date of 14 September 1998. The contract price, just a shade under £2 million, was, however, some £400,000 over the Lottery bid estimate and this reflected the particular difficulties of working in the area.

Tenders in excess of the Lottery bid estimates prepared some years before were not altogether unexpected as the original estimates for each task had been carried out without the advantages of a detail survey so inevitably there were bound to be unforeseen factors which with the best will in the world the estimators would fail to appreciate; this, coupled with the disadvantage of spreading the works over a six-year period during which all sorts of factors both on the waterway and away from it, could drastically alter the delicate financial balance. That the shortfall on completion was only some 3.5% of the total spend reflects great credit on John Laverick and his team. To appreciate just how well the entire project had been managed it is only necessary to call to mind how frequently the completed cost of public works in general bears scant relation to the original estimates.

What was vitally important was that the task should be completed to programme. Throughout the project there was never any thought to dilute the quality of the work, and there was every confidence that if needed the Kennet & Avon Canal Trust would use all its considerable ingenuity to produce the required cash balance to finish the task.

Work on the Bathampton relining contract began with £18,000 being spent diverting the tow path after which the water levels were reduced, fish rescued and the water voles removed to a place of safety. Then, and only then, could the lengthy process of silt removal begin.

On this length three basic methods of lining were used. Some lengths were relined using the PVC and concrete system and then either with a waterway wall or a vegetative shelf on the tow path side and a 'green' bank opposite, while other lengths were partially lined using a bentonite mud sandwich in association with a waterway wall. Bentonite mud is a naturally occurring material which is quarried in the United States. The mud is rolled to a thickness of 7mm (0.25in) and sandwiched between two layers of geotextile. This geotextile material is delivered to the site in rolls weighing 1.25 tons. The sheets are joined with a simple 300mm (12in) overlap filled with either sodium bentonite powder or paste. When wetted the bentonite expands and fuses with the adjoining layers thus forming a watertight joint. Physical protection is then provided to the sheet material with a minimum of 400mm (15in) of excavated material, usually weathered puddle clay and/or imported stone.

Important as the Bath Valley was, the scope was now broadening and work was to start on embankments along the Long Pound between All Cannings and Allington. The contract to reline this section, with a start date of 21 October 1998 and priced at £904,934, was awarded to Morrision Construction Ltd of Sutton Coldfield who also undertook to repair brick bridges, provide additional stop plank grooves and install visitor moorings.

Bentonite sandwich was used as at Bathampton and once again the tow path had to be diverted and fish and reed moved to a place of safety. A special haul road had to be constructed along the tow path and this involved bringing in hundreds of tons of stone.

As was now usual, work started with the removal of the silt which was placed in adjoining fields so as to benefit agriculture. The canal profile was formed then with much of the excavated material being placed carefully to one side so that after the lining material was laid in place it could be returned as protection against mechanical damage; finally a layer of stone was placed on top to give additional protection and form a recognisable barrier against future dredging operations.

Building the pump house
at Wootton Rivers.
(British Waterways)

Using betonite mud. (British Waterways)

Just as the slip at Bathampton had taken everyone by surprise, so did the condition of both banks of the canal on the Horton loop between Bishops Cannings swing-bridge to the east and Horton Chain bridge to the west. BW were aware that this section of the canal leaked, but just how badly was not realised until the vegetation was removed from both banks for a thorough engineering investigation. The leaks were such that action had to be taken immediately if the security of the canal through 1999 was to be guaranteed.

There was insufficient time to draw up a traditional contract so, to speed the process, the dredging contractor who was working to the west of this section was asked to advance into the area and remove all the silt whilst the canal was still in water. This started immediately after Christmas and once the silt had been removed and the fish rescued, Morrison's contract was extended westwards from Allington to Bishops Cannings.

A partial relining scheme was chosen as the leaks were in the upper sections of the banks on either side. Bentomat was laid on the top two thirds of the wall and towed at its lower end into a trench cut in the puddle clay. The top of the bank was then finished with coir rolls which were then backed with reed planting.

A back pumping scheme at Wootton Rivers was built by a Devizes firm, G. Pearce Civil Engineering Ltd. This contract, priced at nearly £600,000 and given a start date of 26 October 1998, was unique in that the firm planned to locally transport most of the required materials by barge. The work required a pump house to be built under the tow path just below Wootton Rivers road bridge and a pipeline to be laid from the pumps, across the main road and along the narrow tow path for 1.6km up to the summit pound just above Cadley Lock where an outfall chamber had been built.

At the same time bye-weirs were constructed at each lock of the Wootton Flight so that, in conjunction with the newly installed pumps, there could be positive control of the water flow. A welcome addition was the provision of landing stages at the head and tail of each lock and, as a final touch, the bank between Wootton Rivers Farm bridge and the pumping station was piled to provide moorings.

G. Pearce also won a £47,979 contract to investigate the twenty-eight culverts located along the Long Pound, starting at the beginning of September 1998. This was an important exercise since culverts represent weak points in the canal structure and need checking and, when necessary, repairing. The techniques employed CCTV and found most of the culverts in remarkably good condition. However, during the winter a culvert running under the canal at Bathampton near the George Inn did collapse and a temporary dam was hurriedly put into place. Bath & North East Somerset Council accepted that as the culvert pre-dated the canal it was their responsibility to carry out repairs.

A rolling programme of dredging operations which had started the previous winter was from now on incorporated into each annual programme. Contracts were sought from five contractors, the award being made to Land & Water Services, one of the two contractors who successfully completed works the year previously. Dredging had to be completed by February as required by the Conservation Plan and its consideration of nesting birds. The lengths dredged were:

1. Bradford-on-Avon Lock to Widbrook bridge.
2. Whadden Grove bridge to Semington Top Lock.
3. Laywood bridge to Horton Chain bridge.
4. Lady's bridge to Bristow bridge.
5. New Mill bridge to Wootton Rivers Farm bridge.
6. Cadley Lock, to a point 0.2km beyond the eastern portal of Bruce Tunnel.

Although for most of the canal a dredged depth of 4ft 6in (1.37m) was specified, on the Long Pound this was increased to 5ft 3in (1.6m) and on the summit 6ft 6in (2m), which was in line with John Rennie's original design that the extra capacity at the summit should act as a reservoir.

Various techniques were used during the dredging process depending on the local geology, ecology and economy of operation as well as the interests of adjoining landowners and businesses. Dredging poses one particular difficulty, namely what to do with the excavated spoil. The most convenient disposal method is to spread it on adjoining land and payments for this use represents a significant part of the overall cost of dredging.

Sadly one or two landowners along the route seemed to think that they had won the Lottery themselves and tried to hold this community project to ransom. As John Laverick later remarked, the attitude of some of the avaricious landowners had filled him with dismay; happily, these mean-spirited people were in the minority.

He found that most riparian landowners behaved in a business-like manner, seeking only appropriate compensation for the right of access and crop loss, while others being particularly enthusiastic and co-operative for the project specifically sought minimal compensation. Of course, after the spoil has been ploughed in, the land is revitalised and returns to full agricultural production.

Aside from the major tasks there were replacement lock gates in the Great Bedwyn area at Longman's Cottage, Beech Grove, Church and Burn Mill; following tender competition the gates were supplied by the Dutch firm of Wijma Kampen BV and fitted by the Devizes BW team.

Swing-bridges were replaced with bridges to John Rennie's original design at Bathampton and Millbrook. The work, which was not completed until later in the year, was undertaken by Sarum Hardwood Structures and followed the pattern and style of the bridges they replaced.

To complete the 1998-1999 winter season a winding (boat turning) hole was completed at Wootton Rivers. As the winter work was being completed there was the passing of yet

There will be many who will miss John Gould's familiar figure, complete with lock windlass and a sheaf of papers, hurrying along the towpath.

another restoration stalwart when, on 19 March 1999, came the sad news that John Gould MBE had died at his home in Rockingham Road, Newbury, aged eighty-five years. For over fifty years John had worked to save and enhance the waterway so it was most fitting that on his last journey he should be carried by boat along the canal to which he had given so much of his time and effort.

After a well-attended service in St Nicolas' Church, his coffin was placed on board the Canal Trust's *Rose of Hungerford* to be taken to his final resting place overlooking his beloved canal at Newbury Lock. That this history could be written at all is testament to the efforts of this determined campaigner of which the canal's revival must be his true and lasting memorial. There will be many who will miss his familiar figure, complete with lock windlass and a sheaf of papers hurrying along the canal towpath intent on his overwhelming determination to further the wellbeing of his beloved waterway.

Although from a construction point of view all was now quiet and peaceful on the canal, in the design offices work proceeded apace planning the tasks for the winter of 2000. Engineers were out and about on the canal undertaking investigations to determine the soil structures whilst ecologists, archaeologists and landscape surveyors assessed the proposals and checked them against the Conservation Plan.

One essential assignment was to negotiate agreements with adjoining landowners for the temporary use of land for access, storage and offices, a task made more difficult as work approached the inner limits of Bath where it would often be necessary to work across the ends of gardens. Although in most cases the end of the garden is owned by BW, the householder who often rents it from BW, quite rightly, wanted to know exactly what is planned, so producing reasons and explanations takes a considerable degree of tact and diplomacy.

Public meetings were arranged to explain details, and an exhibition was held in Devizes of proposed works with drawings and photographs which illustrated with startling clarity just what tremendous tasks lay ahead. To help explain any technical puzzles, experts from all disci-

Work in progress on Bath Top Lock. (British Waterways)

plines of the project were on hand to answer queries. Because the expenditure for the coming programme tended towards Bath, the exhibition was repeated at the Starkis Hotel adjacent to Widcombe Lock.

Work started the first weekend in November 1999 with, as in previous years, the target date for completion set as the weekend before Easter. This gave the team a very narrow window in which to complete works to the value well in excess of £7 million.

The preceding winters had taught the team the vital lesson of carrying out as much pre-planning as possible before the first brick or the first piece of machinery moves onto the site. However, as with any civil engineering project nothing can be completely pre-planned as so much of what will eventually affect the success or otherwise of a job lies buried, waiting to surprise designers who had perhaps forecast something very different.

In accordance with the conditions of the conservation plan and other statutory require-ments, agreement from the Environment Agency and Local Planning Authority has to be obtained and a archaeological study undertaken before any land is used in conjunction with the proposed works. This may be only a desk study or, as for all the sites in Bath, an archae-ological dig requiring a patchwork of trenches to check that the works would not adversely affect any hidden history. Studies undertaken for the Conservation Plan revealed that John Rennie did not have this problem; he took the canal through or very close to a burial ground, through ancient settlements and built the Crofton pumping station on the very edge of a henge.

With planning completed for work in Bath, a £900,000 contract was awarded to Wrekin Construction for the installation of a back pumping system for the Widcombe Lock Flight at Bath, a worthy descendant of an earlier system which fell into disuse some one hundred years before. Two pumping stations had been built, one at Thimble Mill, now part of the Starkis

Hotel, close to Widcombe Lock and another at Abbey View Lock, where all that now remains is a stone chimney.

The new scheme required the building of an underground pumping chamber next to the bottom gates of Widcombe Lock and a small building for the switch gear on the green between the lock and the highway. Additionally, each lock on the flight was fitted with a bye-weir to ensure that flooding of adjacent property could be avoided should any paddles be left in the raised position. Also water is saved as there is now no longer a necessity to empty any locks as a matter of routine when locking uphill. Finally each lock was fitted with landing stages where boats could safely tie-up for lock operations using the bollards which had been placed there – interestingly, it was decided that where boats were welcome to stay for longer periods then mooring rings as opposed to bollards would be provided.

The contract, however, got off to a slow start and proved difficult to keep to programme. The site had limited access and all traffic had to travel along the same length of tow path which, as well as having some thirteen structures being built on it, was at the same time being excavated to lay the pipeline.

A major problem occurred at the temporary dam below Widcombe Lock which relied for its seating on the differential pressure across it. This was set in place with the water level inside the lock on one side lower than the River Avon beyond. A combination of heavy rain and high river overtopped the dam which equalised the levels and the dam became unseated; the delay in being able to re-seat the dam cost much valuable time.

Adjacent to Deep Lock an underground pumping chamber, deep shaft and tunnel were completed. The tunnel, excavated by two miners working by hand in very cramped conditions, is 1.2m in diameter and constructed of pre-cast concrete pipes which pass under the highway and carries both the back pump rising main and the bye-weir pipe around Deep Lock. An underground pipeline connects the pumping station at Widcombe Lock with the outfall structure above Bath Top Lock, and the bank above this lock and as far as Sydney Wharf bridge was piled and faced with a timber rail for visitor moorings.

Building the pumping station at Widcombe Lock. (British Waterways)

Lock chambers throughout the flight were repaired and radial brick walkways were built under the lock balance beams. Further along, through Bath to the east in Sydney Gardens, another contractor, Ellis & Co., repaired the tow path wall and patched the offside wall with Bathstone.

Work also continued on the saga of channel relining in the Bath Valley. During the 1999–2000 winter a section from Bathampton bridge to Darlington Wharf on the eastern outskirts of Bath was tackled at a cost of approximately £1 million per kilometre and was the most expensive single project that year. Essentially the same system as in previous years was employed and savings were made over the expensive tendering exercise by using the same contractor, Alun Griffith who, having climbed the learning curve, was experienced and available for consultation throughout the detailed design process.

Where space and engineering permitted, substantial lengths of green edging were provided on the tow path side with a water depth of 600mm (approx 2in) while landing and mooring sites had a minimum depth of 900mm (approx 3in).

On completion of the whole Bath Valley project all these depths were to be increased by 150mm (6in). As in previous years stringent efforts were made to preserve emergent plants and wildlife. Before work commenced all fish were removed to other parts of the canal and plant life lifted to be stored in purpose-built lagoons. Much of the top soil was also carefully stored with a view to replacing it in much the same position from which it was taken so as to preserve the indigenous flora.

Animal ramps were constructed 200m apart and at known badger crossing points; they have proved to be a great success – not least with domestic pets!

A second lining contract was awarded to Wrekin Construction for a section just west of Ladydown bridge to Parsons bridge at Hilperton Marina. Again much the same techniques were used in a similar section which had also suffered from many leaks and settlements, and that contained the attractive Biss aqueduct which, although not as large as Dundas or Avoncliff, is nevertheless a stunning Rennie design. The aqueduct was relined in a similar manner to the Bath Valley and, in addition, a reinforced concrete slab was formed in the canal bed in order to strengthen the structure, with some 300m of adjacent channel fully lined with PVC and concrete. To complete the operations in the area, lengths of bank were piled in order to preserve and strengthen them thus rendering them waterproof, and a number of bank lengths raised to prevent overtopping.

At Bradford-on-Avon new gates manufactured by the Dutch firm of Wijma Kampen BV were fitted and repairs were carried out to the lock chamber.

Above the lock, reconstruction to the popular visitors' moorings was being undertaken by Dyer & Butler but piling work had to be halted when a band of rock was discovered. The piling team were moved to another location while alternative designs were considered.

Because the piled line of the visitor moorings contained evidence of water vole activity, a similar 300m length of the tow path embankment just to the east of Treenwood bridge was improved as a water vole habitat. This was a mitigation requirement of English Nature under the Wildlife and Countryside Act, the bank being reinforced with willow withes and bundles of hazel fagots at a cost of some £18,000. Under the Act protection of water vole habitat had to be undertaken wherever there was a significant length of piling.

As this legislation came on to the Statute Book after the award of the Heritage Lottery grant, none of this mitigation work was in the original Lottery budget. As there was some 4,000m of piling to be carried out in the programme a similar length of bank would require this mitigation work; inevitably it meant that some lower priority work in the original programme might have to be excluded.

Contractors Dyer & Butler carried out work on the Semington locks; they built bye-weirs, constructed lock landings and carried out repairs to the lock chambers. BW's own team fitted

Bank piling at Trowbridge. (British Waterways)

new gates which enabled Dyer & Butler to complete their work by constructing curved lock operating paths and mooring bollards.

Sells Green saw Greenford Building & Civil Engineering hard at work piling along the embankment. This they carried out down the centre of the tow path with the toes of the piles being embedded in impervious clay some metres below the canal thus effectively stopping the leaks, but avoiding harming the many water voles who regarded this stretch of the canal as home. They did deviate from this line at Spout Lane by piling along the canal edge to form a new visitor mooring.

As an alternative to piling the offside bank, which was very low and had been severely weakened by water voles, John Jackson, HLF Construction Engineer, suggested breaching the bank and flooding the adjoining low-lying land. The land was subsequently purchased and a valuable off-line wildlife habitat was created with what remained of the bank acting as an island and part of the wildlife territory. The overall costs of this environmentally friendly and visually attractive scheme was little more than the cost of piling both banks.

Dyer & Butler also undertook much of that winter's programmed work on the twenty-nine locks at Devizes. The Caen Hill Flight, which is now a scheduled Ancient Monument, was the scene of much activity as work continued apace on all the locks except the middle sixteen.

The contractors provided bye-weirs, lock landings, bollards and paved paths beneath the balance beams. The three bottom ponds of the flight, however, were relined by Ashridge Construction using traditional puddled clay and a new set of gates were fitted to Devizes Top Lock by the local BW team. The middle sixteen locks received minimum intervention works consistent with their scheduled status and were provided with bollards, a second safety ladder and paved walkways beneath the balance beams.

Dredging on the Long Pound. (British Waterways)

Investigations into the continued leaking of the Long Pound revealed that many of the joints in the lining material installed the previous winter had been badly made or damaged as the filling material had been placed on top. The contractor responsible was instructed to return and carry out remedial work and the opportunity was taken to remove any trees which were growing too close to the water's edge and likely to cause damage in the near future.

There was, of course, continuing progress on the rolling dredging programme with work in the lengths between Kintbury and Dreweat's Locks and from Monkey Marsh Lock to Midgham Lock in Thatcham completed early in the winter. Further operations around Frouds bridge and Padworth Lock near Aldermaston were completed before Christmas.

Arrangements were also put in hand to dredge the length from Seend Bottom Lock to Lower Foxhangers, but the portion around Cobblers Lock to Dunmill Lock, in Hungerford, and Burnt Mill Lock to Froxfield Lock near Bedwyn had to be postponed because of concern over the turbid water from the dredged canal finding its way into the River Dun. The work was re-programmed once bye-weirs had been constructed at the appropriate locks which would allow an alternative path for the excess water.

As the 1999-2000 winter's activities closed, plans were already well advanced for the next phase to take place over the winter of 2000-2001, with operations due to start in October.

To inform the public around the eastern end of the waterway, where much activity would take place, an exhibition was held in the Newbury public library where, as in previous years, the Project team and BW staff were on hand to explain the finer details, together with a comprehensive display of maps, drawings and photographs.

The programme this winter saw the last stage of work in the Bath valley with the section from Dundas aqueduct to Bradford-on-Avon being drained. As the water drained away it uncovered a historic piece of engineering from the past. There, lying in the silt in the bed of the canal, the project team found a pair of 200-year-old stop gates thought to be the only examples of its kind. Until needed these Brindley gates were designed to lay flat on the bottom of the canal, one to the left and one to the right of a pair of wooden uprights. When a leak occurred, and depending on the direction, one or other of the gates could be hinged upwards thus shutting off the water flow. Historically, this type of stop gate was known to exist but the last one was thought to have been destroyed many years previously. John Laverick said the find was unique and would be preserved by removing them from Limpley Stoke and immersing them in one of the side ponds on Caen Hill until their final resting place can be determined. Later they were allowed to dry, partly dismantled, and are now on show in the Devizes canal musuem.

Work continued at Dundas throughout the wet winter but on nearing completion was interrupted by an outbreak of Foot and Mouth Disease which closed some of the important access points and resulted in the need to bring split loads of concrete over Dundas aqueduct and along the bed of the canal. This revised need for access delayed the re-filling schedule which on completion raised the water level on the nine-mile pound by some 150mm (6in).

Other work included the complete regating of the Bath Flight with the gates again being supplied by Wijma Kampen BV and installed by the local BW team. The lower gates of Widcombe Lock, however, were a Christmas gift to the Partnership from the Dutch firm of Wijma Kampen BV. The gift attracted much media coverage and was useful in explaining why the Partnership needed to raise match funding or contributions in kind in order to draw down the agreed contribution from the Heritage Lottery Fund; this gift released some £100,000. The completed repairs allowed future smooth operation of this most attractive section.

Winter operations outside the scope of the HLF project were undertaken by BW with remedial works carried out on the weir at Salford Lock and on Avoncliff aqueduct where much of the stonework was thoroughly overhauled and re-conditioned. All this work was paid for by a donation from Hemmings Waste through the Land Fill Tax.

The HLF team continued with other improvement works: Seend Locks had the chambers re-conditioned and were provided with additional safety ladders, lock landings and paved paths under the balance beams, while four locks in the Hungerford area were equipped with bye-weirs and lock landings.

At a number of locations extensive lengths of visitor and permanent moorings were either constructed or improved. Most welcome for the boaters, bridge and lock landings were built in Hungerford, Kintbury, Colthrop, Towney and finally, fulfilling a long-felt need, the lower landing at Woolhampton swing-bridge was extended.

The dredging campaign continued as in previous years but with a startling incident. Work around Wootton Rivers was suspended for a time when a loaded hopper collided with the lock gates at Heathy Close, completely demolishing them and closing the waterway. The BW team at Devizes, however, rushed into action, placing emergency priority orders for the replacements which were made in BW's own workshops.

Early in the new year stabilisation of the remains of Towney original turf-sided lock took place. Steel beams which are hidden from view have been inserted in the earth embankment to hold the wooden planks which in turn hold back the turf sides. This lock was not fitted with gates and now forms the lower channel approach to the adjacent modern steel-piled lock and will be of interest to visitors as a historical feature.

New Year 2001 also heralded the commencement of embankment strengthening and lining work between the Semington road and swing-bridges. Now well into the project, the HLF team had become accustomed to the daily problems which fate would throw at them and learned to expect the unexpected, they even became quite accustomed to the vagaries of the weather but they were not at all prepared for the level of vandalism which struck the Semington site.

Initially machinery was damaged and then later the temporary dam erected near the swing-bridge to hold back the water was sabotaged causing it to collapse and flood the entire drained section. A large excavator parked on the bed of the canal was severely damaged and much time was lost whilst the dam was rebuilt, this time with a clay back-up.

Such a precaution was just as well as the vandals struck again but this time, thanks to the second dam, succeeded in flooding only part of the site. Increased vigilance finally disturbed the miscreants who turned out not to be youngsters up to childish pranks but grown adults who made off before they could be apprehended. This sorrowful affair cost many thousands of pounds, money not only donated from the Lottery fund, but raised by the efforts of the rank and file canal enthusiasts.

This section of the waterway was the subject of a most encouraging sign for the restoration of the Wiltshire & Berkshire Canal when it was announced that following discussions between BW and the Wiltshire & Berkshire Canal organisations a new connection to the revived canal would be made just west of Seend Bottom Lock. This new spur would initially provide off-line moorings to the Kennet & Avon Canal.

After a very busy winter and as the first harbingers of spring heralded the beginning of a new cruising season the waterway opened for business over the Easter weekend of 2001.

The HLF team could look back over not only the wettest winter on record for 400 years but a season in which they encountered landslides and the worst cases of vandalism they had so far experienced, and then as a final test of stamina they had also to overcome the inconvenience caused by the outbreak of Foot and Mouth Disease. As one engineer was heard to remark 'perhaps we have served our apprenticeships for restoration work on the Thames & Severn and the Wiltshire & Berkshire Canals!'

With the end of the project now firmly in sight there was one final drama when it appeared likely that the project would face an overspend of some 3%, due entirely to unforeseen structural problems and the unexpected restraints and conditions which had been imposed on the project after the initial plans and details had been agreed.

Two major causes were the difficulties encountered in the Bath Valley and the extra work which protecting the water vole population had imposed.

There were initial thoughts of approaching the HLF for further funds but this was quickly abandoned in favour of BW taking on the remaining tasks. This was in line with the initial agreement that BW would 'use its best endeavours' to re-classify the revived waterway as a Cruiseway – an expression which by now was somewhat out of date as circumstances had moved on appreciably since the early 1960s parliamentary act.

It, therefore, became necessary during the summer of 2001 for BW, as trustees of the project, to approach the HLF and seek permission to allow this deviation from the original contract. BW would then complete all the scheduled tasks with the expected cash deficit of some £750,000 being found by BW and the Kennet & Avon Canal Trust.

However, work did not cease on the Kennet & Avon but continued, mainly towards the eastern end of the waterway, during the summer months of 2001 and into the winter and summer of 2002.

Works consisted of replacing the sagging lock gates at Little Bedwyn and Potter's along with one close to the summit pound at Brimslade and constructing and refurbishing a further twenty-four weir structures between Crofton Top and Dreweat's Locks.

There was also some public amenity works which included the extension and improvement of canalside car parks, improving facilities at Claverton pumping station and the provision of a further five sanitary stations, while the environmentalists were pleased with the planting of 2km of hedging and 400 trees.

There were improvements for the boating fraternity with the construction of lock landings, visitor moorings and towpath refinements, tasks that were minor in comparison to the scale of the preceding winter projects, but they still had to be carried out to the very high standards which the Heritage Lottery Fund team had set and maintained over the course of the entire restoration project.

Regard to high standards also applied to the finances. Careful analysis of the final accounts showed a list of more than 400 suppliers and contractors with a total spend of some £29,240,000 of which nearly 90% had actually been spent on direct reconstruction costs, and even the remaining 10% largely covered important features such as landowner compensation, land purchase, consultancy engineering and architects fees, power, lock gates, computers, etc. Actual costing interestingly confirms the often-stated assertion that the restoration of a disused waterway will bring a healthy fillip to employment in the area although it is difficult to make an accurate value assessment as the benefit ripples spread far and wide.

The high quality of the work carried out by the HLF team was reflected by the nominations for awards which the team received. During 2000 they were shortlisted by the British Construction Industry Awards 2000 in two categories – 'The Civil Engineering Award' and 'The Construction Best Practice Award' – for reconstruction work between Darlington Wharf and Bathampton in the Bath Valley. From nearly 200 projects originally considered, only five were recognised by the judges which 'best demonstrated an innovative new approach to construction procurement combining faster delivery, improved technological solutions and safety, reduced waste, client satisfaction and better environmental solutions'. To illustrate the competition, one of the five projects chosen was the London Eye.

In 2001 as the team of ten were preparing to disperse, they had the satisfaction of being feted by their peers with a final and very well-deserved accolade by winning the Engineering Council's Environmental Award for Engineers 2001. This was in the Engineering in the Natural Environment Class which was sponsored by Rolls-Royce Plc.

This tribute carried a personal award of £3,000 which the team unanimously decided to present to the Partnership who in turn submitted it to the HLF as match-funding, which released a further grant of £18,000 for spending on the canal. As winners of this award the project is automatically entered for the internationally recognised European Awards for the Environment sponsored by the European Commission and the United Nations Environment Programme.

In addition the conservation plan, which by now had become a model to which the HLF would point future grant applications towards, had itself taken the Strategic Landscape Planning Award 2001 offered by the Landscape Institute.

16 The Future of the Canal and the Canal Trust

Whilst the Heritage Lottery Project had undoubtedly represented a significant part of the overall restoration picture, it would be quite unjust to ignore the increasing level of annual maintenance works carried out at the same time by BW to accommodate the considerable growth in activity on the waterway.

As well as contributing £1.8 million in cash and £0.5 million in management and planning time as match funding, BW also had the responsibility to ensure that, on completion, the revitalised waterway would, in the future, be financially sustainable. They estimated that on completion of the HLF project the annual maintenance costs would rise by 1m per annum, with the income from leisure and tourism increasing over the same period by £750,000. This expected shortfall of £250,000 per annum was the basis for the local authority long-term maintenance agreements, which the Kennet & Avon Canal was the first waterway in the country to secure, helping after 160 years to return the waterway to prosperity – albeit as a non-profit making business reinvesting its many income streams back into further improvements. The original shareholders and proprietors would, however, find today's business structure very different, shareholders have been replaced with stakeholders which include the Government, local communities, businesses as well as many organisations and interested parties.

BW dedication to the HLF project had restricted funds available for improvements to the established cruiseway sections, but future spending enabled cruiseway sections to be brought up to the standard of the newly restored HLF-funded lengths.

Additionally, further Government grants to reduce both national safety-related backlog and arrears of maintenance provided new funds which the Kennet & Avon was able to share. Works in this field included refurbishment of both Dundas and Avoncliff aqueducts as well as reconstruction of weirs on the River Avon and the automation of road bridges.

BW are also sensitive to the needs of everybody who can enjoy the canal for, although boats are fundamental to any inland navigation, by far the largest number of visitors to the waterway just come to watch and enjoy the peace; therefore, the towpath had to be improved to accommodate the wide range of users – walkers, cyclists and anglers.

As the years pass it is hoped that BW will continue to maintain and improve waterway facilities with the same levels of skill and dedication which had so successfully restored this 'jewel in the crown' of Britain's inland waterway network.

During 2003, as the finishing touches to the HLF project were made, it was suggested that the Canal Trust should celebrate its success with a party stretching right along the canal, involving as many revellers as possible at the same time. The date was set for the weekend of 23 and 24 May.

The celebrations began on the afternoon of 23 May when His Highness Prince Charles, greeted by Trust Chairman David Lamb and hosted by Canal manager Michael Goodenough, flew along the length of the canal, stopping for brief walkabouts, firstly at Bradford-on-Avon, then to the Caen Hill flight at Devizes. Finally, before flying home to Highgrove, he stopped off to examine the engines and stoke the boilers at Crofton Pumping Station.

As the Prince's helicopter whirled away from Devizes, far below within the big marquee, erected for the Prince's visit, a tribute was being paid to the Trust's salaried retiring Administrator, Fleur de Rhe-Phillipe. Working at the Devizes headquarters of the Trust, Fleur had, since May 1992, fully immersed herself in the often delicate but essential day-to-day running of the organisation The President of the Trust, Sir Anthony Durant, thanked

Fleur for her eleven years of service and presented her with a cheque and an oil painting subscribed to by members of the Canal Trust.

Amongst the many activities and arrangements made by branches and committees taking place along the length of the waterway that sunny Saturday was the outcome of a suggestion that it would be fun to repeat the carriage along the canal of the widely supported petition sent to Her Majesty the Queen during January 1956 (see page 28). This time, however, there would be an expression of the Trust's gratitude in having the canal restored.

A Declaration of Gratitude and Loyal Address, beautifully hand-scripted on to vellum, was transported along the length of the waterway, gathering signatures on a journey which finished at the celebrations in Devizes on Saturday 24 May. After being exhibited at various functions and gatherings, a deputation from the Canal Trust finally presented the document to Her Majesty the Queen at Buckingham Palace in the early part of November 2003.

With the HLF Project completed and the festivities over everybody could, with considerable satisfaction, look back over fifty years since the original Association's formation in 1949 and view the achievements, all the aims and aspirations of the original founders having been met in full.

Now, as the Canal Trust braced itself for the future, Canal Trust Chairman, David Lamb, decided that it was the right time to announce his intention to stand down from the chair after seven very momentous and successful years. David's resignation was swiftly followed by that of Brian Oram who, as Chairman of the Kennet & Avon Canal Partnership from its conception, also felt his task complete.

Both David and Brian were, to the Canal Trust's great fortune, exactly the right people in exactly the right positions at exactly the right time for the final chapter in this HLF restoration saga, positions which required great tact and skill in melding together all the sometimes conflicting interests and opinions.

For Brian, this not only required liaising with British Waterways on behalf of the Canal Trust and carrying out delicate negotiations with the Heritage Lottery Fund, but also overseeing the extremely important discussions with local authorities and commercial interests, as well as reassuring the ever-worrying environmental lobby who would deftly produce, without warning, the next seemingly impossible demand.

Whilst initially the primary task resting on David's shoulders was chairing the Trust Council and supporting Brian Oram, he also had to hold together all the other important components of the Trust – from Central office and the Branches right down to each individual member, any one of whom could and sometimes did, perhaps with the best of intentions, follow an agenda which did not always chime with the Trust's overall policy.

It is comparatively easy to feel motivated when financially rewarded, but to put in years of unstinting voluntary effort, often at unsocial hours with every possibility of undeserved criticism, is altogether praiseworthy. Both David and Brian join the ranks of those who are owed a great debt of gratitude by everyone who takes pleasure from the waterways.

At a meeting of the Canal Trust's Council, RAF Air Commodore Brian Poulton (retired) was nominated to succeed David. The Council then took the opportunity to express the Trust's sincere thanks to both David and Brian for their successful terms of office.

As Brian Poulton assumed command it was noted with curiosity that he now completed an interesting trio of retired officers, one from each branch of the armed services who had, between them, guided the Trust's course for nearly thirty of its forty-odd years.

The immediate future of the canal looked assured; the repairs which had been carried out over the last six years had elevated the waterway to Cruiseway status in all but name and this, together with the added security of the twenty-one year maintenance agreements arranged with the local authorities, meant that the Kennet and Avon canal was in far better shape now than it had ever been.

There was still much the Canal Trust could do, not in the field of major canal maintenance – that was now very definitely the province of BW – but there still remained a number of areas in which a voluntary body like the Canal Trust had a useful part to play.

With the through route between the two great ports of Bristol and London re-opened, lorry-choked roads and the need to conserve the environment, perhaps the Canal Trust could use its very considerable campaigning expertise to encourage an investigation into the re-introduction of commercial cargo carrying. Using advanced planning techniques and computers to control water and traffic movement who is to know what may be achieved.

On a practical level the Canal Trust could, for instance, help fund special desirable improvements and amenities. It could also act out an essential role as general arbitrator between all the users and BW. Further, whilst words like 'preserve' and 'protect' needed to be used with the greatest caution, a watchful eye was needed to prevent spoiling and destroying what had taken so long to achieve. Additionally, the Canal Trust had over the years acquired a number of obligations which could not be easily disowned.

Besides the head office establishment and its staff, it had in its care the historic pumping station at Crofton, complete with a warden and two cottages, the day-to-day control of the pumping station at Claverton as well as the museum and comprehensive archive facilities in Devizes.

There was also the trading arm which not only ran the trip boats but had leases on a number of shops and tea rooms employing part-time managerial staff.

All this tended to suggest that there was a role for the Canal Trust, if only in a limited capacity, to administer the pumping stations, and to look after the education facilities, museum and archives.

But as modest as these requirements appeared they still needed to be funded by a sizeable number of members. Although a certain amount of 'judiciously cutting the administrative coat to suit the membership supplying cloth' could be helpful, the long-term answer to having any pretence of success was a substantial membership base and this needed the Canal Trust to demonstrate a good, compelling and exciting pioneering element or some other inducement to bring members flocking to join.

Whatever the future holds in store for The Kennet & Avon Canal Trust it is certain, thanks to forty years of voluntary effort, to be assured a place in the history of England's canal system.

The fortunate Lottery grant has guaranteed the future of this beautiful waterway, but the foundations of that success were laid down many years ago by the tenacity of a few far-sighted pioneers. It would be fitting indeed if somewhere along the canal a plaque could be erected to remind all those who take their pleasure or business from the waterway that they do so thanks largely to the dedicated volunteers who fifty years ago set out to restore the waterway, armed only with determination.

One of the most important requirements in canal construction is, of course, an adequate water supply. This presented John Hore with few problems in building the river sections of the waterway – Bristol to Bath via the River Avon and Reading to Newbury using the River Kennet – but when John Rennie came to join the two sections together in the late eighteenth to early nineteenth centuries, he was forced to consider water supplies carefully because the projected route ran through difficult country as far as water supplies were concerned.

As the waterway climbed up from Berkshire towards the Wiltshire summit, Rennie planned to construct a 2.5-mile-long (4km) tunnel between Crofton and Burbage at 410ft (125m) above sea level, this being within the known water table. At the time the canal was constructed, tunnelling was an uncertain and expensive undertaking, so it is not surprising that the canal company looked for a cheaper and more certain alternative. The answer was supplied when it was suggested that instead of a long tunnel the canal height should continue to rise by a further 40ft (12m) by means of ten extra locks, with a pumping engine situated at Crofton, to feed the summit level. As this scheme saved in excess of £40,000 over constructing a tunnel it was approved with enthusiasm by the Canal Company directors who applied for an Act of Parliament to authorize the deviation. (There is a tunnel on the summit, however, which is 502yd (463m) long and was built at the request of the Marquis of Ailesbury for aesthetic reasons).

The Bath end also faced the constructors with water-seeking difficulties with the requirement for a nine-mile level section between Bradford-on-Avon and the flight of locks at Bath. This was also solved by the construction of a pumping station, this time on the site of Claverton Mill which raised water to the level of the proposed canal from the River Avon flowing below.

Crofton Pumping Station

Rennie sited the eastern end pumping station at Crofton and work on the project started in 1800. The pumping station overlooks Wilton Water, an eight-acre reservoir constructed in 1836 by damming the valley in which it sits.

Many engineering parts for the pumps had to be carried to the site by horse and cart, and many more were made on the spot. Rennie was authorised to purchase a Boulton & Watt pumping engine originally intended for the West India Dock Co. This engine, with a wooden beam, a stroke of 8ft (2.5m) and a piston diameter of 3ft (1m) arrived at Crofton in 1807 and by 1809 came into operation with such success that a further Boulton & Watt engine was ordered in 1812.

It is this 1812 engine which holds the distinction of being the oldest working beam engine in the world remaining in its original working position. Both engines were low pressure, working at only 4.5psi with steam supplied from three 'waggon top' boilers standing in the open.

In 1844 Harveys of Hayle installed Cornish boilers and converted both engines to the 'Cornish Cycle' which basically increased the working pressure to 20psi. Later in the same year, the earlier engine was replaced with a Sims combined engine, which gave so much trouble that it was later dismantled. In 1905 the hapless Sims engine was rebuilt as a simple condensing engine and remains as such to this day.

At the same time Lancashire boilers made their appearance, two of which replaced the three Cornish boilers. Both boilers were 27ft (8.3m) long with a diameter of 7.6ft (2.3m) and were manufactured by the Great Western Railway at Swindon.

Both engines continued in service until 1952 with, it is said, the 1812 engine in steam as late as 1958. About this time the chimney was declared unsafe with the top 36ft (12m) being removed. The effect was nothing short of catastrophic as there was now insufficient draught to fire the boilers effectively. Although the authorities contemplated installing a forced draught system, they finally considered that it would be more economical to replace the old steam-driven pumps. This they did using a diesel-engined replacement as a temporary measure before installing permanent modern electric-driven pumps in 1959.

Located at the southern most tip of Savernake Forest and standing some 40ft above the canal and rolling Wiltshire farm land, Crofton pumping station occupies a lonely and isolated spot between Burbage and Bedwyn, about ten miles from Marlborough.

The first thing to be seen, even before one closely approaches the station, is the chimney reaching through the canopy of trees and pointing to the sky. Even at a reduced height the chimney was a landmark but now that it has been rebuilt to its full original height it is an imposing sight, especially when the station is active and plumes of black smoke trail across the landscape as the amateur boiler stokers get to grips with the art of boiler firing.

Crofton in summer is a joy, with magnificent views over Wilton Water and the surrounding countryside, whilst the winter, however, lends a distinct contrast, the open fields allow a bleak and piercing wind to race over the frozen ground, probing with icy fingers every nook and cranny of the buildings and penetrating through to ones very bones. Winter operations in the unfired engine house requires thick pullovers, heavy boots, caps and mufflers to keep the icy cold at bay.

It was on such a cold day during 1966 that a small party of Kennet & Avon Canal Trust members, dispatched to Crofton by the Canal Trust Council on a fact-finding mission, gathered on the rickety bridge which spanned the entrance to the engine house and watched as the resident engineer and caretaker, Frank Wilmott, unlocked the imposing front door and admitted them to the interior.

The party, pleased to be out of the wind, moved into the damp, musty, almost eerie interior of the engine house amongst a jungle of rods and pipes. Here the condensation rolled down the walls and formed clusters of water beads on the heavily greased mechanism while disturbed ranks of spiders scurried away to hide in the nooks and crannies of the rafters.

From the walls surrounding the two massive engines hung huge spanners which, with the pressure and vacuum gauges still carried the original GWR logo. Passing the engines, the party entered the boiler house with its pair of enormous Lancashire boilers gently slumbering in retirement with pressure dial needles resting at zero and the brass work green and dusty. Some time was spent examining the interior before leaving through the massive rear doors to inspect the surrounding grounds.

The purpose of the fact-finding mission was to consider the BWB's offer to sell the pumping station to the Canal Trust so that it could be preserved, possibly restored, and exhibited as an example of nineteenth-century engineering endeavour. However, about a year earlier and unbeknown to the Canal Trust a casual discussion on beam engines between two engineers at the Rolls-Royce Aero factory in Bristol mentioned the two such engines at Crofton. This prompted Roy Simmons and Ian Broom to arrange a visit to the engines during May 1965. From this first visit the idea of recording the engines by photograph and drawings together with researching the engine's history took shape.

Soon the original pair were joined by others and to give the group some substance they elected to call themselves The Crofton Society (much to the disgust, it is reported, of the resident BWB engineer). When the Canal Trust's interest became known they joined forces.

Under the leadership of Nicholas Reynolds, and together with Rodney Law of the Science Museum, the combined party made a number of visits to Crofton.

The negotiations with BW continued until 18 April 1968 when, for the sum of £75, Crofton Pumping station was transferred to the care of the Kennet & Avon Canal Trust and by common assent it was decided that the band of enthusiasts who would oversee the repairs would retain the Crofton Society title and continue to issue the Campaign News letters which had originated in the spring of 1967.

Work could now start and in the space of only a few months the engines were inspected and much vital preparation work undertaken. In the following year work proceeded apace with repairs to the walls and a spring clean of the condenser tank. Work continued throughout 1969 with the restoration diary pages crammed with details of valve gear being stripped, reground and repacked. With cylinders inspected and gauges removed and checked.

By this time there was quite a team of volunteers engaged in restoration which divided into three groups each with a leader to tackle the main elements of engine, boiler and buildings. Many helpers travelled lengthy distances on a regular basis to spend long hours scraping, chipping, wire brushing and polishing the bright work of both engines and boilers.

The greatest task was the boilers which had been without attention since 1958 and as the volunteers started work they found the remains of the old fires left in the furnaces from the last time they were fired. Fortunately frost damage had been averted as water had been drained away and the manhole doors removed from both boilers. After a primary inspection by the boiler insurance company's surveyor to affirm the practicability of repair, work commenced on boiler No.109. Much of the brickwork surrounding this boiler was found to be in such a rotten condition that it had to be shovelled out and dumped. With the boiler shell exposed the seating blocks on which the boiler rested were found also to be in a bad way and were replaced by a specialist company. The outer surface of the boiler was wire scrubbed and painted by a band of scouts from Basingstoke and eight barrow loads of scale were removed from the inside.

It takes a very special breed of volunteer to give up the weekend to lay most uncomfortably in a cold boiler chipping and wire brushing for hours on end with only a wandering lead lamp for company. On the boiler face many knuckles were scarred and bruised drilling out corroded studs and unscrewing rusted nuts, while other workers would spirit away the brightwork fittings to home workshops to be lovingly cleaned, refurbished and polished.

The amount of varied tasks performed over the year from 1969 until the initial steaming on 4 April 1970 was truly impressive and it would indeed fill many pages to record each task in just the slimmest of detail. They ranged from digging a cesspit and providing toilet facilities, building a crew room and providing some rudimentary safety features to overhauling the electrical installations and the inspection of the culvert by a friendly sub-aqua club.

In March 1970 the consulting engineer, Arthur Pyne, checked over No.1 engine, pronouncing it acceptable, whilst the boiler also received a satisfactory report from the boiler surveyor. Early on the morning of 2 April came the great moment to light the fire; gently at first to allow the new brickwork to heat up and to warm the vast amount of water evenly.

On 4 April the fires were pushed the full length of the furnace bars and built up to produce steam, pressure was raised and the stop valve opened for the first time in twelve years. Slowly and somewhat irregularly the engine took a first, few, short hesitant strokes.

Some problems came to light with the feed pumps but the major cause for concern was the engine pump valves which required stripping out and cleaning before the engine could run again.

On 8 May the fires were again lit and on the following day, when the main valve was opened the engine performance was very much better and apart from some minor faults the engine was ready for the formal opening which, watched by Lord Methuen, president of the

Canal Trust, was performed by Sir John Betjeman on Friday 21 August 1970.

With boiler No.109 in good order, attention turned to boiler No.110 which lay on the western side of the building. Here again all the brickwork had to be removed and rebuilt. During the work it became clear that this boiler had a slightly different flue and mounting design so during the restoration smaller flues were built in accord with boiler No.109 thereby giving greater efficiency.

Whilst this work was going on, water was discovered leaking through the brickwork lining of the flue where it passed under the canal feeder channel. The only remedy to this serious problem was to dig out the entire flue and replace the troublesome section with concrete pipes. Work was completed during the 1972-1973 season with a forced draught fan being installed at the point where the two flues meet near the foot of the chimney.

During the early part of 1971, work also started on the No.2 engine which was ready for its first run by November of that year.

Once all was in working order it was then a case of keeping on top of minor maintenance jobs and making gradual improvements. Some of the work was quite easily achieved whilst other tasks were major undertakings. One example was the replacement of boiler No.109 in 1986, originally built in 1903. The replacement boiler was obtained from the Imperial Tobacco Co. factory in Bristol and is fitted with a pair of cross tubes which improve water circulation within the boiler. Also at this time a second boiler was also acquired from the tobacco factory and is now stored at Crofton as a spare. It was the proposed installation of this boiler in the eastern boiler house and the destruction of the boiler in the western boiler house which was to cause such discord in 1991; the details of which are recorded in Chapter 12.

Over the years much time and effort has been expended in keeping the buildings, grounds and equipment in good condition and working order. Since the early 1990s the main burden of this essential work has fallen on a small but dedicated band of enthusiasts who meet, whatever the weather, every Tuesday throughout the year to carry out repairs and improvements. Much of this work being directed towards public safety.

It is pleasing to record that the Tuesday Club, led by Dennis Munson, was awarded the British Waterways John Gould Trophy for 2000 in appreciation of all the effort expended at Crofton since 1990.

Most of the original restoration costs were met from grants from English Heritage and government bodies, both central and local, together with generous donations and national appeals. However the continuing maintenance expenses are now largely funded by the paying public watching the engines operating in steam or lying peacefully at rest.

Although there is a resident warden who welcomes visitors on weekdays, there is still a need for a constant supply of volunteer helpers to open the site on non-steaming weekends thus allowing visitors to wander around the silent engines.

Offers of help will be appreciated. Please contact the chairman of Crofton Branch C/O The Kennet & Avon Canal Centre, Couch Lane, Devizes, Wiltshire, SN10 1EB. Telephone 01380 7271279.

The Kennet & Avon Canal Trust have published a booklet covering the history and operation of the pumping station which is in far greater detail than is possible within the scope of this book. The booklet is obtainable from either the pumping station, or direct from The Kennet & Avon Canal Trust at the Canal Centre, Devizes.

Claverton Pumping Station

Today, the western end pumping station at Claverton differs from the station at Crofton in as much as that it is not owned by the Kennet & Avon Canal Trust but operated by them under a BW licence.

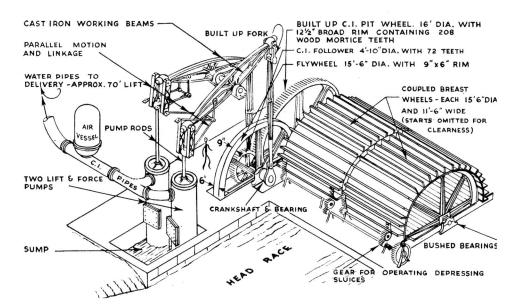

CAST IRON WORKING BEAMS

PARALLEL MOTION AND LINKAGE

WATER PIPES TO DELIVERY -APPROX. 70' LIFT

AIR VESSEL

PUMP RODS

TWO LIFT & FORCE PUMPS

C.I. PIPES

SUMP

BUILT UP FORK

CRANKSHAFT & BEARING

HEAD RACE

BUILT UP C.I. PIT WHEEL. 16' DIA. WITH 12½" BROAD RIM CONTAINING 208 WOOD MORTICE TEETH

C.I. FOLLOWER 4'-10"DIA. WITH 72 TEETH

FLYWHEEL 15'-6" DIA. WITH 9"x6" RIM

COUPLED BREAST WHEELS - EACH 15'6"DIA AND 11'-6" WIDE (STARTS OMITTED FOR CLEARNESS)

BUSHED BEARINGS

GEAR FOR OPERATING DEPRESSING SLUICES

Diagram of Claverton pump.

If the attraction of Crofton pumping station is the romance of roaring boilers and the scent and sound of hissing steam, then Claverton can claim the attraction of an altogether sweeter and softer motion. Rennie solved the water supply problem between Bradford-on-Avon and Bath by powering pumps with a waterwheel driven from the very river from which the water was being extracted. An ingenious, resourceful and pollution-free solution, which today would gladden the heart of even the most virulent member of the green brigade.

Claverton stands on the side of the Bath Valley at the foot of Ferry Lane just off the A36, or can be reached by a walk along the towpath from the Dundas aqueduct. The buildings, started around 1809, were completed in October the following year but it was to be another two years before the machinery, manufactured in Rennie's London workshops, was installed and actual pumping operation commenced. Much of the plant exists today as it was originally constructed; although some modifications have been made over the years much of which have concerned the massive waterwheel which is the motive heart of the complex.

It is reported that during 1952, a log jammed the waterwheel and as a result the rapid deceleration stripped away a large number of the oak gear teeth. This damage, coupled with many years of neglect, effectively brought water-driven operations at Claverton to an end and a diesel-powered pump was employed to maintain the statuary water level in the pound.

During 1968, engineering students at Bath University contacted the Canal Trust with a proposal to carry out a survey on the condition of the machinery and to report on the feasibility and likely cost of restoring the pumping station back to working order. In January of the following year the BWB accepted the recommendation for restoration, this to be carried out jointly by the Canal Trust and Bath University; the estimated cost at this time was given as, what today seems, the almost trifling sum of just £912.

Work started almost straight away, with the students providing the labour and the Canal Trust providing the supervision in the person of John Butt, who in addition to being a qualified technician, had in previous years actually worked on the machinery whilst employed by the GWR. The first task was to make the building safe and remove the accumulation of debris from years of neglect.

Rotten flooring was ripped up and replaced and attention given to the massive waterwheel. To effect repairs to the sluice the pond was drained, but only with great difficulty, as the construction of a temporary dam was required to enable work to commence. Conditions improved with the installation of electric light. Even on a summer's day the interior of the building tended to be distinctly gloomy, which was a stark reminder of the conditions endured by the successions of lone enginemen who had tended the machinery with nothing more than an oil lamp to light their way. During 1970 the task of rebuilding the lower sections of the breast sluice in reinforced concrete was carried out. This with considerable assistance from the training section of the British Aircraft Corporation who manufactured the necessary hardware and also the many local firms who supplied either materials or equipment.

As with the restoration of the pumping station at Crofton the enormity of the task at Claverton and the amount of effort required and the dedication of so many people is really quite overwhelming. Tribute has also to be paid to all the firms and companies without who's assistance the task would have been virtually impossible.

During 1971 some 600ft of 3in x 3in oak was purchased to manufacture the 288 starts that support and hold the float boards to the waterwheel. The complicated machining necessary was undertaken by the apprentices at the BAC plant at Filton where it was seen to be useful training. No trainee was expected to work on more than one or two items so it can be seen that this task alone gave experience to over 100 apprentices.

In 1972 the new sluices and repaired racks were installed but the progress of restoration began to slow down as John Butt, in ill health, was not always able to attend the working parties. Eventually he was obliged to resign and his position was taken by Derrick Dudden, an engineer with Rolls-Royce Aero Engines who became Claverton Restoration Manager. He soon discovered that a number of essential features had been overlooked in the original survey not least of which was making the building clean, safe and fit for public admission. A further cause for concern was the strength of the student working parties which now fell to a very low level; but this was resolved when it became known that other Canal Trust volunteers would be welcomed. A weekend event in October produced some sixty enthusiastic pairs of hands to remove a silt bar blocking the pond and also to clear away quantities of undergrowth and debris together with a vast mound of rubble.

A further oversight on the original survey was discovered when the condition of the supply hatches were examined and extensive restoration was clearly indicated. It had been thought that this work would be undertaken by BWB but on investigation it became clear they had neither the finance or labour to spare. They did agree, however, to providing an estimate for the work to be carried out by contract which would possibly assist the Canal Trust in obtaining a grant from the DoE.

Now that the ball was, as it were, in the Canal Trust's court it was realised that the only successful option would be to replace the entire assembly and plans for this difficult task were drawn up by Derrick Dudden. The work would require some six months of good dry weather to complete from a start date of March 1974. The proceeding months were taken up with making the arrangements and the procurement of all the necessary materials and equipment.

There was some confusion when, in attempting to obtain permission to dam the mill stream, the River Authority assumed that it was proposed to dam the entire River Avon. They were quick to reply that such an action would require an Act of Parliament!

Luckily the misunderstanding was explained with a hastily dispatched note which, with a later site meeting, cleared away any further problems. Meanwhile with only weeks left to the start date the lack of steel piling effected a change of design for the dam; this now had to be built from river gravel and was to cause much concern before it was possible to drain the leat and start work on the hatches. Again, vast quantities of rubbish and a metre of mud had to be removed before the dismantling of the old hatches could begin. As straightforward as this task first appeared, it proved to be deceptively difficult. This so often happens in restoration projects particularly, as in this case, where despite careful planning and observation much of the situation is hidden from view. However, in the end determination and persistence won the day. With the new structure bolted in place a trial operation, carried out in September 1974, rewarded the stalwart labourers by working perfectly. There remained the problem of clearing the leat of mud and silt which was tackled by strenuous efforts of teams of volunteers and the Bath Fire Brigade who arrived with two high-pressure hoses which dispersed the silt with alarming ease.

During 1973, the work, halted in 1971, was resumed on the waterwheel. It is almost impossible to describe or to do full justice in words to the huge task which the restorers had set themselves with the complex and laborious effort to bring the waterwheel back into operation. One can only present a sketchy vignette as a tribute to the hours of dedication and achievement.

Initial work found much effort directed towards de-rusting of all the ironwork. A task made easier with the application of a pneumatic needle gun powered by a petrol engine compressor borrowed from BW; this was later replaced with an electric-motored version loaned to the project by Bristol Pneumatic Co. After the layers of rust and scale had been removed the iron assembly was given a generous coat of red-lead and painted with the appropriate number of green under and top-coats. There followed the replacement of the float and seal boards. Work continued with the fitting of two copper, flow-smoothing sheaths which masked the gap between the fixed and moving members of the sluice and additional work was carried out on the sluice. As it was now possible to rotate the wheel, the remaining oak starts were fitted and the three-wheel bearing was replaced and aligned with great care. With the waterwheel nearing completion, a start was made reconditioning of the pitwheel's wooden gear teeth. Each gear tooth was fashioned from oak planks purchased some years previously. After initial machining each tooth was given a thorough soaking in linseed oil prior to fitting to the wheel and machining each tooth in situ using an ingenious home-made router.

Keen as everyone was to check the performance of the gear assembly, patience was required while maintenance and examination of the remaining pump machinery took place. This required a deal of careful preparation as the pistons were required to be removed and the packing re-placed. Much rust and scale was removed and the cylinders' bores were polished before the a test run could be carried out in February 1976.

As may be expected, the restoration can only be described in but the barest details. The complete story and the list of tasks undertaken far exceeds the original optimistic forecast, with the completed task reflecting great credit to all involved.

Claverton pumping station is open to the public every Sunday during the summer months and in common with the other pumping station has published a comprehensive booklet on its history and restoration. This is obtainable, together with full opening details and volunteer opportunities from The Kennet & Avon Canal Trust, The Wharf, Couch Lane, Devizes, Wiltshire, SN10 1EB. Telephone 01380 721279.

Appendix Two
The Conservation Plan

Conservation has become, perhaps, an oversensitive subject where any query immediately labels the questioner as an anti-environmentalist. But it is perhaps necessary to criticise some aspects of this exercise which many thought carried the potential to put the whole Kennet & Avon Canal project at risk.

It is essential to note that when BW made the original bid application there was included ample provision for an environmental study and conservation plan, which they could and would have carried out as a matter of course. BW has a most conscious environmental policy which is fully supported by an in-house department; the assessment of the environmental impact on any work on any canal was, and remains, central to BW philosophy.

The Kennet & Avon Canal Conservation Plan outlined what is special, what is sensitive, what is vulnerable and what is distinctive. It suggested how this can all be retained, improved and managed and it addressed the problem of how BW might translate these attributes into actual work on the canal bank. It was prepared by a team of BW specialists based on the Oxford Canal at Hillmorton. A wide range of professional skills were required in its production and included ecologists, landscape architects, heritage advisors, engineers and water quality specialists plus other consultant help as and when required.

A specialist building historian was also appointed to review as many documents and archival records as possible which proved quite an undertaking when some details were found as far away as Edinburgh whilst others were lying with such unlikely authorities as the Hampshire County Council.

Working in parallel with the documentary endeavours, a landscape archaeologist researched the historic landscape surrounding the canal including, for example, fields with evidence of ancient settlements. The archaeologist also provided important data to help guide the dredging programme in relation to the deposition of material on to adjoining land. Surveys were made of the flora and fauna, while field workers carried out a full bird analysis. Water resources were also assessed and research carried out on possible visitor numbers and likely boat traffic movements.

A number of initiatives were included in the works as a direct result of observations and research, such as ramps to allow wildlife to escape from the water, measures to protect the water vole population and special areas set aside for fish to spawn. The information gained was assembled into Annual Management plans, approved by the monitors and used to guide the engineering works on a year to year basis.

In the lottery bid, the sum of £158,000 was earmarked for the conservation study which was defined to cover the canal 'corridor'. This phrase clearly meant the canal and the obvious strips of land each side owned by BW but it was also taken as meaning the 'immediate environment' of the canal, this being a less clearly defined width varying, for instance, to the width of a cutting where this was the constriction, through to a sensible intermediate area where the canal ran through more open countryside.

There were conditions placed on the grant in respect to the environment which brought into the picture the agencies of English Heritage, English Nature and The Countryside Commission. This was hardly surprising as spending grant funds from an organisation which was dedicated to help 'Heritage' would bound to attract scrutiny from 'Heritage' experts. However, this logical approach to the heritage expertise was felt by some of those working on the project to falter in some aspects and they questioned the level of guidance given to the staff who, being so dedicated to their expert niche, could, to the detriment of the waterway, easily lose sight of the broader picture.

However, what they deemed potentially more serious was the lack of means for the 'customers', the community at large, to question the experts judgement, thus putting them in a position of being unchallenged dictators of environmental policy with effectively no checks or balances. This was considered to be a vital necessity when, in a situation such as the Kennet & Avon bid, the release of an enormous sum of money – £25 million – hung on the words of such individuals and the failure of the project for the participants was totally unthinkable.

What further added to the problem was the opportunity it gave every other concerned agency to reveal their hidden agendas to milk, for all time, the maximum benefit for their organisation from the project. The very first indication of this came in the definition of the canal corridor; this was now to be from horizon to horizon from the canal line and the impact of the restoration of the navigation in certain countryside areas had to be written into the conservation report.

As Brian Oram, partnership chairman and prime mover of the project for the Canal Trust, was to remark later, 'the aspect of paid experts exercising dictatorial control over most areas of personal and commercial activities has to be subject to challenge and change, without that challenge automatically being used to shore up the contention being questioned,' He thought that 'in this area the management of the Heritage Lottery Fund is as much at fault as the various agencies.' He added that 'the solution to the problem is not, one fears, going to be found in self-regulation but by an eventual political regulation to the problem.'

At the end of two and a half years the cost of the report had grown from the initial budget of £158,000 to £197,000; this extra cost was not funded by extra payments from the HLF and had to come directly from the grant, thus reducing the cash available for the prime purpose of restoring the canal navigation. Although, curiously enough, as the work progressed many of the apparent restrictions placed on the operations by the Conservation Plan actually saved money, a notable example being the requirement for soft edge bank protection using 300mm coir rolls. This supports the bank allowing the vegetation to grow through and as a bonus becomes invisible in but a very few months. The easy alternative would have been to use environmentally hostile sheet piling at a much greater cost.

Many lessons were learnt which will be put to good use in years to come, not only on the Kennet & Avon but on BW canals all over the country. Roger Butler from Waterways Environment Services suggested that the Conservation Plan and its accompanying reports should become the benchmarks against which the Kennet & Avon Canal is managed in the future.

Appendix Three
Lock Data

Lock numbering starts at the Bristol end at Hamham with Lock 1 and ends in Reading at Lock 106, whilst the bridges start in Reading with No.1 and end near Hanham with bridge No.215. Where locks are stated to be always open this excludes normal maintenance

Lock No. Information	Name	Restoration Dates and Opening Ceremony
Lock 106	County	Always usable.
Lock 105	Fobney	Always usable.
Lock 104	Southcote	Always usable.
Lock 103	Burghfield	27 July 1968. Ceremony performed by Lord Methuen, Sir Frank Price and Lionel Munk.
Lock 102	Garston	Always usable.
Lock 101	Sheffield	Always usable. Repaired BWB in 1980.
Lock 100	Sulhamstead	27 July 1968. No ceremony.
Lock 99	Tyle Mill	23 May 1976. Inoperable until the balance beams, which were fitted later, were in place.
Lock 98	Ufton	Ungated. Now disused with the water level raised in adjoining pound.

Lock 97	Towney	1974. Opened officially 23 May 1976 by Dennis Howell, Minister for Sport, Sir Frank Price, General Stockwell and Admiral O'Brien.
Lock 96	Padworth	12 June 1984. Opened by Ian Morgan of Berkshire County Council, Mrs Saunders Rose of Newbury District Coucil & Admiral O'Brien.
Lock 95	Aldermaston	1984. Opened officially 9 Sept 1987 by Dr Robertson, Acting Chairman of BWB, Mr Gimblett, Chairman Berkshire County Council, and Admiral O'Brien.
Lock 94	Woolhampton	9 September 1987. Opened with Aldermaston.
Lock 93	Heales	1989. No official opening.
Lock 92	Midgham	9 September 1987. Opened with Aldermaston but devoid of water.
Lock 91	Colthrop	17 July 1990. Opened by BWB Chairman David Ingham, representatives of Berkshire County Council, and Newbury District Council, and Admiral O'Brien.
Lock 90	Monkey Marsh	17 July 1990. As Colthrop.
Lock 89	Widmead	17 July 1990. As Colthrop.
Lock 88	Bull's	1976. No official opening.
Lock 87	Ham	Always open.
Lock 86	Greenham	Always open.
Lock 85	Newbury Lock	Always open.
Lock 84	Guyer's	Always open.
Lock 83	Higg's	Always open.
Lock 82	Benham	Always open.
Lock 81	Hamstead	Easter Monday 1971. No official ceremony.
Lock 80	Copse	20 May 1972. Opened by Mr Palmer Chairman, Kintbury District Council, Lord Methuen and General Stockwell.
Lock 79	Dreweat's	1972. Opened officially 20 July 1974. No recorded ceremony.
Lock 78	Kintbury	1972. Opened officially 20 July 1974. No recorded ceremony.
Lock 77	Brunsden	1973. Opened officially 20 July 1974. No recorded ceremony
Lock 76	Wire	1973. Opened officially 20 July 1974. No recorded ceremony.
Lock 75	Dunmill	22 Sept 1973. Opening ceremony on 20 September 1974 by Lord Sandford, General Stockwell, Mayor & Constable of Hungerford.
Lock 74	Hungerford	1972. Official opening with Dunmill.
Lock 73	Hungerford Marsh	1975. No official opening.
Lock 72	Cobblers	1975. No official opening.
Lock 71	Picketfield	1975. No official opening.
Lock 70	Froxfield	1976. No recorded official opening.
Lock 69	Froxfield	1976. No recorded official opening.
Lock 68	Oakhill Down	28 August 1977. Opened by General Stockwell, Admiral O'Brien, with representatives from Kennet District Council, and from Great and Little Bedwyn Parish Councils.

Lock 67	Little Bedwyn	1977. No recorded ceremony.
Lock 66	Potter's	1977. No recorded ceremony.
Lock 65	Burnt Mill	1979. No recorded ceremony.
Lock 64	Church	1980. No recorded ceremony.
Lock 63	Beech Grove	29 August 1981.
Lock 62	Longman's	29 August 1981.
Lock 61	Crofton	1980. 'Crofton unlocked' with General Stockwell, Admiral O'Brien, BWB Vice Chairman Sir Frederick Corfield, Tony Durant MP, Charles Morrison MP, Patrick McNair Wilson MP, Chairmen of Berkshire and Wiltshire County Councils, Kennet and Newbury District Councils, and the Mayor of Newbury.
Lock 60	Crofton	1988. Un-official opening on August Bank Holiday 1988. The lock was then closed for re-puddling with the official ceremony held on 6 October 1988.
Lock 59	Crofton	As Lock 60
Lock 58	Sam Farmer	As Lock 60.
Lock 57	Adopters	As Lock 60.
Lock 56	Crofton	As Lock 60.
Lock 55	Crofton Top	As Lock 60.
Lock 54	Cadley	Wootton Rivers Flight reconstructed between 1971–1973. Officially opened 10 June 1973 by Admiral O'Brien, Diana Kendall, Secretary to Lord Methuen, and David Stoddard MP.
Lock 53	Brimslade	As Cadley.
Lock 52	Heathy Close	As Cadley.
Lock 51	Wootton Rivers	As Cadley.
Lock 50	Devizes Top	1980. Opened with the rest of the flight by Her Majesty The Queen on 8 August 1990.
Lock 49	Maton	1990. Opened with the rest of the flight by Her Majesty The Queen on 8 August 1990.
Lock 48	Trust	
Lock 47	Manifold	
Lock 46	A.P. Herbert	
Lock 45	Cave	
Lock 44	Sir Hugh Stockwell	
Lock 43	HM Queen Elizabeth	Opened with the rest of the Devizes Flight by Her Majesty the Queen on 8 August 1990.
Lock 42	Monument	
Lock 41	Boto-X	
Lock 40	Paul Ensor	
Lock 39	Scragg's	
Lock 38	Jack Dalby	
Locks 24-37	Devizes Flight	
Locks 22-23	Foxhangers and Lower Foxhangers	
Lock 21	Seend Top	1980. No Ceremony.
Lock 20	Seend	1980. No Ceremony.
Lock 19	Seend	1979. No Ceremony.
Lock 18	Seend	1978. No Ceremony.
Lock 17	Seend Bottom	1978. No Ceremony.

Lock 16	Harris Semington Top	1979. No Ceremony.
Lock 15	Semington Bottom	1979. No Ceremony.
Lock 14	Bradford-on-Avon	1978. No Ceremony.
Lock 13	Bath Top	
Lock 12	Pulteney Gardens	
Lock 11	Abbey View	
Lock 10	Wash House	5 September 1971. Opened by Sir Christopher Chancellor, Chairman of the Bath Preservation Trust.
Locks 8-9	Bath Deep	
Lock 7	Widcombe	1970. Official ceremony on 16 May 1972 when the lock was opened by Lord Methuen and Sir Frank Price. There was an official opening for the entire Bath Flight on 4 June 1976 by General Stockwell, Admiral O'Brien, Sir Frank Price and the Mayor of Bath. The locks were then closed again until 10 April 1982 when the canal was navigable from Bristol to Dundas.
Lock 6	Weston	Always open. Designated Cruiseway.
Lock 5	Kelston	Always open. Designated Cruiseway.
Lock 4	Saltford	Always open. Designated Cruiseway.
Lock 3	Swinford	Always open. Designated Cruiseway.
Lock 2	Keynsham	Always open. Designated Cruiseway.
Lock 1	Hanham	Always open. Designated Cruiseway.

Appendix Five
Glossary

BWB	British Waterways Board
BW	British Waterways
BTC	British Transport Commission
BTW	British Transport Waterways
D&IWE	Docks & Inland Waterway Executive
GWR	Great Western Railway
HLF	Heritage Lottery Fund
IWA	Inland Waterways Association
IWAAC	Inland Waterways Amenity Advisory Council
K&ACT	Kennet & Avon Canal Trust
MSC	Manpower Services Commission
NACRO	National Association for the Care & Rehabilitation of Offenders